# The Secret of God

*Journey into the Heart of Belief Systems, Comparative Analysis, and Divine Revelation*

# The Secret of God

# Unveiling human spirituality and the path to the true faith

## Julius Bisaso

Xulon Elite

Xulon Press
555 Winderley Pl, Suite 225
Maitland, FL 32751
407.339.4217
www.xulonpress.com

# Xulon ELITE

© 2023 by Julius Bisaso

Edited by Xulon Press

All rights reserved solely by the author. The author guarantees all contents are original and do not infringe upon the legal rights of any other person or work. No part of this book may be reproduced in any form without the permission of the author.

Due to the changing nature of the Internet, if there are any web addresses, links, or URLs included in this manuscript, these may have been altered and may no longer be accessible. The views and opinions shared in this book belong solely to the author and do not necessarily reflect those of the publisher. The publisher therefore disclaims responsibility for the views or opinions expressed within the work.

Unless otherwise indicated, Scripture quotations taken from the King James Version (KJV)–*public domain.*

Scripture quotations taken from the Holy Bible, New International Version (NIV). Copyright © 1973, 1978, 1984, 2011 by Biblica, Inc.™. Used by permission. All rights reserved.

Scripture quotations taken from the English Standard Version (ESV). Copyright © 2001 by Crossway, a publishing ministry of Good News Publishers. Used by permission. All rights reserved.

Paperback ISBN-13: 978-1-66289-106-9
Ebook ISBN-13: 978-1-66289-107-6

# Dedication:

**I DEDICATE THIS** book to my father, Ronald Ssettumba, whose unwavering faith in me and boundless love have been a guiding light throughout my journey. Your dedication has shaped my path, and for that, I am eternally grateful.

To the esteemed Teaching staff of African Bible University (Kampala, Uganda), especially Dr. Jeremiah Pitts- the Vice-Chancellor, and my former teachers, Mr. Sean Kinsella and Rev. Charles Mugasha – your prayers and belief in me have been a source of strength and inspiration.

This dedication extends to the sponsors of African Bible colleges across the continent, whose generosity provides students like me, with limited financial resources, the opportunity to receive a comprehensive university education.

Finally, I dedicate this book to my family, especially to my beloved children, Holy and Eli Jethro Bisaso. May it serve as a guiding light, helping you discover God for yourselves and providing clarity in moments of confusion.

# Table of Contents

Dedication: .................................... v
Introduction ................................... xi
Chapter 1: The Human Quest for Meaning. ............ 1
    The Impact of Doubt and the
    Importance of Seeking Answers .................. 2
    Human's Greatest Need. ........................ 3
Chapter 2: The Journey to Truth .................... 5
    A Worldview ................................. 5
    "Why Am I Here?" ............................ 10
Chapter 3: Unveiling the Divine ................... 15
    Exploring the Harmony
    Between Science and Faith .................... 16
Chapter 4: Religion: ............................ 30
    Religion is Relationship ...................... 35
    My Personal Pilgrimage ....................... 37
    My Silence and Meditations. .................. 43
    My Influential Friends ....................... 46
    Torn between Two. ........................... 48
    Decision time ............................... 50
Chapter 5: Ancient-Modern Paths
           and Sacred Traditions. ................. 51
    Hinduism .................................. 52
    Buddhism .................................. 56

Shintoism . . . . . . . . . . . . . . . . . . . . . . . . . . . . . . . . 59
Taoism. . . . . . . . . . . . . . . . . . . . . . . . . . . . . . . . . . . 62
African Traditional Religions. . . . . . . . . . . . . . . . . . 65
Judaism: . . . . . . . . . . . . . . . . . . . . . . . . . . . . . . . . . 69
Christianity. . . . . . . . . . . . . . . . . . . . . . . . . . . . . . . 72
Islam . . . . . . . . . . . . . . . . . . . . . . . . . . . . . . . . . . . 76
Modern Belief Systems. . . . . . . . . . . . . . . . . . . . . . 79
The Baha'i Faith . . . . . . . . . . . . . . . . . . . . . . . . . . 80
Mormonism . . . . . . . . . . . . . . . . . . . . . . . . . . . . . 83
Jehovah's Witnesses (Watch Tower Society). . . . . . . . . 86
Rastafarianism: . . . . . . . . . . . . . . . . . . . . . . . . . . . 89
Other Modern Belief Systems . . . . . . . . . . . . . . . . . 91

Chapter 6: My Criteria. . . . . . . . . . . . . . . . . . . . . . . . . 96
Section 1: Criteria for Evaluation . . . . . . . . . . . . . . . 98
1.2: Ancient Belief Systems . . . . . . . . . . . . . . . . . . 102
Section 2: Major Abrahamic Religions . . . . . . . . . . . 126
Comparative Analysis. . . . . . . . . . . . . . . . . . . . . . . 162
Section 3: Modern Belief Systems . . . . . . . . . . . . . . 173
Section 4: Contemporary Belief Systems. . . . . . . . . . 197
Comparative Analysis. . . . . . . . . . . . . . . . . . . . . . . 237

Chapter 7: The Mystery . . . . . . . . . . . . . . . . . . . . . . . 242
Section 1: The Universality of God's Plan . . . . . . . . 244
Section 2: Christ Concealed in the Old Testament . . 246
Section 3: The Unveiling of Christ
    in the New Testament . . . . . . . . . . . . . . . . 274
Section 4: Embracing the Inclusiveness
    of God's Covenant . . . . . . . . . . . . . . . . . . . 277
Section 5: Reflection and Application . . . . . . . . . . . 280
Section 6. Christ: Our All-Sufficient
    Inheritance (Colossians 1:27) . . . . . . . . . . . 282
Call to Embrace the Mystery . . . . . . . . . . . . . . . . . . 285

Chapter 8: Foundations of Christian Faith . . . . . . . . . . . 288
    The Trinity . . . . . . . . . . . . . . . . . . . . . . . . . . . . . . . . 290
    The Deity of Jesus Christ . . . . . . . . . . . . . . . . . . . . . 293
    The Holy Spirit . . . . . . . . . . . . . . . . . . . . . . . . . . . . . 295
    The Authority of Scripture . . . . . . . . . . . . . . . . . . . . 297
    Salvation by Grace through Faith . . . . . . . . . . . . . . 299
    Human Depravity . . . . . . . . . . . . . . . . . . . . . . . . . . . 302
    Justification by Faith . . . . . . . . . . . . . . . . . . . . . . . . 304
    The Atonement . . . . . . . . . . . . . . . . . . . . . . . . . . . . . 306
    Eternal Life . . . . . . . . . . . . . . . . . . . . . . . . . . . . . . . . 308
    Resurrection and Ascension . . . . . . . . . . . . . . . . . . . 310
    The Priesthood of Believers . . . . . . . . . . . . . . . . . . . 312
    The Second Coming of Christ . . . . . . . . . . . . . . . . . 315
    The Church . . . . . . . . . . . . . . . . . . . . . . . . . . . . . . . . 317
    Baptism . . . . . . . . . . . . . . . . . . . . . . . . . . . . . . . . . . . 319
    The Lord's Supper (Communion) . . . . . . . . . . . . . . 322
Book Conclusion: . . . . . . . . . . . . . . . . . . . . . . . . . . . . . . 327
Works Cited: . . . . . . . . . . . . . . . . . . . . . . . . . . . . . . . . . 331

# Introduction

**AS A STUDENT** at university, I recall my good friend Jonathan constantly encouraging me to read and try to understand computer notifications and error messages, rather than asking him for assistance every time a dialogue box popped up. Despite being born into a somewhat stable home with some access to computers, I initially lacked the motivation to educate myself about their usage. However, Jonathan's encouragement inspired me to delve deeper into the world of computing and seek knowledge. With time, I became more proficient in using computers and eventually became a trusted resource among my peers, often being referred to as a "consultant." I also found myself at the forefront of introducing and educating my community on the latest technology, such as smartphones. This experience taught me the importance of seeking knowledge and using it to better one's own life and the lives of those around them. Advancements in various fields, including technology, medicine, and human civilization, have emerged as a result of research and study. For example, the discovery of quinine as an effective treatment for malaria is a testament to the impact that dedication to knowledge can have in overcoming challenges and saving lives.

As a scholar and researcher, I have explored the diverse belief systems of the world, both indigenous and international. Through a rigorous comparative analysis and personal criteria, I have embarked on a profound spiritual journey—one that began in the familiar embrace of Roman Catholicism, transitioned into the teachings of Islam during my secondary school years, and ultimately led me to the discovery of a true and transformative relationship with Jesus Christ. It is this journey, rich with experiences and revelations, that I intend to share as I proceed in writing this book.

After my conversion to Christianity, I remained driven by an inward conviction to compare my newfound belief with other belief systems, including Islam, Buddhism, Hinduism, Judaism, Shintoism, and countless others. Guided by a set of criteria that emerged from my own search for truth, I endeavored to weigh these major belief systems against five essential factors: Origin, Longevity, Relevance, Accuracy of Predictions, and The Power and Evidence of God. Throughout the pages of this book, I invite you to join me on this intellectual and spiritual quest, as we explore and evaluate these belief systems on the scales of reason, evidence, and personal conviction. In doing so, it becomes increasingly clear to me that Christianity emerges as the only belief system that withstands rigorous scrutiny and remains resolute in its ability to provide answers to life's deepest questions. This book is a testament to that revelation—an invitation to discover "The Secret of God" and find faith, purpose, and ultimate truth.

# Chapter 1

# The Human Quest for Meaning

**HUMAN BEINGS ARE** unique creatures, driven by an innate desire to find meaning and purpose in their existence. Throughout history, philosophers, theologians, and thinkers of all kinds have grappled with the fundamental questions of life: Who are we? Why are we here? What is our purpose? This chapter explores the depths of the human quest for meaning, exploring the inherent longing for spiritual fulfillment that resonates within each individual.

The Inherent Longing for Purpose: In the depths of every human heart lies a longing for something greater than themselves. From ancient civilizations to modern societies, individuals have sought to understand their place in the grand tapestry of existence. This longing arises from a deep-seated awareness that there must be more to life than mere existence. As Viktor Frankl, the renowned psychiatrist and Holocaust survivor, aptly stated, "Man's search for meaning is the primary motivation in his life and not a 'secondary rationalization' of instinctual drives" (Frankl, 1946, p. 121). It is this search for meaning that drives individuals to explore the realms of spirituality and faith.

## The Impact of Doubt and the Importance of Seeking Answers:

In the pursuit of meaning, doubt often becomes an unwelcome companion on the journey. Doubt can arise from personal experiences, philosophical inquiries, or the challenges presented by a complex and ever-changing world. However, doubt should not be feared or dismissed, for it serves as a catalyst for seeking answers and discovering truth. As the philosopher Descartes famously proclaimed, "If you would be a real seeker after truth, it is necessary that at least once in your life you doubt, as far as possible, all things" (Descartes, 1641, p. 1). Doubt prompts individuals to embark on a quest for knowledge, pushing the boundaries of their understanding and expanding their horizons. It is in this spirit of inquiry and openness that my professor of World Religions, Dr. Travis Campbell, guided me through the exploration of various religious philosophies, preparing me to study deeper into the individual belief systems that await us in the chapters ahead.

Seeking answers is a vital aspect of the human journey. It involves engaging in introspection, exploration, and critical thinking. By seeking answers, individuals actively participate in shaping their own narratives, rather than passively accepting the status quo. This quest for answers becomes a transformative process, enabling individuals to discover their own beliefs, values, and spiritual paths.

# The Human Quest for Meaning

**Human's Greatest Need:**

According to Maslow's hierarchy of needs, the traditional basic human needs are food, shelter, and clothing, followed by necessities like sanitation, education, and healthcare (Maslow, 1943). However, beyond these fundamental requirements, there is an essential need that surpasses the physical and material realm—the need to determine the correct worldview of origin, purpose, morality, and destiny for human fulfillment. American educator, author, and businessman Stephen Covey eloquently captured this sentiment when he wrote that the fundamental needs for human fulfillment are "to live, to love, to learn, and to leave a legacy" (Covey, 1990, p. 21). While Covey's statement did not have a religious motive, it implies humanity's inherent desire to find the correct worldview that encompasses these profound aspects of human existence.

**The Need to Love:** The need to love is a social need that drives humans to relate to other people, to belong, and to be loved. Regardless of individual personality traits, whether extroverted or introverted, all humans share the basic need to experience love, belongingness, and to love others in return. It can be said that "it is a God-given quality for every person to love and to desire to be loved" (Keller, 2013, p. 5). Love fulfills a deep yearning within us, offering a sense of connection, acceptance, and emotional nourishment.

**The Need to Learn:** The need to learn is a mental need that drives curiosity and the desire for personal growth and development. Humans possess an inherent thirst for knowledge and an innate drive to explore and understand their environment and various aspects of life. Theologians argue that "humans will always be curious and seeking to find, for within them is imprinted a profound longing to discover their creator" (Lewis, 1943, p. 21). Learning fuels intellectual curiosity and provides a pathway to expanding our understanding of ourselves, the world, and our place in it.

**The Need to Leave a Legacy:** The need to leave a legacy encompasses the human desire for meaning, purpose, pride, personal satisfaction, and contribution. Humans have an inherent yearning to make a difference, to feel that they have positively contributed to society, and to leave the world a better place. Theologians argue that the desire to be remembered even after death stems from the belief that humans possess eternal souls that transcend the death and decay of the mortal body. They suggest that true fulfillment can only be achieved by finding true purpose, which ultimately requires finding one's creator (Schaeffer, 1972, p. 35).

Conclusion: The human quest for meaning encompasses more than mere physical and material needs. It examines the realms of spirituality, purpose, and the fulfillment of profound human longings. Maslow's hierarchy of needs, expanded to include altruism and spirituality, acknowledges that the self finds its actualization in giving itself to higher goals beyond oneself (Maslow, 1971, p. 406). In the chapters that follow, we will study deeper into the exploration of spirituality, faith, and the search for ultimate meaning, as we seek to uncover "The Secret of God."

# Chapter 2

# The Journey to Truth

**IN THE QUEST** for meaning, individuals encounter the concept of worldview, which plays a pivotal role in shaping their beliefs and understanding of the world. A worldview encompasses a comprehensive framework through which individuals interpret reality, addressing fundamental questions about existence, morality, and the nature of the divine. This chapter probes into the exploration of worldviews, examining their significance in the human journey to truth and their varying perspectives on the existence of God.

## Understanding the Concept of Worldview:

### A Worldview

A worldview serves as a lens through which individuals perceive and interpret the world around them. It encompasses a collection of beliefs, values, and assumptions that form the foundation of one's understanding of reality. As James W. Sire explains, "A worldview is a commitment, a fundamental orientation of the heart, that can be expressed as a story or in a set of presuppositions (assumptions which may be true, partially true or entirely false) that we hold (consciously or subconsciously, consistently or inconsistently) about the basic constitution of reality, and that provides the foundation on which we live and move and have our being" (Sire, 2015, p. 20). Worldviews shape our perceptions, guide our actions, and influence our beliefs about the existence of God.

Examining Different Worldviews: Various worldviews offer diverse perspectives on the existence of God, reflecting the rich panorama of human beliefs and philosophies. While some may argue that the number of worldviews is potentially infinite, it is possible to distill them into six major categories based on different beliefs about God and God's relationship to the world.

1. Agnosticism: Agnosticism is the belief that no worldview can definitively be known as true. Agnostics acknowledge the limitations of human knowledge and maintain that the existence and nature of God are beyond human comprehension. They claim to emphasize intellectual humility and recognize the uncertainty inherent in addressing questions about the divine. Agnosticism prompts individuals to remain open to different possibilities and encourages a continuous search for understanding.

An agnostic would say, "I dont know, and it is impossible to know. The nature of God is beyond our grasp; certainty about the divine is elusive. I embrace intellectual humility, acknowledging that our understanding is limited and ever-evolving."

2. Polytheism: Polytheism asserts the belief in the existence of many divine beings. This worldview posits that the divine realm encompasses multiple gods, each with their own distinct attributes, powers, and spheres of influence.

Polytheistic traditions, such as ancient Greek and Roman religions, Hinduism, and various indigenous belief systems, attribute different aspects of creation and natural phenomena to different deities. Polytheists often engage in rituals, prayers, and offerings to honor and seek favor from these gods.

A polytheist would say, "The divine takes many forms and exists in diverse realms. Each god has distinct attributes and powers, governing different aspects of the world. Through rituals and offerings, we honor and seek the favor of these gods, recognizing their influence in various facets of life."

3. Pantheism: Pantheism embraces the belief that everything in the universe is divine. According to pantheism, the divine essence pervades all aspects of existence, blurring the distinction between the divine and the material world. Pantheists perceive the natural world as a manifestation of God, emphasizing the interconnectedness and interdependence of all things. This worldview finds expression in philosophical systems like Spinoza's pantheism and certain interpretations of Eastern spiritual traditions such as Hinduism, Taoism, Buddhism and more.

A pantheist would say, "God is everything, and everything is God. The entire universe is a manifestation of the divine essence. In every living being, in every rock and river, I see the interconnected threads of a divine mosaic. Nature itself is a sacred expression of God."

4. Panentheism: Panentheism posits the belief in an evolving deity that is co-dependent on or with the cosmos. This worldview holds that God encompasses and transcends the universe, while also being intimately connected to it. Panentheists view the world as an evolving expression of the divine, and they believe that the divine is continuously involved in the processes and development of the universe. Some interpretations of mystical traditions (Hinduism, Buddhism) and certain modern philosophical perspectives align with panentheistic ideas.

A Panentheist could say, "I am a god. God is both transcendent and immanent. The cosmos is an integral part of the divine, and God is intimately involved in the ongoing processes of the universe. The world is a dynamic, evolving expression of the divine, and our connection to God is inherent in every aspect of existence".

5. Theism: Theism asserts the belief in one God who is transcendent and personal. Theistic worldviews, such as Christianity, Islam, and Judaism, hold that there is a singular divine being who created and governs the universe. Theism affirms the existence of a personal God who interacts with humanity, guides human affairs, and establishes moral principles. Theistic traditions often emphasize the importance of faith, worship, and adherence to divine commandments.

A theist would say, "I believe in one God, transcendent and personal. This singular divine being created the universe and continues to guide it. God is a source of moral principles and a loving guide for humanity. Through faith, worship, and adherence to divine commandments, we seek a deeper connection with the Almighty."

6. Atheism: Atheism represents the disbelief or lack of belief in any kind of deity. Atheists claim to reject the existence of God based on various philosophical, scientific, or personal reasons. Atheistic worldviews range from a simple absence of belief in God to active disbelief and the assertion that God's existence is improbable or impossible. Atheists often claim to prioritize reason, empirical evidence, and the pursuit of a naturalistic understanding of the world.

An atheist would say, "I find no reason to believe in any deity. The evidence for God's existence is insufficient, and I prioritize reason and empirical evidence. My worldview doesn't include a divine presence, and I see the natural world as the result of natural processes without a guiding deity."

Conclusion: The exploration of worldviews and their perspectives on the existence of God reveals the vast array of human beliefs and philosophies that shape our understanding of reality. From agnosticism to polytheism, pantheism to panentheism, theism to atheism, each worldview offers unique insights into the human quest for truth and meaning. By examining these worldviews, we embark on a journey of intellectual and spiritual exploration, broadening our perspectives and enriching our understanding of the diverse textile of human thought. In the chapters ahead, we will delve deeper into the examination of different world religions and worldviews, exploring their origins, core principles, and implications for our lives and the search for ultimate truth.

**"Why Am I Here?"**

This profound question often remains unexplored in the rush of daily life. Many individuals traverse their existence as if it were a predetermined cycle: education, career, family, retirement, and eventually, death. It's a path frequently marked by personal accomplishments and societal commendations, yet it often leads to bewildering outcomes. Relationships crumble, an unsettling emptiness pervades, and a profound sense of wasted time and purposelessness looms.

In the scriptures, King Solomon, the author of Ecclesiastes, provides us with a poignant perspective. He possessed unparalleled wealth, wisdom, numerous relationships, luxurious estates, and every imaginable form of pleasure. Yet, he summarized a life lived solely in the material realm, devoid of spiritual depth, as meaningless. In his words, "Meaningless! Meaningless! . . . Utterly meaningless! Everything is meaningless" (Ecclesiastes 1:2, paraphrased). This phenomenon is not confined to Solomon alone but extends to many in our modern world, including celebrities in various fields who appear to lead lives of excitement yet grapple with depression and even contemplate suicide. It raises the question: Is there something more profound, something beyond the material and the visible that gives life true meaning?

Deep within our hearts, an intuition persists that there exists a reality beyond what our senses perceive. This inner knowing tells us that we are more than mere mortal bodies, that we are, in some way, connected to eternity. The Bible illuminates this concept by stating that God has "set eternity in the hearts of men" (Ecclesiastes 3:11) and that humans are created in the image and likeness of God (Genesis 1:26). This profound truth suggests that our essence transcends the limits of our mortal existence, hinting at life beyond the earthly realm.

Before humanity's fall from grace, before sin disrupted our relationship with our Creator and tainted the world, several key aspects characterized our existence:

1. **Social Design**: God created humanity to be social beings, designed to interact and connect with one another (Genesis 2:18–25).

When we examine the creation account in Genesis 2:18–25, we discover a fundamental truth about human nature: we are inherently social beings. God, in His divine wisdom, recognized that it was "not good for man to be alone." Therefore, He created a suitable partner for Adam, Eve. This act of companionship reflects the divine intention for human interaction and connection.

In this social design, we find the essence of community, partnership, and the importance of relationships. Humans were crafted to thrive in the context of meaningful connections with one another. The family unit, often considered the cornerstone of society, is a testament to this social design. It embodies the idea that we are not isolated individuals but interconnected members of a greater whole.

2. **Purposeful Work**: Work was an inherent part of human life, designed to provide fulfillment and purpose (Genesis 2:15).

In Genesis 2:15, we encounter another crucial aspect of human existence—work. Far from being a punishment or a burden, work was woven into the fabric of human life as a source of fulfillment and purpose. God placed Adam in the Garden of Eden "to work it and take care of it." This divine assignment reveals the inherent value of purposeful labor.

Work, in this context, represents more than mere toil; it is a means through which humans can contribute to the world, exercise stewardship over creation, and find satisfaction in their endeavors. It underscores the dignity of human effort and the potential for creativity and innovation. Purposeful work, rooted in cooperation with God's creative order, offers individuals a sense of fulfillment and meaningful contribution to the world around them.

3. **Divine Fellowship**: God shared a close fellowship with humankind (Genesis 3:8).

Prior to the introduction of sin, humanity enjoyed a close and intimate fellowship with the Creator. In Genesis 3:8, we read about God walking in the garden in the cool of the day, seeking to commune with Adam and Eve. This divine fellowship reflects the deep, personal relationship that God desires to have with His creation.

Divine fellowship highlights the spiritual dimension of human existence. It signifies that humans are not limited to the material realm but possess the capacity for a profound connection with the divine. This relationship is characterized by communion, trust, and open communication. It is a source of guidance, comfort, and spiritual nourishment, emphasizing that the human journey is not solely a physical one but a spiritual odyssey as well.

4. **Stewardship of the Earth**: Humans were entrusted with dominion over the earth (Genesis 1:26).

In Genesis 1:26, God entrusts humanity with a remarkable responsibility—the dominion over the earth. This stewardship signifies that humans were appointed as caretakers and custodians of God's creation. It underscores the importance of our role in preserving the natural world and ensuring its flourishing.

The concept of stewardship implies a sense of accountability and responsibility. It implies that humans are called to exercise their dominion with wisdom and care, recognizing the intrinsic value of the environment and the creatures within it. This role as stewards aligns with the idea that human existence is intertwined with the welfare of the earth. It emphasizes that our actions have far-reaching consequences, not only for ourselves but for the entire ecosystem.

In sum, these key aspects of humanity's existence before the fall underscore the profound truths about our nature and purpose. They reveal that humans are inherently social, designed for meaningful relationships; work is a source of fulfillment and contribution; divine fellowship offers spiritual nourishment and guidance, and stewardship of the earth highlights our responsibility in preserving and nurturing God's creation. Understanding these foundational principles provides insights into the intrinsic value of human life and the purpose for which we were created.

These aspects were intended to enrich and define our lives on Earth, contributing to our sense of purpose and fulfillment. Innately, we seek something greater than ourselves, often acknowledging the existence of a superior power or searching for meaning beyond the visible world. This innate longing is evident in the fact that approximately 84 percent of the world's population aligns with one of the five major religions: Christianity, Islam, Hinduism, Buddhism, or various forms of folk religion. In a world brimming with diverse belief systems, spanning approximately 10,000 distinct religions, the quest for truth and meaning is both universal and intricate.

However, the diversity among these belief systems poses a pressing question: amidst the array of religious and spiritual paths, which one holds the ultimate truth? They cannot all be simultaneously true, for such a paradox would imply collective delusion. A closer examination of these belief systems reveals profound differences and contradictions, with only a few shared elements.

To navigate this spiritual labyrinth and discover the genuine and worthy form of worship, I developed a set of criteria that is presented in the chapters that follow. These criteria offer a lens through which we can scrutinize and discern the path that leads to true and meaningful communion with our Creator.

## Chapter 3

# Unveiling the Divine

**IN THE PURSUIT** of meaning and truth, the exploration of the existence of God holds profound significance. This chapter delves into the unveiling of the divine, engaging with philosophical arguments and evidence that support the existence of God. Additionally, we will explore the harmony between science and faith, examining scientific discoveries that point towards a higher power, revealing a deeper understanding of the mysteries of the universe.

Throughout history, philosophers have presented compelling arguments that provide intellectual frameworks for contemplating the existence of God. These arguments offer rational insights and logical reasoning, inviting individuals to critically examine the nature of reality and consider the possibility of a divine presence.

One prominent philosophical argument is the cosmological argument, which posits that the existence of the universe implies the existence of a necessary and transcendent cause, commonly referred to as the "First Cause" or "Uncaused Cause." As Thomas Aquinas articulates in his famous "Five Ways," the cosmological argument asserts that the chain of causes and effects cannot extend infinitely into the past and must ultimately originate from an uncaused, self-existent being (Aquinas, Summa Theologiae, I, Q.2, A.3).

Another significant argument is the teleological argument, also known as the argument from design. This argument contends that the intricate order, complexity, and purpose observed in the natural world indicate the existence of an intelligent designer. From the intricate workings of biological systems to the fine-tuning of the physical constants in the universe, proponents of the teleological argument assert that such evidence suggests a deliberate and purposeful creation (Paley, Natural Theology).

Furthermore, the moral argument highlights the existence of objective moral values and duties as evidence for the existence of God. This argument posits that moral principles and obligations, which are inherent in human consciousness, require a transcendent source to ground their objectivity and universality (Craig, Reasonable Faith, 170-190).

**Exploring the Harmony Between Science and Faith:**

Contrary to popular misconceptions, science and faith are not inherently at odds with each other. For many years, science and religion have been seen as opposing forces, with scientists often challenging the religious beliefs of a creator and the idea of a single beginning as described in the Bible. However, in recent times, there have been statements from learned scientists that support the biblical view of creation, leading to the question: Has science finally discovered God?

Eminent inventors and innovators like Albert Einstein were skeptical about the possibility of science discovering God, but this might be the greatest scientific discovery of all time. So, what are these new discoveries that have perplexed the greatest scientific minds of the past century and caused them to reconsider the origin of our universe?

These discoveries stem from advancements in technology, particularly the development of powerful telescopes that have unveiled mysteries about our universe, providing new scientific insights into the origin of life. These discoveries raise questions about the existence of a God—a designer and creator of the universe—even in the face of science suggesting that a higher power is unnecessary to explain the universe. What is it about these discoveries that fundamentally differs from previous findings and has astounded the scientific community?

One significant discovery lies within the field of molecular biology, where scientists have uncovered the sophisticated coding within DNA. Many scientists now acknowledge that the universe and life itself seem to be part of a grand design. And Many scientists, when they admit their views, incline toward the design argument. Surprisingly, many scientists discussing God have no religious beliefs themselves. It is intriguing to examine deeper into these remarkable discoveries that have prompted scientists to speak of God.

Four revolutionary discoveries from the fields of astronomy and molecular biology stand out among many:

1. The universe had a beginning.
2. The universe is perfectly designed for life.
3. DNA coding reveals intelligence.
4. The human conscience is eternal.

The statements made by leading scientists about these discoveries may be surprising, as many align with the creation story presented in the Bible's book of Genesis. Scientists have strived to prove what theologians and Bible scholars have long believed. Renowned astronomer Robert Jastrow, who had no Christian agenda, put it this way:

"For the scientist who has lived by his faith in the power of reason, the story ends like a bad dream. He has scaled the mountains of ignorance; he is about to conquer the highest peak; as he pulls himself over the final rock, he is greeted by a band of theologians who have been sitting there for centuries." (Jastrow, God and the Astronomers, 116).

1. **The universe had a beginning:**

The notion that the universe had a one-time beginning challenges the long-held belief that the mass, space, and energy of the universe had always existed. Edwin Hubble, an astronomer in the early 20th century, discovered that the universe is expanding. By mathematically rewinding this process, he concluded that everything in the universe, including matter, energy, space, and time, had a beginning (Proceedings of the National Academy of Sciences of the United States of America 15, 168-173.)

This revelation was met with resistance from scientists, including Einstein, who actively tried to evade the idea of a universe with a beginning, later referring to it as "the biggest blunder of my life." British astronomer Sir Fred Hoyle, another opponent of the idea, sarcastically dubbed the creation event the "big bang." However, theologians of the time argued that what Hoyle called the "big bang" referred to the resounding voice of God that brought all of creation into existence as recorded in Genesis 1.

Sir Fred Hoyle, Einstein, and other scientists clung to the steady-state theory, believing that the universe had always existed. But as evidence for a universe with a beginning grew overwhelming, the logical conclusion emerged: "Someone or something beyond scientific investigation must have started it all."

The biblical statement, "In the beginning God created..." aligns with the scientific discovery that the universe had a finite beginning.

## 2. The universe is perfectly designed for life:

Furthermore, the fine-tuning of the universe for life has captivated the attention of scientists, revealing a remarkable harmony and precision that raises profound questions about its origins. The fundamental physical constants and parameters, such as the strength of gravity, the speed of light, and the masses of particles, appear to be finely tuned to allow for the emergence and sustenance of life. The slightest deviations in these values would lead to a universe inhospitable to the development of galaxies, stars, planets, and ultimately life itself.

Consider, for example, the cosmological constant, which represents the energy density of empty space. If this constant were even slightly different, the expansion rate of the universe would be vastly different, making it inhospitable for the formation of galaxies and the emergence of life. Similarly, the ratio of the electromagnetic force to the gravitational force is exquisitely balanced to allow for the formation of stable atoms and the existence of complex chemistry necessary for life. These examples illustrate the delicate interplay of physical constants that must be precisely fine-tuned to create the conditions suitable for life as we know it.

The existence of such fine-tuning has prompted scientists to consider two possible explanations. One possibility is that it is purely coincidental, a result of chance within a vast multiverse where different universes with varying physical constants exist. However, this explanation raises further questions about the origin and nature of the multiverse itself, as well as the remarkable coincidence that we find ourselves in a universe with the right conditions for life.

Another explanation is that the fine-tuning is indicative of intelligent design. The precise calibration of physical constants and conditions to allow for life suggests the presence of a cosmic designer who intentionally set the stage for the emergence and development of life in the universe. This perspective aligns with the concept of teleology, which posits that there is purpose and intentionality behind the organization and order found in the natural world.

The anthropic principle, which acknowledges the apparent fine-tuning of the universe for the existence of intelligent life, adds further weight to the argument for intelligent design. It recognizes that we, as conscious observers, are intricately connected to the specific values of the fundamental physical constants and conditions that allow our existence. The anthropic principle suggests that the universe, with its precise tuning, seems tailored to accommodate and support life, leading to the inquiry of whether this fine-tuning is a mere coincidence or a deliberate act of a cosmic designer and Creator.

The Bible provides insights that resonate with the idea of the universe being carefully designed for life. In the book of Psalms, it is written, "The heavens declare the glory of God; the skies proclaim the work of his hands" (Psalm 19:1). This verse highlights the notion that the beauty and order observed in the heavens are a testimony to the divine craftsmanship behind the universe. It suggests that the intricacies and fine-tuning of the cosmos serve as a reflection of God's glory and creative power.

Additionally, the apostle Paul, in his letter to the Romans, speaks of the evidence of God's invisible attributes being clearly seen through His creation. He writes, "For since the creation of the world, God's invisible qualities—his eternal power and divine nature—have been clearly seen, being understood from what has been made" (Romans 1:20). This passage emphasizes that the intricacies and fine-tuning of the natural world are not random happenstance but rather deliberate manifestations of God's attributes.

The recognition of the fine-tuning of the universe for life aligns with the biblical concept of divine intentionality and purpose in creation. The book of Isaiah reminds us that God's wisdom and understanding are unfathomable, stating, "Who has measured the waters in the hollow of his hand, or with the breadth of his hand marked off the heavens? Who has held the dust of the earth in a basket, or weighed the mountains on the scales and the hills in a balance?" (Isaiah 40:12). This verse underscores the idea that the intricacies of the universe are the product of divine craftsmanship and wisdom beyond human comprehension.

Physicist Paul Davies, in his book "The Goldilocks Enigma," expresses the overwhelming impression of design that arises from the fine-tuning of the universe. This sentiment echoes the awe and wonder felt by many scientists as they explore into the mysteries of the cosmos, discovering the delicate balance and intricate organization that underpins the emergence of life.

In conclusion, the fine-tuning of the universe for life presents a compelling argument for the existence of a cosmic designer. The remarkable precision and delicate balance of the fundamental physical constants and parameters necessary for the emergence and sustenance of life raise profound questions about the origin and nature of our universe. While alternative explanations such as chance within a multiverse have also been presented, the overwhelming impression of design and purpose calls for a deeper exploration of the possibility of intelligent design. The fine-tuning of the universe invites us to contemplate the existence of a cosmic designer who crafted the universe with meticulous care, setting the stage for the beauty, complexity, and wonder of life. This resonates with biblical passages that speak of the glory, wisdom, and intentionality of God's creation, such as Psalm 19:1, which declares, "The heavens declare the glory of God; the skies proclaim the work of his hands," and Romans 1:20, which states, "For since the creation of the world, God's invisible qualities—his eternal power and divine nature—have been clearly seen, being understood from what has been made." As we research into the mysteries of the cosmos, the recognition of intelligent design invites us to explore the profound connection between scientific inquiry and faith, as we marvel at the beauty, complexity, and purpose embedded within the universe.

3. **DNA coding reveals intelligence:**

The discovery of the intricate coding within DNA has revolutionized our understanding of life and has opened up a fascinating realm of inquiry. DNA, or deoxyribonucleic acid, serves as the blueprint for all living organisms, containing the instructions that dictate their development, growth, and functioning. The remarkable complexity and sophistication of the genetic code embedded within DNA have astounded scientists and led them to ponder the presence of intelligence (a Creator) in its design.

The DNA molecule consists of a sequence of nucleotide bases—adenine (A), cytosine (C), guanine (G), and thymine (T)—that form a precise order, similar to the way letters in a language create meaningful words and sentences. This precise arrangement of genetic information is responsible for the incredible diversity and intricacy of life on Earth. The DNA code not only determines an organism's physical characteristics but also governs its physiological processes, behavior, and overall functioning.

The level of information contained within DNA is staggering. Each human cell carries approximately three billion base pairs of DNA, forming a complex web of instructions that orchestrates the development of a human being from a single fertilized egg. This level of complexity is far beyond what could arise through random or accidental processes alone. The intricacy of the DNA code, with its precise sequences and functional patterns, strongly suggests the involvement of intelligence in its formation.

Artificial intelligence (AI) has been employed to study the genetic code and its structure, enabling scientists to gain a deeper understanding of DNA and its implications (Darrin S. Joy, Article). However, the genetic code is textbook scientific knowledge that was soundly established without resorting to AI (Joiret, Leclercq, et al. Article). The discovery that DNA codes information in a digital form points decisively back to a prior intelligence, as information always comes from an intelligence, whether it's hieroglyphic inscription or a paragraph in a book (Biola Magazine Staff, 2010).

The recognition of intelligence in DNA's design has led scientists to contemplate the existence of a higher intelligence, such as a divine creator, in the origin of life. They argue that the vast amount of information and the intricate coding within DNA are best explained by the presence of an intelligent mind behind its creation. This perspective aligns with the concept of intelligent design, which proposes that certain features of the natural world, including the complex information systems within DNA, are best explained by an intelligent cause rather than solely by natural processes.

Moreover, the remarkable similarities in the genetic code across different species further support the idea of a common designer. Scientists have discovered that the genetic code is nearly universal, meaning that the same coding principles apply to various organisms, from bacteria to plants to humans. This suggests a shared blueprint and a common source of design, pointing towards an intelligent creator (perhaps singular) who crafted life with purpose and intention.

Jewish scriptures provide insights that resonate with this notion. Psalm 139:14 (NIV) states, "I praise you because I am fearfully and wonderfully made; your works are wonderful, I know that full well." This verse acknowledges the awe-inspiring intricacy and complexity of human beings, implying the presence of a divine hand behind their creation. The sophisticated genetic code within DNA serves as a testament to the remarkable design and purpose woven into every individual.

In Genesis 1:27 (NIV), it is written, "So God created mankind in his own image, in the image of God he created them; male and female he created them." This verse suggests that humanity possesses a unique reflection of God's attributes. The intricate information system encoded within DNA reflects the intelligence and creativity of its Creator, reinforcing the idea that life is not a product of random chance but rather a deliberate design.

The recognition of intelligence in DNA's coding aligns with the concept of intelligent design, which is also supported by Romans 1:20 (NIV): "For since the creation of the world God's invisible qualities—his eternal power and divine nature—have been clearly seen, being understood from what has been made, so that people are without excuse." This verse emphasizes that the natural world bears witness to God's existence and attributes. The intricate coding within DNA serves as a tangible example of the complexity and order present in the universe, pointing towards an intelligent Creator.

Furthermore, in Jeremiah 1:5 (NIV), God declares, "Before I formed you in the womb I knew you, before you were born I set you apart; I appointed you as a prophet to the nations." This verse highlights God's intimate involvement in the formation of each individual. The intricate genetic instructions encoded within DNA reflect God's foreknowledge and purpose for every person, further emphasizing the presence of intelligence in its design.

It is important to note that to some scientists, the recognition of intelligence in DNA's coding does not provide definitive proof of a divine creator, as some insist that Scientific inquiry focuses on empirical evidence and natural explanations, while the question of a higher intelligence falls within the realm of faith, spirituality, and metaphysics. However, the intricate nature of DNA's design and the presence of information-based coding within it serve as thought-provoking indications that invite further contemplation, exploration, and the necessity of logical deductions into the mysteries of life's origins.

In conclusion, the discovery of the intricate coding within DNA has revealed the presence of intelligence in its design. The complexity, specificity, and information content of the genetic code raise intriguing questions about the origin of life and the involvement of a higher intelligence, such as a divine creator. While scientific inquiry provides valuable insights, the ultimate nature of life's origins and the existence of a divine creator remain profound mysteries that invite both scientific exploration and philosophical contemplation.

### 4. The Human Consciousness is Eternal:

The concept of the human conscience has long fascinated both scientists and philosophers. The Merriam-Webster dictionary defines conscience as "the sense of the moral goodness or blameworthiness of one's own conduct, intentions, or character together with a feeling of obligation to do right or be good." According to theologians, conscience is equated with the soul, which can be defined as the invisible spirit inhabiting the human body, or the mental abilities of a living being, such as reason, character, feeling, consciousness, memory, perception, and thinking.

While the study of ethology, which is the scientific and objective study of animal behavior, has not yet considered the fact that man's behavior is modeled after the character of one's inward soul, scientific evidence seems to prove that humans have an indwelling, invisible (spiritual) intellect that lives on after the death of the body.

One theory on consciousness is that it is information stored at a quantum level. Anesthesiologist and professor Stuart Hameroff, known for his studies of consciousness, suggests that the operations of microtubules in brain cells are critical to the existence of eukaryotic cells, including humans. "Hameroff argued that these subneuronal cytoskeleton components could be the basic units of processing rather than the neurons themselves." (Hameroff, S. 2023, October). British physicist Sir Roger Penrose believes that protein-based microtubules, a structural component of human cells, carry quantum information that is stored at a subatomic level, and that consciousness is based on non-computable quantum processing performed by qubits formed collectively on cellular microtubules. His theory, known as "Orchestrated Objective Reduction" (Orch-OR), posits that consciousness is significantly amplified in the neurons. Hameroff and Penrose reviewed their theory in 2014, stating that "the evidence now clearly supports Orch OR," and that there have been more and more experimental confirmations of the Orch-OR theory.

This scientific phenomenon suggests the possibility of life after death, as the quantum information is released from the microtubules into the universe when a person temporarily dies. If the person is resuscitated, the quantum information is channeled back into the microtubules, sparking a near-death experience. If the person is not revived, the quantum information can exist outside the body, perhaps indefinitely, as a soul (Life after death: Soul continues on a QUANTUM level, https://www.express.co.uk/news/science/1005845/life-after-death-what-happens-when-you-die-soul-quantum). This idea of the eternal nature of the human soul is often discussed by theologians who claim that humans are not only flesh, blood, and bones, but also living souls that return to their maker for judgment after death. Dr. Hans-Peter Dürr, former head of the Max Planck Institute for Physics in Munich, claimed that "what we consider the here and now, this world, it is only the material level that has reality. Ultimate reality is spiritual" (qtd. in Charan, 2017).

These discussions on consciousness, quantum information, and the eternal nature of the human soul add another layer of complexity to the questions surrounding existence, the afterlife, and the possibility of realms like heaven and hell. They invite us to explore the boundaries of science, philosophy, and spirituality in our quest for understanding the mysteries of life and death.

In conclusion, recent scientific discoveries have reignited discussions about the existence of God. While some scientists have acknowledged the possibility of a divine creator based on the remarkable discoveries in fields such as cosmology and molecular biology, these findings do not provide definitive proof of God's existence. Science operates within the realm of empirical evidence and natural explanations, whereas the concept of God pertains to matters of faith, spirituality, and metaphysics. Different scientists hold varying views on the relationship between science and God, with some finding compatibility between their scientific endeavors and religious beliefs, while others maintain a more skeptical stance, viewing science and religion as separate domains that address distinct aspects of human experience.

It is important to note that although science has made significant progress in understanding the natural world, there are still vast phenomena and aspects of nature that remain unexplained. Some scientists point to these gaps in scientific knowledge and the intricate design found in the universe as evidence of a higher power. They argue that the complexity and orderliness of the natural world suggest an intelligent designer, subtly proclaiming the existence of God.

However, it is crucial to recognize that these assertions are based on inherent personal interpretation and philosophical perspectives, rather than empirical evidence, for it seems like God wants us to research and discover him not only by a physical undeniable proclamation of "Here I am, I am God the creator), but to be perceived at a heart level of submission. Science, by its nature, seeks to explain phenomena through natural causes and observable evidence, while matters of faith and spirituality often transcend the boundaries of scientific inquiry.

One Bible verse that aligns with this idea is found in Jeremiah 29:13, which states, "You will seek me and find me when you seek me with all your heart." This verse emphasizes the importance of a sincere and wholehearted search for God. It suggests that the discovery of God goes beyond empirical evidence and requires an earnest pursuit fueled by faith and a deep desire for connection with the divine. The verse encourages individuals to seek God not merely on a surface level but with a genuine and submissive heart, acknowledging that the understanding of God's existence and presence often surpasses the limitations of scientific investigation.

Therefore, while scientific discoveries may raise questions and offer glimpses into the mysteries of existence, the ultimate nature of God and the existence of a divine creator remain beyond the scope of scientific inquiry. The exploration of science and the contemplation of spiritual and philosophical questions continue to be ongoing pursuits for individuals seeking to understand the nature of our existence. Ultimately, the existence of God remains a matter of personal belief, shaped by a combination of scientific knowledge, philosophical reasoning, and individual experiences.

## Chapter 4

# Religion:

**RELIGION, WITH ITS** vast array of beliefs, rituals, and traditions, has profoundly shaped the human experience since time immemorial. It is a profound expression of our search for meaning, purpose, and connection to something greater than ourselves. In this chapter, we embark on a captivating journey to unravel the essence of religion, exploring its significance in human life and the intrinsic inclination that drives us towards its embrace.

Defining Religion and Its Significance: Delving into the complexities of defining religion is no small task. It encompasses a myriad of beliefs, practices, and customs that bind individuals and communities together in their shared quest for transcendence. From ancient belief systems to modern spiritual movements, religion encompasses a vast spectrum of ideologies, rituals, and values that shape our understanding of the world and our place within it. Religion is a cultural system of worship that relates humanity to the supernatural or transcendental, and it is characterized by designated behaviors and practices, worldviews, texts, places, ethics, and organizations (Geertz).

The Innate Human Inclination: Intriguingly, the yearning for the divine seems to be an integral part of the human condition. Throughout history, across cultures and civilizations, humans have exhibited a deep-seated inclination towards religious beliefs and practices. This innate longing manifests in our relentless pursuit of answers to existential questions, our rituals of worship, and our search for moral guidance and spiritual fulfillment.

The Importance of Studying Religion: To truly comprehend the complexities of human culture and spirituality, the study of religion becomes an indispensable endeavor. Religion, as a cultural phenomenon, provides profound insights into the values, norms, and aspirations of societies throughout time. By examining various religious traditions, we gain a deeper understanding of the human experience, unravel the intricacies of social dynamics, and appreciate the diversity of beliefs that shape our global community.

Embarking on this captivating voyage of discovery, we navigate through the diverse landscapes of religious thought and practice, unraveling the intricate embroidery of human spirituality and our relentless quest for truth and meaning. While the world is home to an estimated 10,000 distinct religions, it is noteworthy that the five largest religions- Christianity, Islam, Hinduism, Buddhism, and forms of folk religion- encompass a staggering 84% of the global population (Pew Research Center). Christianity, with approximately 32% of the world's population, stands as the largest religious affiliation, closely followed by Islam at 23% and Hinduism at 15%. These figures provide insight into the profound influence and prevalence of these major traditions.

However, it is crucial to acknowledge the emergence and growing prominence of modern religions, particularly in the Western world. New religious movements, spiritual practices, and secular belief systems are gaining traction and claiming a significant share of the world's population. These diverse belief systems, ranging from atheism to alternative spiritualities, pose new challenges and opportunities for understanding the complexities of human faith and belief.

The escalating diversity in religious affiliations and beliefs emphasizes the imperative for meticulous scrutiny and thorough examination of various belief systems. Scholars assert that the clashes and conflicts prevalent in the world frequently originate from divergent religious perspectives and interpretations. Consequently, comprehending the intricacies of these belief systems, encompassing their doctrines, values, and practices, assumes utmost significance in fostering a constructive dialogue regarding the indispensability and implications of these diverse beliefs. By delving into the intricacies of these systems, we can unravel the profound necessity of their tenets and assess their impact on societal harmony and individual spiritual growth. Moreover, some scholars contend that the intricate tapestry of religious diversity is not only a source of conflict but can also contribute to societal challenges such as crime. Careful examination and comparative analysis of belief systems can shed light on the underlying causes and potential solutions to these issues.

In light of these complexities, it becomes evident that a comprehensive study of religions, both ancient and modern, is vital in navigating the intricate fabric of human belief. By undertaking a scholarly exploration of religious traditions, we can foster a greater understanding of one another, promote dialogue, and strive for a world that embraces purity and truth amidst the vast arras of religious thought and practice.

**The Term Religion**

For many years, religious differences have caused disparity and anarchy around the world. However, the term "religion" as it is used today was not utilized by early believers. The word "religion" originates from the Latin word religio, which in the ancient and

Religion:

medieval world referred to individual virtue of worship, not as doctrine, practice, or an actual source of knowledge (Beckford). Max Müller, a philologist, stated that "religion" originally meant "reverence for God or the gods, careful pondering of divine things, piety" (Müller). Ancient cultures such as Egypt, Persia, and India also had similar beliefs about religion as an individual virtue. Medieval Japan had a comparable relationship between "imperial law" and universal or "Buddha law" that later became independent sources of power (Beckford). In other words, these ancient cultures, now referred to as religion, aimed to instill lawfulness, direct and maintain order among the natives, and were not solely associated with beliefs.

There is no Hebrew equivalent for "religion," and Judaism does not clearly distinguish between religious, national, racial, or ethnic identities. One of its central concepts is "Halakha," the Jewish Bible, meaning the "walk" or "path" that guides religious practice, belief, and daily life. The word "religion" was never known to them (Sacks). On the other hand, many religious sects of Abrahamic descent such as Islam, Christianity, Rastafarian, Samaritans, Druze, and others refer to themselves more as religions than faiths.

The current concept of "religion" as an abstraction involving distinct sets of beliefs or doctrines is a modern invention in the English language. This usage began with texts from the 17th century, as a result of the splitting of Christendom during the Protestant Reformation, and more prevalent colonization or globalization during the age of exploration, which involved contact with numerous foreign and indigenous cultures with non-European languages (Beckford). Some languages have words that can be translated as "religion," but they may use them differently, and some have no word for religion at all. The term "religion" received its modern shape in the 17th century, despite the fact that ancient texts like the Bible, the Quran, and other ancient "sacred" texts did not have a model of religion in the original languages, and neither did the people or the cultures in which these sacred texts were written (Beckford). The Greek word "threskeia," used by Greek writers such as Herodotus and Josephus, and found in texts like the New Testament, is sometimes translated as "religion" today, although it was well understood as "worship" in the medieval period.

The Arabic word "din" in the Quran is often said to mean "religion" in modern translations. However, up to the mid-1600s, translators expressed din as "law." In the 1st century AD, Josephus used the Greek term "ioudaismos," which some translate as "Judaism" today, even though he used it as an ethnic idiom, not one related to modern abstract concepts of religion as a set of beliefs (Beckford).

Terms like "Buddhism," "Hinduism," "Taoism," and "Confucianism" first emerged in the 19th century. Japan, throughout its long history, had no concept of "religion" because there was no corresponding Japanese word or anything close to its meaning. However, when American warships appeared off the coast of Japan in 1853 and forced the Japanese government to sign a treaty that opened the country to foreign trade, the Japanese were suddenly exposed to the idea of "religion."

The Japanese had no clear concept of religion prior to this, but they were soon introduced to the Western concept of "religion" as a formal system of beliefs and practices held to be true by its adherents. At first, the Japanese were confused by this idea, as the Japanese had no formal religious beliefs or practices. As the Japanese began to encounter foreign religions, they started to find ways to classify them in terms of their own understanding of the world.

The Japanese started to use terms such as "Buddhism," "Hinduism," "Taoism," and "Confucianism" to refer to these foreign religions. Such terms were created to help the Japanese categorize and understand these new religions. These terms were also used to distinguish between the various religious beliefs and philosophies of Japan and those from abroad.

**Religion is Relationship:**

Religion, as I have come to understand it, is fundamentally about nurturing and maintaining a relationship between God or gods and humanity. When people inquire about one's religion, they are essentially asking about their connection with a higher power that demands worship and models an individual's way of living. The Creator desires a harmonious relationship with us, and we, in turn, are called to cultivate a meaningful bond with Him. Looking back to the accounts in the holy books, such as the Book of Genesis in the Bible and Surat Al-Baqarah in the Quran, we learn that when God created Adam, the first man, He made him in His own image. Notably, God did not prescribe any specific religion to Adam. Adam and Eve had the freedom to explore and engage in everything except eating from the forbidden tree. Adam was not a Muslim, Christian, Buddhist, or adherent of any of today's known religions. The only Prophet he knew was God Himself.

Adam did not know about the Prophet Muhammad or practice circumcision, making him neither a Muslim nor a Jew. Observance of the Sabbath was not instructed to Adam, so he was not a Seventh-Day Adventist. He did not know Jesus as the Christ, so he was not a Christian. Adam never encountered Buddha, hence he was not a Buddhist. I do not aim to criticize religions, but it is worth noting that Adam had a perfect relationship with God without the presence of any of these religions, some of which have unfortunately caused strife and conflict that has claimed many lives. Adam's relationship with God was based on mutual understanding and friendship- a fellowship between two beings. God desired Adam to feel comfortable, which is why He provided him with a companion in the form of Eve (known as Hawa in Arabic).

In the Garden of Eden, God would visit Adam and Eve, and one might assume that His presence would evoke fear and prompt Adam to hide. However, their conversations were intimate, akin to a conversation between two friends. In one instance, as recounted in the Bible, God entered the Garden of Eden and did not see Adam rushing to welcome Him, as one might expect. Instead, God called out, "Adam, where are you?" (Genesis 3:9). Of course, God knew Adam's location, but He desired to engage with him on a personal level. This demonstrates that God yearns for a relationship of peace and harmony with humanity- that is the essence of true religion.

Following Adam, there were other notable individuals who enjoyed a commendable relationship with God, such as Abel, Enoch, and the prophet Noah. These individuals did not adhere to the religious practices as we understand them today; rather, they sought to know the one true God. Remarkably, God did not instruct them to undergo circumcision or provide them with the Ten Commandments. All they offered God was their love and a willing heart to know Him more deeply.

Abraham was declared righteous and pleasing before God, despite not having an extensive set of laws to obey (Genesis 15:6). The act of circumcision, for Abraham and his household, symbolized a spiritual commitment rather than a strict legal requirement.

It signified their separation from the moral impurities of the world and their dedication to a righteous and pure God. In an epistle to the Hebrews (Hebrews 11), we discover that it was not circumcision itself that made them righteous; rather, it was their unwavering faith in the invisible God. This faith continued to guide subsequent generations, including Isaac, Jacob, and the Israelites, leading them to the eventual reception of the Law of Moses and the Ten Commandments.

**My Personal Pilgrimage**

In my pursuit of truth and a deeper understanding of God and religion, I embarked on a journey filled with questions and introspection. Growing up in a strict Catholic family, I was raised with a devout adherence to Catholicism. Our home was filled with rituals of catechism reading and recitation, and attending Mass on Sundays was non-negotiable. My father ensured that we sat close to him, expecting our undivided attention and discipline throughout the service.

My aunt, Divine Kalibakya, a staunch Catholic and cousin to my father, often stayed with us for extended periods each year and took it upon herself to educate us about the fundamentals of Catholicism. Even before enrolling us in the parish, she introduced us to the seven sacraments, teaching us about their significance. Every evening, we would gather in the bedroom to pray the holy rosary and discuss the lessons from catechism.

From the young age of ten, I was well-versed in the doctrine of the sacraments, even before completing my Confirmation and Holy Communion at the St Maria Gorreti Cathedral. Catholicism was the only reality we knew and were permitted to explore. However, as my parents decided to send us to boarding schools, my exposure to different religions broadened. I encountered students from various religious backgrounds, including Protestantism, Islam, and Hinduism.

My first experience in a boarding school with a Muslim foundation occurred when I was eight years old. Although the school was under the ownership of a Protestant family at that time, Islam and Protestantism were the dominant religious influences. Throughout my secondary and high school education, I attended several schools, some religious and others not.

During my adolescence, I formed friendships with peers who possessed an interesting sense of humor but were also rebellious. Influenced by older students, I became increasingly defiant toward teachers, staff, and even my own parents. As a result, my father transferred me from one school to another, seeking an institution that would bring me down to my knees. He sent me to remote country schools, hoping that the experience would change my unruly behavior. Little did he know that these schools harbored even more stubborn individuals, sent there by their own parents as a means of discipline transfer.

In these schools, students formed gangs based on common interests such as sports, appearance, or the display of wealth. The gangs indulged in various illicit activities, treating crime as a source of entertainment. Physical altercations between students and teachers became commonplace and intriguing news for us. Drug abuse, violence, pornography, and sexual immorality were prevalent evils within these educational institutions and also posed constant unhealthy temptations to the students.

Upon completing my lower secondary education with better results than my father had anticipated, he granted me the freedom to choose the school where I would pursue my upper secondary academics. Seeking advice, I consulted some of my school friends, and together we agreed on attending a newly advertised school that had gained prestige and popularity through its extensive TV and radio campaigns. The prospect of being a student in such a renowned and impressive institution seemed appealing.

Accompanied by my father, I enrolled in the school and joined my peers, eagerly anticipating the journey ahead. Due to the extensive advertising efforts, the school received an overwhelming number of applicants, leading to the construction of additional classrooms and dormitories to accommodate the influx of students. The large student population worked in our favor, as it became increasingly difficult to stand out or be singled out among the sea of students all dressed uniformly in white shirts, white trousers, and green coats. Lower-level students, who were required to attend all classes (with no electives), found it easier to blend in with the upper secondary students and sneak into the student lounge during class time. The lounge was always bustling with activity, and the temptation to spend more time there than necessary grew stronger. Succumbing to this temptation, a few of my peers and I began skipping numerous lessons and evading tests for which we were unprepared.

The school administration was unaware of our actions until the visitation day, when parents were invited to review their children's classwork books and test results. On that particular Sunday visitation day, I found myself without any good test results to show my father, and we ended up in the headmistress's office, where I was labeled as one of the troublemakers among the senior five students.

One evening, while already asleep in my bed, I was awakened by the sound of students shouting outside the dormitory. Chaos ensued as students attempted to strike, prompting the intervention of the police. That very night, we were abruptly roused from our beds and instructed to kneel on the rough gravel floor. Interrogations commenced as we endured hours of pain, pressured to reveal the ringleaders of the strike. The following day, the school closed, and reports were issued to the students to take home. However, I did not receive mine as I had not taken the midterm exams.

My father, who was abroad on a business trip at the time, contacted me and instructed my elder sister to accompany me back to the school to meet with the headmistress and address the situation. It seemed that the headmistress had been assigned the task of compiling a list of suspected students to be expelled in connection with the strike. During our meeting, she attempted to manipulate us by asserting that I would be expelled if I did not admit to participating in the strike. Recognizing her tactics, I chose to remain silent in response. Consequently, we returned home, and my father instructed my sister Grace to find another school for both me and my sibling who was also attending the same school.

A year had passed since my lower secondary school graduation when we set off with our elder sister to a rural school, as per our father's decision. The journey took us through villages, towns, forests, and swamps, lasting several hours. As we arrived at the school, a sinking feeling settled in my heart, realizing that this was not the kind of institution I had envisioned attending. I attempted to propose the idea of exploring other schools to my sister Grace, but she hesitated due to strict orders and a limited budget, as every school required an application fee.

Reluctantly, we paid the required fees and completed the application and registration forms, accepting the reality that I would be joining an Islamic school located far from home and the capital city. When it was time for the school year to commence, my father had already returned home and provided us with everything necessary for school. He expressed his anger towards us for suggesting that Grace should seek out a better school than the rural Muslim school we were about to join. He sat us down to counsel us, but his rage seemed to consume him, as he began uttering negative and abusive words. As I sat in the living room, tears streaming down my face, his words made me question if he truly was my father.

The following day, my father drove us to his workplace and openly discussed my "stupidity" with anyone who would listen, including friends and relatives. The embarrassment and deep emotional wounds inflicted upon my sibling and me were overwhelming. Tears continued to flow uncontrollably from my eyes. I found myself questioning the very essence of our relationship, and I confided in one of my father's male employees, whom we affectionately called Uncle Kizza, about my doubts. In truth, that was the turning point when I started regarding my father as an adversary. It is with regret that I admit developing a strong, intense hatred towards him.

During the arduous journey to the new school, which stretched from the afternoon until late in the evening, and even into the night, my thoughts were consumed by my father. Hatred had consumed me to such an extent that I desired nothing from him, not even his financial support.

Eventually, we arrived at the school around 10 p.m., and the gatekeeper granted us entry. Several teachers, who were on duty, warmly received us and called upon some students to assist us in finding our way to the dormitories. Their kind assistance was a relief. The following morning, I awakened with an unprecedented determination. My sole objective was to excel academically and secure a scholarship, ensuring that I would no longer rely on my father's financial assistance. I resolved to do whatever it took to enhance my academic performance and survival skills. Being near my father under any circumstances was the last thing I desired.

I vividly recall an incident that occurred during the first week at the new school when the water supply ran short. In such situations, students were permitted to fetch water from a nearby borehole located just outside the school gate. As I seized the opportunity to fill a jerrycan, I caught a glimpse through the staff room windows of a fellow student enduring a severe caning administered by the head teacher. Intrigued, I asked a classmate about the offense committed, and I was astonished to learn that the student's infraction was simply failing to tuck in their shirt. My classmate further revealed that receiving twenty lashes was the minimum punishment for any transgression, and depending on the severity of the offense, a student could endure up to a hundred lashes. Even a Christian student leader, who happens to be my friend until now, had received a hundred lashes for engaging in nightly prayers near the dormitory.

The revelation of such stringent disciplinary measures left me in a state of shock. I pondered how I would react if I were subjected to twenty, forty, or more lashes. In my heart, I temporarily resolved that if faced with twenty lashes, I would refuse and willingly accept expulsion from the school. After all, I had already been labeled the worst son by my father. Although I had never been expelled from any school before, I was certain that my father would not be surprised if it were to happen. I chose, in my heart, to embrace that negative perception.

Nevertheless, driven by my earnest desire to secure a scholarship and distance myself from my father, I forced myself to adhere strictly to the school's rules and regulations. I diligently tucked in my shirt, attended all classes and study sessions, ensured punctuality, and demonstrated unwavering obedience to the school staff. Unexpectedly, this unwavering discipline garnered popularity among my peers and the admiration of the teachers.

My plan was to excel academically, earn a scholarship, graduate from high school, and subsequently join the military. In truth, my father did love me deeply, although he was not one to express it openly. I acknowledge that I had caused him much distress and pain. At that moment, however, I failed to consider the emotional, psychological, and financial toll my actions had taken on him. While his outpouring of negative words was excessive, perhaps both of us would have benefited from counseling during that trying period.

**My Silence and Meditations:**

Due to the emotional pain caused by my father, I made a conscious decision not to make any new friends at the new school. My focus was solely on my own studies and preparing to leave the campus. I attended classes attentively, always sitting in the front row to give my full attention to the teachers. I carried out most of my activities alone and refrained from engaging in casual conversations with fellow students. In the quiet moments I had, I found myself contemplating and reflecting on my life. I would sit in silence, pondering over my past, my present circumstances, and my future prospects. It gradually dawned on me that I had been a troublesome and directionless young man, with little hope of realizing my dream of becoming a successful international rapper. Thoughts and questions about how I could improve my life resonated loudly within me, and achieving a successful education seemed like the most ideal path.

At the school, students were divided into three religious sects: Muslims, Catholics, and "others," who gathered in the chapel where the Pentecostals held the most influence. Initially, the Catholic students were not given separate facilities for worship, but eventually, some Catholic teachers managed to obtain permission for them to have their own space. Islam was the only officially recognized religion at the school, while the rest were categorized as "others."

Being a teenager who wasn't particularly religious, I wasn't interested in becoming deeply involved in religious activities. My passions revolved around rap and hip-hop music, movies, and basketball, and attending church was not a regular part of my life.

However, all non-Muslim students were required to attend chapel prayers every Sunday morning, while the Muslim students gathered in the school mosque for their Darasa lessons. As a result, I had no choice but to go to the chapel and sit there, attempting to pass the time. On my first Sunday in the chapel, I arrived early, and as student leaders were organizing the seating arrangement. Moses and Bridget, whom I later came to know as the student pastors of the day, exchanged curious glances and engaged in a silent debate from a distance; it became clear that they had something to tell me. Eventually, Moses decisively approached me with a smile. He greeted me with a smile and asked a question that had never been posed to me before: "Are you born again?" Wanting to leave a positive impression, I smiled back and replied, "No, I am only a Christian." Moses seemed a little satisfied with my response and walked away. His approach left me with the sense that he wanted me to experience a born-again transformation, even though I didn't fully comprehend what it entailed.

At that time, my mother was the only clear example of a born-again Christian in my life. She had separated from my father eleven years prior and had joined the Pentecostal faith. Although I had accompanied her to a few church services, I didn't feel compelled to switch from Catholicism to Pentecostalism. The Pentecostal pastors often preached about deliverance from demonic oppression, sickness, and poverty, but I didn't believe I belonged to any of those categories. I didn't consider myself oppressed or sick, and as a seventeen-year-old, I didn't perceive myself as poor since I wasn't actively seeking employment or facing financial struggles.

I held deep affection for my mother, and while I had briefly contemplated embracing her faith, I was fearful of ending up in the same poverty-stricken situation she had experienced since becoming born again. When I was around ten years old, my mother had a successful hardware shop for building materials, earning her the nickname "Hardware" in the local area. However, when I visited her at the age of twelve, I discovered that she was always at home and only left in the evenings to go to church. I felt a great deal of pity for her because I knew she had very little money and yet had to support us when we visited her during holidays. This circumstance likely contributed to my father's explicit instructions not to ask her for anything.

As I observed my mother's devout prayers and consistent church attendance, I began to question why her life remained perpetually difficult. I started to feel that our prayers were merely acts of religious conformity and remained unanswered. My mother had no stable income apart from the small amount she received from renting out rooms in her house. She often borrowed money from tenants to manage her increased expenses when we visited her. Contemplating her hardships, I convinced myself (although it was merely my own interpretation) that her struggles were a result of her being born again. Consequently, I held the belief that becoming born again was akin to embracing self-destruction.

Given these preconceptions, you can understand the internal conflict that arose when Moses and Bridget aimed to guide me toward a born-again experience. During my evening walks to study sessions in vacant classrooms, I would often encounter a group of born-again Pentecostal students singing and praying fervently in some of the secluded classrooms. Their passionate preaching and prayers intrigued me, and I found myself captivated, stopping to listen and watch them for a few minutes. Gradually, I began to develop a growing awareness of the Christian faith, particularly the practices of the Pentecostals.

Simultaneously, as I pursued my "winter" revision sessions in the silent hours of the night, I couldn't help but overhear the loud audio cassettes playing Islamic teachings through the mosque speakers at dawn. Being alone, my mind inevitably wandered, contemplating the teachings I heard from the mosque and drawing connections to my previous knowledge of Christianity. Although unintentional, I found myself evolving into a quietly religious person, becoming more receptive and tolerant of God's purpose and sovereignty in my life.

**My Influential Friends:**

During my attendance at the Sunday chapel services, I maintained a distant and disinterested demeanor. My primary focus was checking the time, eagerly anticipating the moment when I could leave. However, one aspect that consistently captured my attention was the choir. Their beautiful voices, joyful expressions, and theatrical performances were a source of intrigue. Their songs never grew old for me, and they became the sole reason for my presence at the chapel. Gradually, the messages conveyed through their music began to resonate with me, igniting a desire for personal transformation and the aspiration to become a better individual.

It was through Kefa, my dormitory neighbor and a senior leader of the chapel choir known as "Echoes of Chariots," that I inquired deeper into religious beliefs. Kefa and I developed a somewhat close friendship through our daily interactions. He frequently sought my help in polishing his shoes, often borrowing my shoe brush for the task. It was during these moments that he shared insights into his Seventh-Day Adventist background, revealing that he had received his singing training in Seventh-Day Adventist schools and churches. Kefa, an affable and well-liked individual, had a diverse group of friends, including Isa, a Muslim classmate who occupied the bed next to his. Over time, I also developed a friendship with Isa. These two individuals became my first acquaintances in the Muslim school, although our relationships had yet to deepen.

Through conversations with Kefa, I probed further into the tenets of the Seventh-Day Adventist faith. It was during these discussions that I encountered the concept of certain dietary restrictions imposed on Christians. This was an entirely new idea for me, as I had grown up without any restrictions on my food choices. Surprisingly, Kefa and Isa, despite their different religious backgrounds, found common ground in their belief in dietary prohibitions such as avoiding pork. This shared conviction seemed to solidify their bond, and religion never became a contentious topic between them. Intrigued by their shared beliefs, I adopted similar dietary practices, yet I did not fully identify as either a Muslim or a Christian. In my perception, Islam and Christianity represented distinct but parallel forms of worship directed towards the same divine entities—Allah for Muslims and Jehovah or Elohim for Christians.

Emboldened by my curiosity, I embarked on an exploration of both the Bible and the Quran. Within these texts, I discovered a remarkable overlap in the reverence bestowed upon key figures such as Abraham, Isaac, Jacob, Joseph, King David, Solomon, Noah, Isaiah, Elisha and an array of prophets. In the Arabic Quran, these figures were referred to as Ibrāhīm, Isḥāq, Ya'qūb, Yūsuf, King Dāwud, Sulaymān, Nūḥ, Ilyās, al-Yasa', and many others. This realization deepened my fascination with the interconnections between Islam and Christianity, leaving me in awe of the shared narratives and veneration of these influential individuals.

**Torn between Two:**

I became increasingly fascinated with Islam and began accompanying my friend Isa to the mosque on Fridays and Sundays. I found myself captivated by the vivid stories and prophecies depicted in the Quran and the teachings found in the Hadiths. Many of these teachings invoked a sense of fear within me, leading me to question whether Islam held superiority over Christianity and other religions. The descriptions of multiple beautiful companions in Allah's Jannah (paradise) were alluring and motivating, while the accounts of the terrifying events of the end times and the Day of Judgment (Yawm al-Din and Yawm al-Qiyamah) filled me with a sense of dread and apprehension.

Isa took it upon himself to guide me in practicing the Islamic prayer rituals. Thankfully, this was not a difficult transition for me, as I had been exposed to Islam since my first years in boarding school at the age of 8. I easily familiarized myself with the ablution process and followed the group in performing the physical acts of bowing, kneeling, and standing during mosque prayers.

As I engaged in discussions with my fellow Christian Religious Education students, I couldn't ignore the numerous similarities between Islam and Christianity. These shared elements seemed to suggest that various religions and forms of worship ultimately directed their reverence towards the same God. However, my perspective was challenged by a classmate- nicknamed "Fidem", who boldly stated that I could not be both a Christian and a Muslim simultaneously. He asserted that I had to choose between believing in the authenticity of either the Bible or the Quran while considering the other as false.

His argument revolved around the contrasting views on Jesus. According to the Bible, Jesus is the Son of God who died on the cross to save mankind, and He is proclaimed as the sole path to truth and eternal life (John 14:6). In contrast, the Quran denies Jesus' divinity and asserts that he did not die on the cross (Quran 5:72–75). This contentious debate propelled me into a phase of intense research as I sought to uncover the truth about religion.

I felt a profound emptiness, realizing that my journey of character transformation would hold no meaning if I did not worship the true God. I found myself at a critical crossroads, torn between uncertainty about both Islam and Christianity. I sensed an impending inner turmoil and the weight of making the right decision, knowing that my entire life hinged on it. I recognized the need for an informed and reliable choice, as the consequence of my decision carried eternal implications. It became evident that humanity, as a created existence, must navigate life in a manner worthy of their maker, with the destination being either heaven or hell.

Through my extensive studies, I gradually comprehended the vast differences that set Christianity and Islam apart. These disparities created a significant divide between the two religions or faiths, as I now perceived them. I couldn't help but acknowledge how hastily I had reached conclusions with such limited research, especially considering that the eternal destiny of my soul hung in the balance. My mistakes could lead me to everlasting damnation, while the accuracy of my findings could potentially grant me eternal peace. It became apparent that I had been viewing everything through a veil, compelling me to rise to the challenge and uncover the mysteries behind religion and God.

This realization prompted me to embark on a journey of extensive research across different realms of faith, religion, and science. My aim was to discover the true, genuine, and righteous path to the one true God. Along this transformative path, I finally came to the profound understanding that religion, far beyond mere spiritual practices and norms, encompasses a genuine, evidential relationship between humankind and their Creator.

**Decision time:**

While I turned to the Quran and the Bible in search of answers, I couldn't ignore the undeniable presence of a gift of faith already residing within my heart. As I studied the scriptures, I encountered distinct perspectives on the concept of the Judgment Day, with the Quran presenting a different account than the biblical book of Revelation. It was a unique experience for me to read through extensive passages without the anticipation of tests or exams as I had in the past. It felt as though I was studying for the ultimate examination of my soul, placing the weighty volumes of destiny—the Bible and the Quran—on the scales of truth, while my very soul was also being measured on that same balance of truth. Deep within, I carried a resolute conviction that compelled me to continue my research, as if I had established a connection with a higher power that demanded my voluntary surrender and worship. After a few days and nights of intense exploration, I found myself in the quietness of the dormitory, surrounded by slumbering peers. Kneeling on my bed, I made a heartfelt confession of faith—the result of which I will share in greater detail in the forthcoming chapters of this book.

Chapter 5

# Ancient-Modern Paths and Sacred Traditions

**AS WE EXPLORE** the historical evolution of religions and their teachings, we unveil the intricate and diverse landscape of human spirituality. From the ancient foundations of Hinduism, Buddhism, Shintoism, Judaism, Christianity, Islam, and Taoism to the various modern belief systems, we unearth profound insights into the myriad paths individuals have trodden in their quest for meaning, purpose, and a connection with the divine. These time-tested traditions offer not just wisdom but a compass to navigate the complexities of human existence, illuminating the spiritual journey. To safeguard our souls, we must earnestly study these belief systems, for it is through understanding their teachings that we can make informed decisions about the paths we choose to follow, ensuring the well-being of our innermost selves.

Tracing the historical development of religions and their teachings provides valuable insights into the diverse beliefs and practices that have shaped human spirituality throughout the ages. By examining the origins and evolution of ancient belief systems, we can better understand the common threads and distinctive aspects that have influenced religious thought and guided people's quest for meaning and transcendence.

## Hinduism

One significant ancient belief system is Hinduism, which has a rich history dating back thousands of years. The Vedas, the oldest sacred texts of Hinduism, contain hymns, rituals, and philosophical insights that offer glimpses into the religious and cultural practices of ancient Indian society (Easwaran 22). The Upanishads, another important component of Hindu scriptures, plumb into profound metaphysical questions and explore the nature of the self and ultimate reality (Olivelle 12). These ancient texts provide a foundation for Hindu teachings and spiritual practices, highlighting the importance of dharma (moral and ethical duty), karma (the law of cause and effect), and moksha (liberation from the cycle of birth and death) in seeking enlightenment and union with the divine.

## Common Beliefs and Practices in Hinduism:

1. **Polytheism:** Hinduism is known for its belief in a multitude of deities, with each representing various aspects of the ultimate divine reality, Brahman. The most prominent gods and goddesses include Brahma (the creator), Vishnu (the preserver), Shiva (the destroyer), Lakshmi (goddess of wealth), Saraswati (goddess of knowledge), and Durga (goddess of power), among many others.
2. **Reincarnation:** Hindus believe in the cycle of birth, death, and rebirth (samsara). The quality of one's next life is determined by their karma, the accumulated moral and ethical consequences of their actions in previous lives.

3. **Karma:** Karma is the law of cause and effect. It asserts that one's actions, intentions, and thoughts have consequences, shaping their current life and future rebirths. Good karma leads to better circumstances, while bad karma can result in suffering.
4. **Dharma:** Dharma refers to one's moral and ethical duties and responsibilities in life. It varies based on a person's age, caste, gender, and occupation. Fulfilling one's dharma is seen as essential for leading a righteous life.
5. **Moksha:** Moksha is the ultimate goal of Hinduism, representing liberation from the cycle of samsara and union with Brahman, the supreme reality. Achieving moksha involves transcending the ego and realizing one's true nature, which is identical to Brahman.
6. **Yoga and Meditation:** Hinduism introduced the practices of yoga and meditation to the world. Yoga, through various paths like Hatha, Bhakti, Karma, and Jnana, offers techniques for spiritual growth, self-realization, and mental and physical well-being. Meditation is used to attain inner peace and self-awareness.
7. **Temples and Worship:** Hindus worship in temples where they offer prayers, perform rituals, and make offerings to deities. They often engage in aarti (ceremonial light offering), bhajans (devotional songs), and pujas (rituals) as part of their worship.
8. **Festivals:** Hinduism has numerous festivals, celebrating various deities and aspects of life. Diwali (Festival of Lights), Navaratri (Nine Nights Festival), Holi (Festival of Colors), and Ganesh Chaturthi (Ganesha Festival) are some of the most widely observed festivals.

9. **Ahimsa (Non-Violence):** Hinduism emphasizes the principle of ahimsa, or non-violence, as a core ethical value. This extends to respect for all living beings, which has influenced the vegetarianism practiced by many Hindus.
10. **Pilgrimage:** Hindus undertake pilgrimages to sacred sites across India, believing that visiting these places can cleanse the soul and accrue spiritual merit. Famous pilgrimage destinations include Varanasi, Rishikesh, and Amarnath Cave.
11. **Caste System:** Although officially abolished in modern India, the caste system has historically played a significant role in Hindu society, influencing social hierarchies and roles. It was initially based on occupational divisions, with people assigned specific roles in society based on their skills and professions. According to traditional Hindu scriptures, there are four main varnas or broad categories: Brahmins (priests and scholars), Kshatriyas (warriors and rulers), Vaishyas (merchants and farmers), and Shudras (laborers and service providers). Beyond these varnas, there were numerous subgroups, known as jatis or castes, which were even more specific and occupation-based. The caste system is hierarchical, with Brahmins traditionally considered the highest caste and Shudras the lowest. Outside of this system were the Dalits (formerly called Untouchables), who were considered so impure that they were excluded from the caste hierarchy and often subjected to severe discrimination. The caste system determined one's occupation, social status, and even whom they could marry or interact with. It created a rigid social order where mobility between castes was highly restricted.

12. **Iconography and Symbolism:** Hinduism employs a rich array of symbols and iconography, such as the Om symbol, the lotus flower, and the third eye of Lord Shiva, each carrying deep spiritual significance.

Hinduism's diversity is evident in the wide range of beliefs and practices within its fold, and individuals may emphasize different aspects based on their personal inclinations and cultural influences. Despite this diversity, the overarching goal remains the pursuit of spiritual realization, enlightenment, and union with the divine.

While Hinduism is undoubtedly one of the world's most ancient and diverse belief systems, it is not without its critiques and challenges. One notable concern is the historical caste system, which has led to social hierarchies, discrimination, and inequalities. Although officially abolished in modern India, its remnants still persist in some areas. Additionally, the multitude of deities and rituals within Hinduism can be overwhelming, and the belief in karma and reincarnation may raise questions about justice and suffering in the world. However, it's essential to approach any critique with fairness and an understanding of the cultural and historical contexts in which Hinduism has evolved. In my forthcoming analysis, I will apply a comprehensive five-level criteria to objectively assess the strengths and weaknesses of Hinduism as a belief system, providing a balanced evaluation.

## Buddhism

Another prominent ancient belief system is Buddhism, originating in ancient India and propagated by Gautama Buddha. The early Buddhist scriptures, known as the Tripitaka, consist of the Vinaya Pitaka (rules for monastic discipline), the Sutta Pitaka (discourses of the Buddha), and the Abhidhamma Pitaka (philosophical analysis) (Rhys Davids 67). These ancient texts elucidate the Four Noble Truths, which address the nature of suffering, its causes, and the path to liberation from suffering (Maha-parinibbana Sutta 11). Buddhism emphasizes mindfulness, compassion, and the cultivation of wisdom as essential practices for attaining enlightenment and breaking the cycle of rebirth (Walpola Rahula 89). By studying the ancient teachings of Buddhism, we gain insights into the principles of impermanence, interdependence, and the potential for liberation that continue to guide Buddhist practitioners worldwide.

## Common Beliefs and Practices in Buddhism:

### 1. The Four Noble Truths:
- *The Four Noble Truths are foundational to Buddhism. They articulate the nature of human suffering (dukkha), its causes (tanha or craving), the possibility of its cessation, and the path leading to its cessation. These truths provide a framework for understanding the human condition and the pursuit of liberation.*

## 2. The Eightfold Path:

- *The Eightfold Path is the practical guide to living a life that leads to the cessation of suffering. It consists of right understanding, right intention, right speech, right action, right livelihood, right effort, right mindfulness, and right concentration. Buddhists seek to cultivate these qualities in their daily lives.*

## 3. Karma and Rebirth:

- *Buddhists believe in the law of karma, which asserts that one's intentional actions have consequences. Good actions lead to positive outcomes, and bad actions lead to negative ones. Karma also influences one's future rebirths in the cycle of samsara, the cycle of birth, death, and rebirth, until liberation is achieved.*

## 4. Meditation:

- *Meditation is a core practice in Buddhism. It includes mindfulness meditation (Vipassana), concentration meditation (Samatha), and loving-kindness meditation (Metta). Meditation is a means to develop inner peace, insight, and wisdom.*

## 5. Impermanence (Anicca):

- *Buddhism teaches that all phenomena are impermanent and subject to change. Understanding impermanence is essential to overcoming suffering since attachment to things that change inevitably leads to dissatisfaction.*

### 6. No-Self (Anatta):
- *The concept of anatta, or "not-self," asserts that there is no permanent, unchanging self or soul. Instead, the self is seen as a combination of ever-changing mental and physical elements. This understanding is crucial to reducing ego-driven suffering.*

### 7. Compassion (Karuna) and Loving-Kindness (Metta):
- *Buddhists emphasize compassion for all sentient beings, aiming to alleviate their suffering. Loving-kindness meditation is a practice of sending goodwill and loving thoughts to oneself and others. Compassion and loving-kindness are seen as antidotes to negative emotions and sources of inner peace.*

### 8. Refuge in the Three Jewels:
- *Buddhists take refuge in the Three Jewels: the Buddha (the enlightened teacher), the Dharma (the teachings), and the Sangha (the community of monks and nuns). These provide guidance, inspiration, and support on the path to liberation.*

### 9. Ethical Precepts:
- *Lay Buddhists often follow ethical precepts, such as refraining from killing, stealing, lying, sexual misconduct, and intoxicants. Monastics follow additional precepts, including celibacy and minimalism.*

### 10. Dharma Wheel (Dharmachakra): 
- The Dharma Wheel, with eight spokes, represents the Noble Eightfold Path and serves as a symbol of Buddhism. It signifies the continuous cycle of teachings, practice, and enlightenment.

11. **Vesak (Buddha's Birthday):** - Vesak is a major Buddhist festival celebrating the birth, enlightenment, and death (parinirvana) of Gautama Buddha. Buddhists worldwide commemorate this day with acts of generosity, meditation, and reflection on the Buddha's teachings.

Buddhism is a diverse tradition with various schools and interpretations, but these common beliefs and practices serve as the foundation for Buddhist spirituality and ethics. Buddhists seek to understand the nature of suffering, cultivate virtuous qualities, and ultimately attain enlightenment, breaking free from the cycle of rebirth and suffering.

While Buddhism offers a profound and well-structured system for understanding suffering and pursuing liberation, there are areas where criticism and further examination are warranted. One notable aspect is the concept of karma and rebirth, which, while central to Buddhist teachings, can be challenging to reconcile with empirical evidence and scientific understanding. Additionally, the idea of "no-self" (anatta) might raise philosophical questions about personal identity, consciousness, and accountability. As a researcher, I'll apply a comprehensive five-level criteria to objectively assess the strengths and weaknesses of Buddhism in a forthcoming analysis. This will provide a balanced evaluation, allowing us to better understand the intricacies of this ancient belief system.

## Shintoism

Shintoism, deeply rooted in the cultural and spiritual heritage of Japan, offers a unique perspective on religion and reverence. This indigenous belief system, which has evolved over millennia, reflects a profound connection between the Japanese people, their land,

and the unseen forces of nature. Shintoism, often intertwined with Japan's rich history and traditions, emphasizes the veneration of kami, spirits or deities that inhabit natural elements, sacred places, and ancestors. Through rituals, shrines, and a deep sense of harmony with the environment, Shintoism embodies a profound respect for the spiritual dimensions of the world, making it a captivating subject of exploration for those interested in diverse religious traditions.

**Common Beliefs and Practices in Shintoism:**

1. **Kami:** Central to Shintoism is the belief in kami, which are spirits or deities. These kami are believed to inhabit various elements of the natural world, such as mountains, rivers, trees, and even ancestors' spirits.
2. **Reverence for Nature:** Shintoism places a strong emphasis on the veneration of nature. Practitioners believe that natural elements are inhabited by kami, and thus, nature is to be respected and preserved.
3. **Shrines:** Shinto shrines, known as "jinja," are sacred places where people can connect with kami. These shrines can vary in size and significance, from small roadside shrines to major pilgrimage destinations like the Ise Jingu.
4. **Rituals and Ceremonies:** Shinto rituals and ceremonies are conducted to honor and communicate with kami. These rituals often involve offerings, purification, prayers, and various forms of worship.
5. **Purity and Cleansing:** Purification rites, such as washing hands and rinsing the mouth before entering a shrine, are common in Shinto practices. These rituals symbolize physical and spiritual purity.

6. **Festivals:** Shintoism has a rich calendar of festivals, or "matsuri," celebrated throughout the year. These festivals often involve processions, music, dance, and offerings to kami.
7. **Ancestor Worship:** Ancestor veneration is an integral part of Shintoism. Ancestors are believed to become kami after death, and families often maintain household shrines to honor their ancestors.
8. **Harmony and Community:** Shintoism promotes the idea of living in harmony with others and with nature. It places value on community, both in terms of local communities and the broader Japanese society.
9. **Emperor Worship:** Historically, the Japanese emperor has been closely associated with Shintoism, and the emperor was considered a symbolic figure connecting Japan with the divine.
10. **Amulets and Talismans:** Many Shinto shrines offer amulets and talismans, known as "omamori," that are believed to provide protection, luck, or blessings to those who possess them.
11. **Visiting Shrines:** It is common for individuals to visit Shinto shrines for various life events, including weddings, births, and festivals. Shrines are also visited for guidance and blessings during challenging times.
12. **Coexistence with Other Belief Systems:** Shintoism has historically coexisted with other belief systems in Japan, such as Buddhism, and many Japanese people practice both Shintoism and Buddhism simultaneously.

Shintoism, with its focus on the reverence of kami and the natural world, offers a unique perspective deeply embedded in Japanese culture and history. While it celebrates harmony with nature and ancestral veneration, there are aspects that may warrant further examination. One such aspect is the concept of kami, which, being spirits or deities inhabiting natural elements, might be seen as somewhat elusive and subjective in comparison to more structured theological frameworks. Additionally, the coexistence of Shintoism with other belief systems, such as Buddhism, raises questions about the compatibility of these diverse traditions. As a critical researcher, I'll employ a five-level criteria to assess the strengths and weaknesses of Shintoism, providing a balanced evaluation of this distinctive belief system in due course. This will allow for a deeper understanding of Shintoism and its place in the spiritual landscape.

**Taoism**

Taoism, also known as Daoism, is a profound and ancient philosophical and spiritual tradition that has left an indelible mark on Chinese culture and beyond. Rooted in the concept of the "Tao" or "Dao," meaning "the Way" or "the Path," Taoism offers a unique perspective on the nature of existence, human life, and our relationship with the universe. With a history spanning thousands of years, Taoism has influenced diverse aspects of Chinese life, including art, medicine, martial arts, and governance. At its core, Taoism seeks to harmonize individuals with the natural order, advocating simplicity, spontaneity, and a deep appreciation for the mysteries of existence.

**Common Beliefs and Practices of Taoism:**
1. **The Tao (Dao):** Central to Taoism is the belief in the Tao, often translated as "the Way" or "the Path." It represents the fundamental, unnameable, and unknowable source of all existence. Tao is both the ultimate reality and the guiding principle of the universe.
2. **Wu Wei:** Wu Wei, often translated as "non-action" or "effortless action," is a key concept in Taoism. It suggests that one should align with the natural flow of the Tao rather than striving against it. It's about achieving goals through minimal interference and effort.
3. **Yin and Yang:** Taoism emphasizes the balance and interplay of opposites, symbolized by the concept of Yin and Yang. Yin represents the receptive, yielding, and passive aspects, while Yang symbolizes the active, assertive, and dynamic aspects of existence. Harmony is found in their constant interaction.
4. **The Tao Te Ching:** The Tao Te Ching, attributed to Laozi, is a foundational Taoist text. It consists of 81 short chapters offering wisdom on living in harmony with the Tao, humility, simplicity, and the art of governing through non-interference.
5. **Nature and Simplicity:** Taoism encourages a deep connection with nature and simplicity in life. Nature is seen as a reflection of the Tao, and by observing it, individuals can gain insights into the Way. Simple living and a minimalistic approach to life are highly valued.
6. **Meditation and Contemplation:** Taoist practices often include meditation and contemplation to quiet the mind, align with the Tao, and gain spiritual insights. These practices promote inner peace and self-awareness.

7. **Health and Longevity:** Taoism places importance on physical and spiritual health. Practices like Tai Chi and Qigong, which involve gentle movements, meditation, and breath control, are aimed at promoting vitality and longevity.
8. **Immortality and Inner Alchemy:** Some Taoist traditions explore the pursuit of physical or spiritual immortality. Inner alchemy (Neidan) involves transforming one's inner energy (Qi) to attain higher levels of consciousness and spiritual insight.
9. **Respect for Ancestors:** Ancestor worship and veneration are common in Taoist communities. It involves paying respects to deceased family members and seeking their guidance and blessings.
10. **Taoist Deities and Spirits:** While Taoism is generally non-theistic, it incorporates a pantheon of deities and spirits, each representing different aspects of the Tao and nature. The most well-known deity is the Jade Emperor.
11. **Feng Shui:** Feng Shui, meaning "wind and water," is a Taoist practice that involves arranging the environment to harmonize with the flow of Qi and the principles of Yin and Yang. It is often used in architecture and interior design.
12. **Taoist Ethics:** Taoism advocates virtues such as compassion, humility, frugality, and simplicity. Ethical behavior is seen as a way to align with the Tao and achieve personal and societal harmony.

These common beliefs and practices reflect the essence of Taoism—a spiritual and philosophical tradition that seeks to guide individuals on a path of inner peace, harmony with the universe, and a deep understanding of the Way. It is a philosophy that continues to inspire individuals in their quest for meaning and balance in life.

Taoism, with its profound philosophy centered around the Tao, undoubtedly offers a unique perspective on existence and our place in the universe. However, when placed in a comparative context, it might encounter some challenges, especially from a Christian standpoint. One notable point of contention lies in the non-theistic nature of Taoism, which, while appealing to those seeking a secular spirituality, deviates significantly from the monotheistic core of Christianity. Additionally, the pursuit of immortality and inner alchemy within Taoism could be perceived as an alternative to seeking salvation through Christ in Christian doctrine. The emphasis on simplicity and non-action, while fostering harmony and balance, may also raise concerns about passivity in addressing moral and social issues. Nevertheless, it is crucial to approach these critiques with respect for the rich mosaic of human spiritual beliefs and practices. In the subsequent analysis, I will subject Taoism to a comprehensive evaluation using a five-level criteria to assess its compatibility and coherence as a belief system.

**African Traditional Religions**

In the tapestry of world religions, African Traditional Religions (ATRs) may not always be prominently featured, but their significance and cultural richness cannot be underestimated. These belief systems, originating from various ethnic groups across the vast and diverse continent of Africa, have a historical legacy that predates many of the world's major religions. Despite facing significant challenges from the introduction of Christianity, Islam, and Western ideologies during colonial eras, African Traditional Religions remain deeply rooted in the hearts and lives of countless people. African Traditional Religions should be considered part of the world's major belief systems, acknowledging their enduring influence, unique practices, and profound beliefs.

## Common Practices and Beliefs in African Traditional Religions

African Traditional Religions encompass a wide array of belief systems practiced by diverse ethnic groups across the African continent. While the specifics of these religions vary significantly from one community to another, there are some common beliefs and practices that provide a foundational understanding of ATRs:

1. **Ancestral Worship:** Central to ATRs is the veneration of ancestors. Ancestors are believed to be intermediaries between the living and the divine realm. Rituals and offerings are made to seek their guidance and blessings.
2. **Belief in a Supreme Deity:** Many ATRs recognize the existence of a supreme, all-powerful deity. However, this belief may vary in emphasis from one tradition to another.
3. **Nature and Animism:** ATRs often incorporate animistic beliefs, viewing natural elements, animals, and plants as possessing spiritual significance. There is a profound connection to the natural world.
4. **Rituals and Ceremonies:** ATRs are rich in rituals and ceremonies, including initiation rites, agricultural celebrations, and healing ceremonies. These rituals are a means of connecting with the divine and addressing various life challenges.

5. **Oral Tradition:** ATRs rely heavily on oral tradition for passing down religious knowledge, myths, and legends. Griots, or storytellers, play a crucial role in preserving and transmitting this cultural and spiritual heritage.
6. **Community and Communal Living:** A strong sense of community is integral to ATRs. Spiritual practices often involve the entire community, reinforcing social cohesion and unity.
7. **Diverse Pantheon:** Some ATRs have a pantheon of deities, each associated with specific aspects of life, such as fertility, war, or wisdom. These deities are often invoked for various purposes.
8. **Sacrifices and Offerings:** Ritual offerings, such as food, drink, livestock, and in some cases- human sacrifices, are made to deities and ancestors as acts of devotion and to seek favor or protection.
9. **Divination:** Diviners or priests are consulted to interpret signs and messages from the spiritual realm. Divination is used for guidance on important decisions and to understand the causes of misfortune.
10. **Masks and Artifacts:** Intricate masks and artifacts hold significant spiritual symbolism in ATRs. They are used in rituals, ceremonies, and celebrations to connect with the divine.

While these common beliefs and practices provide a broad overview of African Traditional Religions, it's essential to recognize the diversity within ATRs. Each ethnic group and region may have its unique variations and interpretations, making African Traditional Religions a complex and rich fabric of spiritual expression.

As we move further into the intricacies of African Traditional Religions (ATRs), it's essential to approach our examination with fairness and respect for the rich cultural heritage and spiritual practices they encompass. ATRs undoubtedly hold immense historical and cultural significance, providing a deep sense of identity and community for millions across the African continent. However, in the spirit of critical analysis, we must acknowledge certain aspects that may raise questions.

One area of scrutiny might be the diverse and sometimes conflicting beliefs within ATRs. With countless ethnic groups practicing their variations of these religions, there can be significant differences in beliefs, rituals, and even the number and nature of deities. This diversity, while reflecting the complexity of Africa's cultural landscape, may also pose challenges when seeking a coherent and unified understanding of ATRs.

Furthermore, ATRs often rely on oral tradition, which can make it challenging to preserve and transmit religious knowledge accurately over time. This can lead to variations in myths, legends, and rituals within and across different communities.

In the forthcoming evaluation using the five-level criteria, we will explore these and other aspects of African Traditional Religions more thoroughly. This process aims to provide a comprehensive assessment of the belief system, shedding light on its strengths and potential areas for reflection within the context of contemporary society. Stay tuned for this in-depth analysis, which will offer a balanced perspective on ATRs.

**Judaism:**

Similarly, ancient Judaism offers a unique perspective on spirituality and morality. The Hebrew Bible, known as the Tanakh, encompasses the Torah (the five books of Moses), the Prophets, and the Writings, collectively revealing the historical and theological development of Jewish faith (Coogan 36). The Hebrew Bible recounts the covenant between God and the Israelites, emphasizing the significance of obedience to divine commandments and the pursuit of justice and righteousness (Deuteronomy 10:12-13). The ancient Jewish tradition values communal worship, study of sacred texts, and acts of loving-kindness as integral aspects of spiritual life (Neusner 45). Through exploring these ancient teachings, we gain a deeper understanding of the moral foundations and ethical principles that continue to shape Jewish identity and religious practice.

**Common Beliefs and Practices in Judaism:**
1. **Monotheism:** Judaism is firmly rooted in the belief in one God, known as Yahweh or Jehovah. This belief in the one, all-powerful, and all-knowing God is central to Jewish faith.
2. **Covenant:** The concept of a covenant, a sacred agreement, is fundamental in Judaism. The Hebrew Bible, particularly in the Torah, outlines the covenant between God and the Jewish people. This covenant entails the Jews' commitment to obeying God's commandments and living according to His laws.
3. **Torah:** The Torah, comprising the first five books of Moses (Genesis, Exodus, Leviticus, Numbers, and Deuteronomy), holds special significance in Judaism. It contains not only religious laws (mitzvot) but also the history and narratives of the Jewish people.

4. **Synagogue Worship:** Jews gather in synagogues for communal prayer and worship. The synagogue is not just a place of prayer but also serves as a center for community activities, education, and social gatherings.
5. **Study of Sacred Texts:** The study of sacred texts is highly valued in Judaism. Beyond the Torah, Jews study other texts such as the Talmud, Mishnah, and Midrash, which provide interpretations, commentaries, and discussions of religious laws and traditions.
6. **Shabbat (Sabbath):** Shabbat, observed from Friday evening to Saturday evening, is a day of rest and reflection. Jews attend synagogue services, light candles, share special meals, and refrain from work to honor and observe the Sabbath.
7. **Kosher Dietary Laws:** Kosher dietary laws dictate what foods are considered permissible for Jews to eat. These laws are based on the Torah and include guidelines on how animals are slaughtered, which animals are considered clean or unclean, and the separation of meat and dairy products.
8. **Circumcision (Brit Milah):** Circumcision is a significant religious rite for Jewish boys on the eighth day of life. It symbolizes the covenant between God and the Jewish people, as mentioned in the Torah.
9. **Acts of Loving-Kindness (Tzedakah):** Charity and acts of loving-kindness are essential values in Judaism. Jews are encouraged to help those in need, support their communities, and engage in social justice initiatives.
10. **Passover (Pesach) and other Festivals:** Jewish festivals, including Passover, Hanukkah, Rosh Hashanah, and Yom Kippur, commemorate historical events and religious themes. Passover, for instance, celebrates the Israelites' liberation from slavery in Egypt.

11. **Bar and Bat Mitzvah:** Jewish boys and girls become responsible for observing Jewish commandments at the age of 13 (Bar Mitzvah for boys) and 12 (Bat Mitzvah for girls). This milestone is marked with a ceremony and often involves reading from the Torah.
12. **Zionism:** While not strictly a religious belief, the Zionist movement, which advocates for the establishment and support of a Jewish state in Israel, holds significance for many Jewish communities worldwide.

These common beliefs and practices underscore the rich fabric of Judaism, emphasizing faith, community, ethical conduct, and a deep connection to sacred texts and traditions. They continue to play a vital role in shaping Jewish identity and guiding the lives of Jewish individuals and communities across the globe.

Judaism, with its profound monotheism, rich history, and ethical principles, offers a unique perspective on spirituality and morality. However, from a broader perspective, there are aspects that may warrant closer examination. One such aspect is the exclusivity of the covenant between God and the Jewish people, which can raise questions about inclusivity and how Judaism interacts with other faiths in a diverse world. It's akin to Judaism being in a wrestling match, facing challengers like Taoism and Shintoism. The challenge becomes even more formidable when Christianity, another opponent, lends its voice, alleging that Judaism is not fully inclusive. Additionally, the strict adherence to kosher dietary laws and certain rituals may pose challenges in a modern, multicultural society. However, it's essential to approach these questions with sensitivity and respect for the deep-rooted traditions and beliefs of Judaism. In due course, we will employ a five-level criteria to evaluate Judaism fairly, seeking to better understand its strengths and potential areas for reflection within the context of contemporary society. This examination will provide insights into the enduring significance of Judaism in shaping the lives and identity of Jewish individuals and communities.

**Christianity**

Christianity, one of the world's major monotheistic religions, traces its roots to the life and teachings of Jesus Christ. Christianity unites the Jewish Tanakh, known as the Old Testament, with the life and teachings of the Jewish Prophet Jesus (in the New Testament), forming the basis of its sacred scriptures- the Bible. Jesus, often referred to as the Messiah, is seen as the culmination of prophetic traditions in Judaism, and his life's mission was profoundly influenced by the Jewish faith. Christianity's foundation rests on the life, death, and resurrection of Jesus Christ, who lived in the region of ancient Judea in the first century CE. His teachings, as recorded in the New Testament of the Bible, emphasize love, forgiveness, and the establishment of the Kingdom of God. Central to Christian doctrine is the concept of salvation, which involves faith in Jesus as the means to redemption and eternal life. The Christian faith encompasses a wide spectrum of denominations and traditions, each with its interpretations of scripture and liturgical practices. Notable branches include Roman Catholicism, Eastern Orthodoxy, Protestantism, and modern Pentecostalism, each with its distinct beliefs and customs.

**Common Beliefs and Practices in Christianity:**

1. **Belief in the Holy Trinity:** At the core of Christian belief is the doctrine of the Holy Trinity, which states that there is one God in three persons: God the Father, God the Son (Jesus Christ), and God the Holy Spirit.
2. **The Bible:** Christians regard the Bible as their sacred scripture, which is divided into the Old Testament (shared with Judaism) and the New Testament. The New Testament contains the teachings and life of Jesus Christ and writings of early Christian leaders.
3. **Salvation through Faith:** Christians believe in the concept of salvation, which is achieved through faith in Jesus Christ as Lord and Savior. This faith involves accepting Jesus's sacrificial death on the cross for the forgiveness of sins. Christianity maintains that humanity possesses an inherent sinful nature and cannot attain salvation through righteous deeds alone. Instead, salvation is received as a divine gift from God, achieved through faith in Jesus Christ, who is regarded as the ultimate atonement for sin (John 3:16, Ephesians 2:8-9, Romans 3:23-24).
4. **Worship Services:** Christians gather for worship services in churches. These services typically include prayers, hymns, scripture readings, sermons, and the observance of sacraments, particularly the Eucharist or Holy Communion.
5. **Sacraments:** Many Christian denominations practice sacraments, which are sacred rituals. Baptism (Matthew 3:13-17) and Holy Communion (Matthew 26:26-28) (also known as the Lord's Supper or Eucharist) are the two most widely recognized sacraments. Baptism

symbolizes initiation into the Christian faith, while Holy Communion commemorates the Last Supper of Jesus with his disciples.

6. **Prayer:** Prayer plays a central role in the Christian life (Matthew 6:5-15; Philippians 4:6-7). Believers communicate with God through personal and communal prayer, seeking guidance, strength, and a deeper relationship with the divine.
7. **Christian Holidays:** Key Christian holidays include Christmas (celebrating the birth of Jesus), Easter (commemorating the resurrection of Jesus), and Pentecost (marking the descent of the Holy Spirit upon the apostles). These holidays hold significant religious and cultural importance for Christians.
8. **Moral and Ethical Teachings:** Christianity emphasizes ethical conduct and moral values, often guided by the Ten Commandments (Exodus 20:1-17) and the teachings of Jesus, including the Sermon on the Mount (Matthew 5-7).
9. **Service and Charity:** Christians are encouraged to engage in acts of service, charity, and compassion (Matthew 25:35-40). Many Christian organizations and individuals actively participate in humanitarian and social justice efforts.
10. **Church Leadership:** Christian denominations have various forms of church leadership, including clergy (ordained ministers, priests, and pastors) and laity (non-ordained members). Church leadership roles and hierarchy vary among denominations.

11. **Mission and Evangelism:** Christians are called to spread the message of Christianity, often referred to as evangelism (Matthew 28:19-20). Missionary work aims to share the faith with those who have not yet heard the Gospel.
12. **Creeds:** Many Christian traditions affirm their faith through creeds, such as the Nicene Creed and the Apostles' Creed, which summarize key Christian beliefs.
13. **The Second Coming:** Christians anticipate the Second Coming of Jesus Christ, a future event when they believe Christ will return to judge the living and the dead (1 Thessalonians 4:16-17).
14. **Variety of Denominations:** Christianity is characterized by a rich diversity of denominations, each with its distinct beliefs and practices. Major branches include Roman Catholicism, Eastern Orthodoxy, Protestantism, and modern Pentecostalism, with numerous denominations within each branch.

These common beliefs and practices illustrate the foundational principles of Christianity, emphasizing faith in Jesus Christ, worship, moral values, and the importance of scripture. While there is considerable diversity within the Christian faith due to various denominations and traditions, these core elements serve as unifying factors for millions of Christians around the world.

In the realm of belief systems, it's essential to foster fairness and respect while maintaining a critical eye, especially considering the various contenders that are willing to engage Christianity in a thoughtful sparring match. Each belief system offers its unique perspective on spirituality and morality, exemplifying the diverse range of human thought and culture. These challengers, including Taoism, Shintoism, Islam, and many others, come prepared with their distinct attacks on aspects of Christian doctrine and practice. Yet, as we subject Christianity to a rigorous evaluation using a five-level criteria, we not only unravel its strengths and potential areas of improvement but also witness how it stands resilient in the face of these challengers' criticisms. Join us in this exploration as we observe these spiritual contenders step into the ring with Christianity, each with their unique moves and strategies.

**Islam**

Rooted in the Arabian Peninsula and founded in the 7th century AD, Islam has a rich history, complex theology, and a diverse array of traditions and practices that have evolved over centuries. Islam, while drawing from elements of Judaism and Christianity, offers a distinct perspective by presenting a subtly revised narrative that centers around the prophethood of Muhammad and the final revelation of the Quran. At the heart of Islam lies a profound monotheism—the belief in one God, known as Allah in Arabic. Muslims, the followers of Islam, regard this belief as the central tenet of their faith. But Islam is far more than a simple monotheistic religion; it encompasses a comprehensive way of life that guides the spiritual, moral, and social aspects of its adherents. The Quran, Islam's holy scripture, is considered by Muslims to be the literal word of God as revealed to the Prophet Muhammad over a span of 23 years. Alongside the Quran, the Hadiths, which are collections of the sayings and actions of the Prophet Muhammad, provide further guidance on how to live a righteous life in accordance with Islamic principles. Islam is not a monolithic faith; it comprises various denominations and schools of thought, the two largest being Sunni and Shia Islam. These denominations, while sharing core beliefs, have some theological differences and historical divisions.

**Common Beliefs and Practices in Islam:**

1. **Monotheism (Tawhid)**: Islam's foundational belief is the absolute monotheism, proclaiming the oneness of God (Allah). This central concept underscores that there is no deity but Allah and that He has no partners or associates.
2. **Prophethood**: Muslims believe in the prophethood of Muhammad, the final prophet sent by God. They also recognize earlier prophets such as Adam, Abraham, Moses, and Jesus, considering them as messengers of God.
3. **The Quran**: The Quran is regarded as the literal word of God, revealed to Muhammad. It serves as the primary source of guidance, addressing various aspects of life, including morality, law, and spirituality.
4. **Prayer (Salat)**: Muslims engage in ritual prayers five times a day, facing the Kaaba in Mecca. These prayers are an essential act of worship and serve to maintain a close connection with Allah.
5. **Charity (Zakat)**: Muslims are obliged to give a portion of their wealth, known as zakat, to assist the less fortunate and support various charitable causes within their community.
6. **Fasting (Sawm)**: During the holy month of Ramadan, Muslims fast from dawn to sunset, refraining from food, drink, and other physical needs. This practice fosters self-discipline and empathy for the hungry.
7. **Pilgrimage (Hajj)**: Muslims who are physically and financially able are required to undertake the pilgrimage to Mecca at least once in their lifetime. The Hajj is a profound spiritual journey that unites Muslims worldwide.

8. **Respect for Family**: Islam places great importance on the family unit, emphasizing the roles and responsibilities of family members. Respect for parents and the care of children are highly regarded.
9. **Modesty and Humility**: Muslims are encouraged to embody qualities of modesty and humility in their actions, dress, and interactions with others.
10. **Community (Ummah)**: The concept of the Ummah underscores the unity of the global Muslim community. Muslims are encouraged to support and assist fellow believers.
11. **Diversity of Interpretation**: Islam encompasses a wide range of interpretations and schools of thought. While the core beliefs remain consistent, there are variations in practice and jurisprudence, with the two major branches being Sunni and Shia Islam.

These common beliefs and practices form the spiritual and ethical foundation of Islam, guiding the lives of over a billion Muslims worldwide. Despite its diverse expressions, Islam's core principles revolve around submission to the will of Allah and the pursuit of righteousness and community building.

In fairness, it's crucial to recognize that Islam, like any belief system, is not without its questions and complexities. As with any religion, interpretations of its teachings can vary, leading to different understandings and practices among its followers. Additionally, there can be challenges and criticisms related to various aspects of Islamic belief and practice, just as there are within Christianity and other faiths. In the spirit of fairness and intellectual exploration, we will later subject Islam to a comprehensive evaluation using my five-level criteria. This process will help us better understand how

Islam addresses contemporary challenges and stands as a credible and meaningful belief system for its adherents. Stay tuned for this in-depth analysis, which aims to provide a balanced perspective on the faith.

## Modern Belief Systems

In our increasingly interconnected world, where cultures converge and ideas transcend borders, a plethora of modern belief systems have emerged, showcasing the dynamic nature of human spirituality. Among these, a few stand out as particularly notable in their influence and distinctiveness. Alongside the Bahá'í Faith, Mormonism, Jehovah's Witnesses, and Rastafarianism we find an array of contemporary worldviews, each offering its unique perspective on life's meaning, ethics, and the mysteries of existence. Notable among these diverse belief systems are New Age Spirituality, Atheism, Agnosticism, Secular Humanism, Skepticism, Pastafarianism (Church of the Flying Spaghetti Monster), Raelism, the Church of the SubGenius, Scientology, Wicca and Neopaganism, Jediism, Transhumanism, Environmentalism and Eco-Spirituality, African Traditional Religions, and the Spiritual but Not Religious (SBNR) movement. Each of these belief systems draws inspiration from various sources, be it holistic healing, rationalism, skepticism, satire, science fiction, or nature worship, reflecting the evolving landscape of spirituality and philosophy in our contemporary world. In the following discussions, we will extend into the beliefs, practices, and impact of the Bahá'í Faith, Mormonism, Jehovah's Witnesses (Watch Tower), and later other modern belief systems with their common beliefs and practices.

## The Baha'i Faith

In the wide textile of world religions and belief systems, the Baha'i Faith stands as a relatively young yet profoundly impactful spiritual tradition. Rooted in the belief of the essential oneness of humanity, the Baha'i Faith presents a vision of unity, peace, and social justice that transcends the boundaries of nationality, ethnicity, and creed. Emerging in the mid-19th century, this faith has steadily gained recognition and adherents, resonating with those seeking a path that promotes global harmony and the betterment of the human condition.

The Baha'i Faith's teachings, inspired by the words of its founder, Baha'u'llah, emphasize the fundamental principles of unity, equality, and the elimination of prejudice. Its adherents, known as Baha'is, are encouraged to strive for the betterment of society through acts of service and the promotion of justice. As we research into the depths of the Baha'i Faith, we will uncover its core beliefs, practices, and its unique perspective on the spiritual and moral evolution of humanity. Join me on this enlightening journey as we explore the essence of the Baha'i Faith and its relevance as a growing belief system that attempts to give a message of hope and unity for a fractured world.

### Common Beliefs and Practices in the Baha'i Faith:

1. **Oneness of God:** Baha'is believe in the existence of one, all-powerful, and unknowable God who is the source of all creation.
2. **Oneness of Religion:** Baha'is believe that all major religions are part of a single, progressive process of divine revelation, with each religion providing guidance appropriate for its time and context.

3. **Oneness of Humanity:** Central to the Baha'i Faith is the concept of the oneness of humanity. Baha'is believe that all humans are equal in the sight of God, regardless of race, nationality, gender, or background.
4. **The Baha'i Prophets:** Baha'is recognize Baha'u'llah, born in 1817, as the latest in a line of prophets that includes Abraham, Moses, Buddha, Jesus, and Muhammad. Baha'is believe that Baha'u'llah fulfills the promises of these previous prophets and brings a new message for the modern world.
5. **Independent Investigation of Truth:** Baha'is are encouraged to seek truth through independent investigation of religious and spiritual principles. Blind imitation of religious beliefs is discouraged.
6. **Unity in Diversity:** Baha'is emphasize the importance of unity in diversity, celebrating the richness that different cultures, races, and traditions bring to the global community.
7. **Progressive Revelation:** Baha'is believe that God's guidance to humanity is progressive and that new messengers and teachings will continue to appear throughout history.
8. **Universal Education:** The Baha'i Faith places great importance on education for all, promoting literacy and knowledge as essential tools for personal and societal development.
9. **Service to Humanity:** Baha'is are encouraged to engage in acts of service and social action to promote the betterment of society, alleviate suffering, and work towards world peace.
10. **Prayer and Meditation:** Baha'is are encouraged to pray and meditate daily to foster a closer connection with God and seek guidance for their lives.

11. **The Nineteen Day Feast:** Baha'is gather on the first day of each month of the Baha'i calendar for a community meeting that includes worship, consultation, and socializing.
12. **The Baha'i Calendar:** Baha'is follow a unique calendar with 19 months of 19 days each, plus an additional period of "Intercalary Days" to reach a total of 365 days in a year.
13. **Fasting:** Baha'is observe a 19-day fast from sunrise to sunset during the month of Ala (March 2 to March 20). This period is a time of spiritual reflection and renewal.
14. **Marriage and Family:** Baha'i marriages are considered spiritual unions and should be conducted in accordance with local laws. Baha'is are encouraged to raise their children in an environment of love, unity, and spiritual education.
15. **Consultation and Consensus:** Decision-making in the Baha'i community often involves consultation and striving for consensus rather than voting.

The Baha'i Faith, with its emphasis on the unity of humanity and the promotion of peace and justice, undoubtedly offers a unique and admirable perspective on spirituality. However, as we explore its teachings, it's essential to approach them with a critical yet respectful lens. One point of potential critique lies in the concept of progressive revelation, which suggests that new messengers and teachings will continue to appear throughout history. While this idea can be seen as a way to adapt spiritual guidance to the changing needs of humanity, it might also raise questions about the finality of religious truth. Additionally, the notion of the oneness of religion, while fostering unity, might encounter challenges in reconciling the doctrinal differences among various faiths. These are aspects we will explore as we subject the Baha'i Faith to a comprehensive evaluation using a five-level criteria, seeking a deeper understanding of its strengths and potential areas for reflection within the context of contemporary spirituality and religion. Stay tuned for this insightful examination.

**Mormonism**

Mormonism, formally known as The Church of Jesus Christ of Latter-day Saints (LDS Church), is a distinctive and relatively young belief system that emerged in the early 19th century in the United States. Rooted in the teachings of Joseph Smith, its founding prophet, and the Book of Mormon, this faith has grown into a significant religious movement with millions of members worldwide. Mormonism offers a unique perspective on Christianity, claiming to be a restoration of the original Church as established by Jesus Christ. With its distinctive doctrines, practices, and a strong sense of community, Mormonism has captured the attention of scholars, theologians, and seekers of spiritual truth. In this exploration, we will delve into the core beliefs and practices that define the Mormon faith, shedding light on its history, teachings, and its place in the diverse tapestry of world religions.

**Common Beliefs and Practices in Mormonism**

1. **The Book of Mormon:** Mormons believe in the Book of Mormon as a sacred scripture alongside the Bible. They consider it to be an additional testament of Jesus Christ and believe that it was translated by Joseph Smith from ancient golden plates.
2. **Joseph Smith as a Prophet:** Mormons revere Joseph Smith as a prophet of God, through whom the faith was

restored. They also honor subsequent prophets, including the current president of the LDS Church.

3. **Restoration of the Priesthood:** Mormons believe that the priesthood authority, which they consider essential for performing sacred ordinances, was restored to Joseph Smith by heavenly messengers.
4. **Temples:** Temples hold great significance in Mormonism. These buildings are used for various religious ceremonies, including baptisms for the dead, marriage ceremonies, and endowment rituals.
5. **Baptism for the Dead:** Mormons practice baptism for the deceased, believing that it offers the opportunity for those who have passed away to accept the gospel in the afterlife.
6. **Family and Genealogy:** The importance of family is central in Mormonism. Mormons engage in extensive genealogical research to perform proxy baptisms and other ordinances for their ancestors.
7. **Latter-day Revelation:** Mormons believe in the continuous revelation from God to their leaders. They consider the President of the LDS Church to be a prophet who receives divine guidance.
8. **Tithing:** Mormons are required to tithe, contributing ten percent of their income to the LDS Church. These funds are used for various purposes, including building and maintaining temples and churches.
9. **Missionary Work:** Active proselytizing is a hallmark of Mormonism. Young men and women often serve as missionaries, spreading the faith's message globally.

10. **Word of Wisdom:** Mormons adhere to a health code called the Word of Wisdom, which includes abstaining from alcohol, tobacco, coffee, and tea.
11. **Eternal Progression:** Mormons believe in the concept of eternal progression, where individuals have the potential to become gods in the afterlife and continue learning and growing.
12. **Three Degrees of Glory:** Mormons have a unique belief in three degrees of glory in the afterlife: the Celestial Kingdom, Terrestrial Kingdom, and Telestial Kingdom, with varying levels of glory and reward.

These common beliefs and practices form the foundation of Mormonism, a faith that has grown and evolved since its inception, leaving a significant mark on the religious landscape of the United States and the world.

As a spiritual researcher and writer, it's essential to approach the beliefs of the Mormon faith with respect and fairness while also critically examining its tenets. Mormonism is a unique belief system with distinctive teachings that set it apart from traditional Christianity. Some concerns and criticisms that have been raised about the Mormon faith include questions about the authenticity of the Book of Mormon and the historical accuracy of Joseph Smith's translations, particularly given the lack of archaeological evidence supporting certain claims. Additionally, the hierarchical structure of the LDS Church and the unquestioning obedience expected of its members have been points of contention for some. However, it's crucial to acknowledge that every belief system faces scrutiny, and these concerns should be explored with a spirit of open inquiry.

In the spirit of intellectual exploration and fairness, I will later subject the beliefs of the Mormon faith to a comprehensive evaluation using a five-level criteria. This process will help us better understand how Mormonism addresses existential questions, moral dilemmas, and its overall coherence as a belief system in the contemporary world. Stay tuned for this in-depth analysis, which aims to provide a balanced perspective on this unique faith.

**Jehovah's Witnesses (Watch Tower Society)**

Jehovah's Witnesses, often recognized by their distinctive door-to-door evangelism and literature distribution, represent a distinct belief system with a worldwide presence. Founded in the United States in the late 19th century, this Christian denomination has evolved over the years, developing its unique interpretations of the Bible and theological doctrines. Jehovah's Witnesses are characterized by their fervent commitment to spreading their message, their particular understanding of God's name, and their rejection of certain traditional Christian beliefs. In this exploration, we will examine the core beliefs and practices of Jehovah's Witnesses, shedding light on their distinctive worldview and religious practices.

**Common Beliefs and Practices of Jehovah's Witnesses (Watch Tower Society):**

1. **Monotheism:** Jehovah's Witnesses firmly believe in the existence of one God, Jehovah, whom they consider the only true God.

2. **Rejection of the Deity of Jesus:** Jehovah's Witnesses reject the traditional Christian belief in the deity of Jesus Christ. They view Jesus as a created being, not as part of the Godhead. According to Jehovah's Witness theology, Jesus is identified as Michael the Archangel, a prominent angelic being.
3. **The Bible:** They regard the Bible as the inspired Word of God, but they edit a few verses to suit their narrative, emphasizing its literal interpretation and relying primarily on the New World Translation of the Holy Scriptures, a translation specifically produced by the Watch Tower Bible and Tract Society.
4. **God's Name:** Jehovah's Witnesses place a strong emphasis on using God's name, "Jehovah," and consider it crucial to their worship. They believe that restoring God's name to the Bible is essential.
5. **End Times and Eschatology:** Jehovah's Witnesses have a distinct eschatological belief system. They teach that Armageddon is imminent, and only faithful Witnesses will be saved, with the rest of humanity facing annihilation. After Armageddon, a paradise on Earth will be established.
6. **No Trinity:** Jehovah's Witnesses reject the Christian doctrine of the Holy Trinity, asserting that the Father, Jehovah, is the only true God, and Jesus Christ is a separate created being.
7. **Salvation:** Salvation in Jehovah's Witness theology is attainable through faith, active participation in evangelism, and adherence to Watch Tower Society teachings. They do not believe in the concept of eternal hellfire.

8. **Blood Transfusions:** Jehovah's Witnesses abstain from blood transfusions, believing it goes against biblical teachings regarding the sanctity of blood. They have developed alternative medical treatments when blood transfusions are necessary.
9. **Political Neutrality:** They maintain strict political neutrality, refusing to participate in political activities, salute flags, or serve in the military.
10. **Rejection of Holidays and Celebrations:** Jehovah's Witnesses do not celebrate holidays or birthdays, considering them of pagan origin or non-biblical.
11. **Kingdom Halls:** Their places of worship are called Kingdom Halls, where they gather for meetings, Bible study, and worship services.
12. **Door-to-Door Evangelism:** Jehovah's Witnesses are well-known for their door-to-door ministry, where they distribute literature and engage in conversations about their faith.
13. **Disfellowshipping:** The practice of disfellowshipping involves excommunicating members who violate Watch Tower Society doctrines or moral standards. Shunning is applied to those who are disfellowshipped.
14. **Leadership:** The Watch Tower Bible and Tract Society, headquartered in New York, plays a central role in the governance and decision-making of Jehovah's Witnesses.

Jehovah's Witnesses, often referred to as the Watch Tower Society, present a unique perspective within the landscape of non-Christian belief systems. It is crucial to approach any critique of their faith with fairness and respect for their deeply held convictions. One notable point of contention lies in their rejection of the traditional Christian doctrine of the deity of Jesus Christ and their identification of Him as Michael the Archangel. This stance challenges fundamental Christian beliefs about the nature of Jesus. Furthermore, the tight-knit and structured nature of the Jehovah's Witness community raises questions about individual autonomy and critical thinking. In the following analysis, I will apply a five-level criteria to the Jehovah's Witness belief system to assess its coherence and compatibility as a faith tradition. This process aims to offer a comprehensive and balanced evaluation of their beliefs, keeping in mind the importance of respectful dialogue in matters of faith.

**Rastafarianism:**

Rastafarianism, a distinct and vibrant belief system, emerged in the early 20th century in Jamaica, and it has since grown into a global movement with followers known as Rastafarians. Rooted in a unique blend of spirituality, cultural identity, and resistance against societal oppression, Rastafarianism offers a perspective on life, divinity, and the human experience that sets it apart from mainstream religious traditions. In this exploration, we will delve into the core beliefs and practices that define Rastafarianism, shedding light on its history, teachings, and its place in the diverse tapestry of world religions.

**Common Beliefs and Practices in Rastafarianism**
1. **Haile Selassie I:** Rastafarians regard Haile Selassie I, the former Emperor of Ethiopia, as a messianic figure and the earthly representation of Jah, the supreme deity. They believe in his divinity and view him as the fulfillment of biblical prophecies.

2. **Marijuana (Ganja):** The sacramental use of marijuana is prevalent in Rastafarian rituals. Rastafarians believe that the consumption of marijuana aids in spiritual enlightenment and facilitates a connection with the divine.
3. **Dreadlocks:** Rastafarians often grow their hair into dreadlocks, symbolizing a covenant with God mentioned in the Bible (Numbers 6:5, Leviticus 21:5). The growing of locks represents a commitment to a natural way of life and a rejection of societal norms.
4. **Reggae Music:** Reggae music, particularly the works of artists like Bob Marley, plays a central role in Rastafarian culture. The lyrics often convey spiritual messages, social commentary, and a call for justice.
5. **Ital Diet:** Rastafarians adhere to an "Ital" diet, which consists of natural, unprocessed, and pure foods. This dietary practice aligns with the principles of living in harmony with nature.
6. **Afrocentrism:** Rastafarianism embraces an Afrocentric worldview, emphasizing the pride, heritage, and identity of people of African descent. It advocates for social and economic empowerment within the African diaspora.
7. **Repatriation:** Many Rastafarians express a desire for repatriation to Africa, particularly Ethiopia, believing it to be the promised land and the homeland of Haile Selassie I.
8. **Rejecting Babylon:** Rastafarians often reject the socio-political system, known as "Babylon," that perpetuates oppression, inequality, and injustice. The term is symbolic of oppressive forces that hinder the progress of marginalized communities.

These common beliefs and practices form the foundation of Rastafarianism, a belief system deeply intertwined with cultural identity, resistance, and a profound connection with the divine. As we explore Rastafarianism, it's essential to approach its tenets with an understanding of its historical context, cultural significance, and the spiritual aspirations that guide its followers.

In the upcoming sections, I will subject the beliefs of Rastafarianism to a comprehensive evaluation using a five-level criteria. This process aims to provide a balanced perspective on this unique faith, considering its responses to existential questions, moral dilemmas, and its overall coherence in the contemporary world. Stay tuned for an in-depth analysis that seeks to appreciate the diversity and richness of Rastafarianism while critically examining its foundational principles.

## Other Modern Belief Systems

As we research further into the fabric of modern belief systems, we encounter an array of worldviews that span the spectrum of human thought and experience. Beyond the Baháʼí Faith, Mormonism, and Jehovah's Witnesses, we encounter a myriad of contemporary perspectives that challenge convention and offer unique interpretations of the human condition and our place in the cosmos. These belief systems encompass New Age Spirituality, Atheism, Agnosticism, Secular Humanism, Skepticism, Pastafarianism (Church of the Flying Spaghetti Monster), Raelism, the Church of the SubGenius, Scientology, Wicca and Neopaganism, Jediism, Transhumanism, Environmentalism and Eco-Spirituality, African Traditional Religions, and the Spiritual but Not Religious (SBNR) movement. Each of these belief systems contributes to the rich embroidery of human spirituality and philosophy, reflecting the diverse and ever-evolving nature of our collective quest for meaning, ethics, and understanding in the modern world.

1. **New Age Spirituality**: This eclectic belief system combines elements from various religious and spiritual traditions, emphasizing personal growth, holistic healing, and the interconnectedness of all things.
2. **Atheism**: Atheism is the rejection of belief in deities or gods. Atheists assert that empirical evidence should be the basis for beliefs, and they often promote secular humanism and rationalism.
3. **Agnosticism**: Agnostics maintain that the existence of gods or the supernatural is uncertain or unknowable. They neither affirm nor deny the existence of deities and often tend to focus on skepticism and critical thinking.
4. **Secular Humanism**: This worldview emphasizes reason, ethics, and the well-being of humanity without the need for religious beliefs. It promotes human rights, secular government, and social justice.
5. **Skepticism**: Skeptics approach claims and beliefs with doubt and a critical mindset. They seek empirical evidence and reject supernatural or pseudoscientific explanations.
6. **Pastafarianism (Church of the Flying Spaghetti Monster)**: A satirical religion that criticizes the teaching of creationism and advocates for the separation of church and state.
7. **Raelism**: Founded by Claude Vorilhon (Rael) in the 1970s, Raelism teaches that life on Earth was created by an extraterrestrial species called the Elohim.

8. **Church of the SubGenius**: A parody religion that satirizes religion, conspiracy theories, and consumerism, often described as "a religion for the sarcastic."
9. **Scientology**: Established by L. Ron Hubbard, Scientology combines elements of self-help, science fiction, and spirituality, emphasizing the pursuit of personal enlightenment.
10. **Wicca and Neopaganism**: These modern pagan belief systems draw inspiration from ancient polytheistic traditions, focusing on nature worship, magic, and rituals.
11. **Jediism**: Inspired by the Star Wars franchise, Jediism incorporates the Jedi philosophy into a belief system that values peace, mindfulness, and self-improvement.
12. **Transhumanism**: This movement advocates for the use of science and technology to enhance human abilities, including life extension, artificial intelligence, and merging with machines.
13. **Environmentalism and Eco-Spirituality**: These belief systems emphasize the sacredness of nature and advocate for ecological sustainability and the protection of the environment.
14. **African Traditional Religions**: Some African belief systems, such as Yoruba and Vodou, have seen a resurgence and adaptation in modern contexts, often blending with Christianity or Islam.
15. **Spiritual but Not Religious (SBNR)**: Many individuals identify as spiritual but not religious, seeking a personalized spiritual path outside traditional religious institutions.

These belief systems reflect the diversity of human thought and the evolving nature of spirituality and philosophy in the contemporary world. They often provide alternative perspectives (without using holy books) on life's meaning, ethics, and the mysteries of the universe.

In the arena of belief systems, there exists a tension that cannot be ignored. The world's largest religions, such as Judaism, Christianity, and Islam, find it challenging to reconcile their faith in a supreme creator and lawgiver with the seemingly contradictory embrace of modern belief systems. These modern worldviews often reject the existence of such a divine entity while advocating for unity and acceptance of all systems. It raises questions about coherence — how can one follow the path of science yet dismiss evidence of intelligent design pointing to a creator? Can one truly appreciate the multitude of world systems while denying the very foundation upon which these religions stand? This apparent paradox explains why major world religions often eye modern belief systems with skepticism, ready to scrutinize their claims.

However, it's vital to acknowledge that modern belief systems, like any belief system, come with their set of challenges and areas of ambiguity. Take, for instance, New Age Spirituality, celebrated for its eclecticism but occasionally criticized for the lack of a solid theological foundation. This leads to a wide range of interpretations and practices, raising questions about its core tenets. Similarly, Atheism and Agnosticism, champions of rationalism and skepticism, sometimes face inquiries regarding the nature of morality and the purpose of human existence in a universe devoid of divine guidance.

In the spirit of intellectual exploration and fairness, we are poised to undertake a comprehensive evaluation of these modern belief systems using a five-level criteria. Through this rigorous process, we aim to gain deeper insights into how these worldviews tackle profound existential questions, grapple with moral dilemmas, and maintain overall coherence in the contemporary world. Join me for this profound analysis, which seeks to provide a balanced perspective on the ever-evolving landscape of human spirituality and philosophy.

Delving into the historical evolution of religions and their teachings reveals the intricate and diverse landscape of human spirituality. From the ancient foundations of Hinduism, Buddhism, Shintoism, Judaism, and Christianity to the various modern belief systems, we unearth profound insights into the myriad paths individuals have trodden in their quest for meaning, purpose, and a connection with the divine. These time-tested traditions offer not just wisdom but a compass to navigate the complexities of human existence, illuminating the spiritual journey. To safeguard our souls, we must earnestly study these belief systems, for it is through understanding their teachings that we can make informed decisions about the paths we choose to follow, ensuring the well-being of our innermost selves.

## Chapter 6

# My Criteria

**THE QUEST FOR** understanding the existence of God and the pursuit of genuine worship and true religion have intrigued humankind for centuries. I firmly believe that every individual must embark on their own personal quest for knowledge and truth, enabling them to cultivate a robust and unshakable worldview. I am delighted to share my own perspective based on the methodology I have found satisfying in shaping my own worldview and belief system. It's essential to emphasize that every individual is free to establish their own set of criteria. In light of the enigmatic nature of these profound matters, I have formulated a set of criteria—a collection of guiding principles—to assist in the discernment of authentic religious belief systems. These criteria serve as a tool for evaluating and judging various faiths, helping us sift through the complexities of the spiritual landscape. They are designed to facilitate a thoughtful examination, even though the sheer multitude of belief systems in the world may make a comprehensive assessment a daunting task.

To navigate this intricate terrain, we will employ a method akin to "cluster sampling." This technique involves categorizing the diverse array of belief systems into clusters that are recognizable and comprehensible. Our primary clusters encompass:

## My Criteria

1. Ancient Belief Systems: This cluster includes belief systems such as Shintoism, Taoism, Confucius, and African Traditional Religions. These ancient faiths have deep historical roots and are often associated with specific cultures or regions.
2. Major Abrahamic Religions: This cluster encompasses Judaism, Christianity, and Islam. These are transcultural and international faiths with significant global followings. Judaism, in particular, holds a unique position as both an indigenous and a world religion due to its Abrahamic roots and its profound influence on major world faiths like Christianity and Islam.
3. Large Modern Belief Systems: In this cluster, we find belief systems such as the Bahai Faith, Mormonism, Jehovah Witnesses (Watch Tower), and other contemporary faiths. These belief systems have emerged more recently and have gained substantial followings in the modern world.
4. Other Modern Belief Systems: This diverse cluster includes belief systems such as New Age Spirituality, Atheism, Agnosticism, Secular Humanism, Skepticism, Pastafarianism (Church of the Flying Spaghetti Monster), Raelism, the Church of the SubGenius, Scientology, Wicca and Neopaganism, Jediism, Transhumanism, Environmentalism, Eco-Spirituality, African Traditional Religions, and the Spiritual but Not Religious (SBNR) movement. These belief systems often reflect contemporary philosophies and worldviews that address a wide range of spiritual and secular concerns.

By categorizing these belief systems into these distinct clusters, we aim to facilitate a more structured and comprehensible examination, allowing us to explore the complexities of the spiritual landscape with greater clarity and precision.

New-age religions, in contrast, may not explicitly identify as "religions" but rather as "collections of thought systems." They encompass a wide array of spiritual philosophies and often reject what some see as the exclusivity of Christianity, which teaches Jesus Christ as the sole path to eternal salvation. These thought systems aim to harmonize various religious beliefs and philosophies, claiming to promote religious tolerance, moral diversity, and moral relativism. They advocate for "pluralism" and "feel-goodism," claiming to emphasize personal well-being without causing harm to others.

**Section 1: Criteria for Evaluation**

My criteria for evaluating these belief systems consist of five fundamental elements: origin, longevity, relevance, accuracy of predictions, and the presence of evidence for God. For me, these criteria are vital in scrutinizing the authenticity and coherence of any religious belief system. They provide a structured framework for assessing the historical roots, contemporary significance, predictive accuracy, and theological foundation of each faith.

It is crucial to acknowledge that my five-level criteria are not the sole means of examining and evaluating world religions. I have benefited from the wisdom and expertise of scholars, including my esteemed American university professor, Dr. Travis Campbell, who has imparted valuable insights into other multifaceted aspects of assessing diverse belief systems. From him, I recognize that each belief system is built upon distinct worldviews, and there

## My Criteria

are alternative methods for their evaluation. However, the criteria I present here are the result of my personal analysis and spiritual-intellectual journey—a journey driven by a profound desire to discover a true, reliable, and dependable belief system upon which to anchor my soul's eternal security.

Throughout this journey, we must approach our task with the utmost respect and objectivity, recognizing that every belief system has its own unique perspective and significance. Our aim is not to diminish the value of any faith but rather to engage in thoughtful analysis, guided by principles grounded in reason and faith. Let us explore each of these criteria, understanding their significance in our quest for authenticity.

1. **Origin:** The origin of a belief system carries immense weight in assessing its validity. We must explore the historical roots, the circumstances surrounding its emergence, and the figures who brought it to light. Origin allows us to trace the lineage of faith, unraveling the narrative that underpins its existence. Through this lens, we can better understand the foundations upon which a belief system is built. It's akin to a building, where, no matter how beautiful it might appear on the inside or outside, it cannot be trusted if it is on a shaky foundation. Similarly, a belief system, for it to be authentic, must rest on a sure foundation with a credible origin. Just as a solid foundation ensures the stability of a structure, a well-established origin provides the groundwork for the authenticity and reliability of a belief system.
2. **Longevity:** The enduring nature of a belief system provides valuable insight into its resilience and relevance across time. Longevity is a testament to the enduring power of a faith

to sustain and guide generations. It prompts us to examine how a belief system has adapted, evolved, or endured over centuries and millennia. Additionally, I felt that a credible belief system should be one that was revealed to the earliest inhabitants of the earth or one close to such. This is because, in my perspective, people in the contemporary world might not necessarily have a superior connection with their creator compared to those in ancient times. The idea is that a belief system that has withstood the test of time, reaching back to the earliest generations, holds a unique position of authenticity and connection with the human experience throughout history.

3. **Relevance:** In an ever-changing world, relevance is a crucial factor in assessing a belief system's ability to address the pressing questions and challenges of our time. We must consider how a faith engages with contemporary issues, offering wisdom and guidance that resonate with the needs of today's society. Furthermore, I felt that the true form of religion should be one that genuinely cares about the worshippers and its adherence. It should be capable of satisfactorily answering the most important questions of humanity and offering reasonable guidance to the soul. In my evaluation, a belief system's relevance lies not only in its historical or doctrinal aspects but also in its capacity to provide meaningful answers and support to individuals navigating the complexities of modern life.

4. **Accuracy of Predictions (Prophecies):** A belief system's claims about the future, particularly its prophecies and predictions, provide a unique lens through which we can evaluate its credibility. We must scrutinize the accuracy of these claims and their fulfillment in history, for they

reflect a belief system's divine guidance and insight. In my assessment, for any belief system to claim authenticity, it must have reliable wisdom for the present life and the future. It must have a well-documented record of fulfilled predictions and also those of the future, both near and far. This is a critical aspect that underscores the legitimacy and trustworthiness of a belief system, as it directly correlates with its ability to navigate the complexities of human existence and illuminate the path ahead.

5. **The Power or Evidence of God:** Ultimately, the presence of divine power and evidence within a belief system is a central criterion for its authenticity. We must explore the manifestations of the divine within the faith, seeking to understand the profound experiences and encounters that affirm its truth. This is because growing up in Africa, I saw many people that were supposedly oppressed by demons and others living with highly deteriorated health and with little or no help. There was always a need for supernatural intervention in the lives of the African people. I, therefore, thought to myself that a true form of religion should be able to meet the needs of the suffering people and to do more than what human beings can do for themselves. And this would be the evidence of God through that form of religion. The lame should walk, the sick healed, the fatherless comforted, and perhaps the dead raised back to life. This tangible and transformative evidence of divine power is a testament to the authenticity and efficacy of a belief system, indicating its ability to bring about meaningful change and alleviate human suffering in ways that surpass human capacity.

Each of these criteria, while not exhaustive, forms an integral part of our framework for evaluation. They provide us with the tools to embark on a journey of discovery—a journey that transcends personal analysis and taps into the collective wisdom of generations. It is important to note that these criteria do not represent the sole means of examining and evaluating world religions. However, they represent a path—a path forged through personal analysis and intellectual exploration, driven by a deep desire to discover a true, reliable, and dependable belief system that can anchor our eternal security.

## 1.2: Ancient Belief Systems

In the tapestry of human history, ancient belief systems weave intricate patterns that have shaped cultures, philosophies, and spiritual landscapes across the globe. It is essential to acknowledge their significance in the broader context of religious diversity, for they have profoundly impacted humanity's understanding of the divine and the human experience.

These belief systems, including Buddhism, have left an enduring legacy, influencing not only the spiritual realm but also culture, philosophy, and ethics. Their contributions to the mosaic of human thought cannot be denied, and it is with this acknowledgment that we approach the task of evaluation. It is our intent to engage in a respectful and objective analysis, recognizing the historical and cultural value these faiths hold.

## 1.2.1. Buddhism

**Origin:** Buddhism, tracing its roots to Siddhartha Gautama, emerged in the ancient Indian subcontinent. While its origin is indisputable, the circumstances surrounding Siddhartha's enlightenment and the absence of historical documentation leave room for interpretation and skepticism. The absence of concrete evidence regarding the Buddha's life and teachings during his time raises questions about the reliability of its origin story. Additionally, Buddhism does not claim to know the actual origin of the universe. It has no recorded text or passage indicating the creation or formation of the known universe and creatures. This, for me, feels like following Buddhism, I would be a blind follower.

Example of Limitation: For instance, the story of Siddhartha's enlightenment under the Bodhi tree, while profoundly inspiring, lacks empirical evidence. This lack of historical documentation leaves room for doubt and the possibility of mythologization over time. The absence of a clear narrative on the origin of the universe further adds to the limitations, as it leaves followers without a foundational understanding of their existence and purpose within the broader cosmic context.

**Longevity:** Buddhism's longevity is undeniable, spreading across Asia and evolving into various schools of thought. However, the enduring nature of Buddhism has not always translated into unchanging teachings. The proliferation of sects and interpretations highlights the fluidity of Buddhist doctrine, which can be viewed as both a strength and a weakness. Despite its long history, Buddhism fails to provide recorded texts or passages indicating the actual formation or creation of the known universe and all its inhabitants, raising questions about its status as the earliest form of worship.

*Example of Limitation:* The existence of numerous Buddhist sects, each with its own interpretation of Buddhist teachings, raises questions about the consistency and authenticity of Buddhist doctrine. This diversity can lead to confusion among adherents and skeptics alike. The lack of a clear narrative on the origin of the universe further adds to the limitations, as it leaves followers without a foundational understanding of their existence and purpose within the broader cosmic context.

**Relevance:** Buddhism's teachings on mindfulness, compassion, and inner peace have undeniably found resonance in the modern world. Yet, the relevance of Buddhism varies across cultures and regions. Its philosophical intricacies can be challenging for some to integrate into their daily lives, and the practical application of Buddhist principles may not universally address the contemporary issues and challenges we face.

*Example of Limitation:* While mindfulness and meditation have gained popularity, the complex metaphysical aspects of Buddhism, such as the cycle of rebirth and karma, may be challenging for individuals in non-Buddhist cultures to fully embrace and apply in their lives. Moreover, the fundamental concept of "anatta," or the denial of self, can present a significant limitation.

*Limitation of Denial of Self:* One notable limitation arises from Buddhism's core concept of "anatta," the doctrine that denies the existence of a permanent, unchanging self. While this philosophical idea may lead to a sense of detachment and inner peace, it can also raise ethical concerns regarding accountability for one's actions.

The denial of self can be interpreted as negating personal responsibility and individual agency. If one asserts, "I do not exist" without a clear reference to the self ("I"), it potentially erodes the foundation of moral accountability and the basis for law and order in society. In many cultures, legal and ethical systems rely on the notion of personal responsibility, where individuals are held accountable for their actions. Buddhism's denial of self, in this context, may be seen as incompatible with the principles that underpin systems of justice and governance in many societies.

While Buddhism's emphasis on compassion and mindfulness has its merits, the philosophical complexities, coupled with the denial of self, pose significant challenges in terms of addressing fundamental aspects of human existence, including personal responsibility and accountability for one's actions. These limitations underscore the importance of considering the broader implications of certain metaphysical philosophies within ancient belief systems.

**Accuracy of Predictions (Prophecies):** Buddhism lacks explicit prophecies or predictions in the way some other belief systems do. Instead, it offers insights into the nature of suffering and the path to liberation. However, these insights are open to interpretation, and the subjective nature of enlightenment experiences leaves room for skepticism regarding the accuracy of its spiritual claims.

*Example of Limitation:* The absence of specific prophetic elements in Buddhism can be viewed as a limitation for those seeking clear, verifiable predictions about the future, which are more commonly found in some other religious traditions such as Abrahamic belief systems.

**The Power or Evidence of God:** Buddhism does not revolve around a personal deity or a divine presence in the same way as some other religions. While it acknowledges various celestial beings, the absence of a central God figure raises questions about the presence of divine power or evidence within Buddhism. Its emphasis on self-realization may not satisfy those seeking a personal connection with a higher power.

Example of Limitation: For individuals seeking a personal relationship with a deity or a clear divine presence, Buddhism's focus on individual enlightenment and the absence of a personal God can be seen as a limitation. The idea that one must discover oneself as a god for self-actualization might be insufficient for those in vulnerable and confused states, such as teenagers in need of guidance. Suggesting that individuals are gods who need self-discovery could lead to more questions and confusion, as it contradicts the concept of a God who is perfect, all-powerful, and all-knowing.

In our evaluation of Buddhism, it becomes evident that while it has its merits, it largely presents limitations and ambiguities. The Buddha's teachings, while profound, leave room for interpretation and skepticism, especially in matters related to origin and divine presence. As we continue our exploration of ancient belief systems, we will encounter further complexities and nuances that will contribute to our overall assessment of these faiths.

## 1.2.2. Hinduism

**Origin:** Hinduism, often hailed as one of the world's oldest religious traditions, boasts a rich and diverse fabric of beliefs and practices. However, this very diversity poses a significant challenge when it comes to tracing its origins. While Hinduism is deeply rooted in the Indian subcontinent, it lacks a specific historical founder or a single foundational text. This absence of a clear and documented origin story raises questions about the reliability of its historical roots and the authenticity of its claims.

Example of Limitation: The complexity of Hinduism's origin is exemplified by the vast array of scriptures, philosophies, and traditions it encompasses, making it challenging to pinpoint a single, concrete origin or a central figure like those found in some other religions.

Similar to Buddhism, Hinduism also does not claim to know the actual origin of the universe. It lacks a recorded text or passage indicating the creation or formation of the known universe and creatures. This aspect may raise concerns for those seeking a belief system with a more explicit and documented understanding of the origin of existence. The absence of such clarity might make followers feel like they are following without a clear foundation.

**Longevity:** Hinduism's enduring influence on Indian culture and spirituality over thousands of years is undeniable. However, this longevity comes with its own set of limitations. While some may view this continuity as a testament to its strength, others might argue that the lack of significant change or evolution within the religion raises questions about its adaptability and relevance in a rapidly changing world.

*Example of Limitation:* The persistence of certain practices within Hinduism, such as the caste system, raises ethical concerns and may be seen as a limitation. Despite efforts at reform, the caste system continues to impact millions of people, leading to social inequality and discrimination. This presents a stark contradiction between the ideals of equality and compassion often associated with Hinduism and the harsh realities of social hierarchies ingrained in certain segments of its practice.

*Another Limitation:* Some individuals attribute Hinduism's remarkable longevity not to its inherent spiritual strength but to extraterrestrial beings, such as the ancient fallen angels. This perspective arises from the belief that Hinduism's plethora of deities with unconventional forms—combining human and animal features, multiple limbs, and surreal appearances—may have been inspired or influenced by beings from beyond Earth. While this interpretation remains speculative and calls for the search for empirical evidence, it underscores the complexity and mystery surrounding the religion's origin and continued existence.

Moreover, because Hinduism, like Buddhism, fails to show any recorded texts or passages indicating the actual formation of the known universe and all its inhabitants, some may find it challenging to consider Hinduism as the earliest form of worship. For me, the Bible's narrative provided a more logical foundation, emphasizing the idea that the creator would reveal himself to the creature, a concept that Hinduism appears to lack.

**Relevance:** Hinduism's philosophical concepts, rituals, and practices have undoubtedly left an indelible mark on Indian culture and spirituality. However, assessing its relevance in contemporary society beyond the Indian subcontinent can be a complex endeavor. Hinduism's multifaceted belief system, with concepts like karma, dharma, and reincarnation, may not always easily align with the worldview of individuals from different cultural backgrounds.

*Example of Limitation:* While yoga and meditation, rooted in Hinduism, have gained global popularity, the broader metaphysical aspects of the religion, such as belief in multiple gods and the intricate cosmology, may be challenging for individuals from non-Hindu cultures to fully grasp and integrate into their lives.

**Accuracy of Predictions (Prophecies):** Hinduism presents a unique challenge in terms of evaluating predictions or prophecies, as it lacks a centralized system of prophetic claims. While the Vedas contain glimpses of future events and cycles of time, these predictions are often subject to interpretation and symbolic representation.

*Example of Limitation:* The Vedas' prophetic elements, such as the concept of Yugas (cosmic ages), are highly symbolic and open to diverse interpretations. This ambiguity may make it challenging to assess their accuracy or relevance in a concrete, verifiable manner.

**The Presence of Divine Beings:** Hinduism's polytheistic nature, with its multitude of deities and manifestations of the divine, raises questions about the nature of divinity and the presence of God. The variety of gods and goddesses, while rich in symbolism and mythology, can lead to theological complexity and ambiguity.

*Example of Limitation:* The diversity of deities within Hinduism, while a source of spiritual richness for many, can also be viewed as a theological limitation. It may raise questions about the nature of ultimate reality and the challenge of reconciling monotheistic perspectives with Hinduism's polytheistic framework.

In our evaluation of Hinduism, we find that while it possesses a rich cultural and spiritual heritage, it also presents significant limitations. The complexity of its origin, coupled with the persistence of certain practices that perpetuate social inequality, raises ethical concerns. The multifaceted nature of Hindu beliefs and rituals can pose challenges to its universal relevance. Additionally, the ambiguity surrounding prophetic elements and the theological intricacies of multiple deities contribute to the complexities and limitations of Hinduism as a belief system.

**1.2.3: Shintoism**

**Origin:** Shintoism, as the indigenous religion of Japan, possesses a unique historical context. Its roots are deeply intertwined with Japanese culture and mythology, tracing back to the earliest recorded history of the Japanese archipelago. However, the very nature of Shintoism as a collection of beliefs, rituals, and practices without a centralized sacred text or a single founder raises questions about its historical origins.

*Example of Limitation:* The absence of a single origin story or a central religious figure can make it challenging to establish a clear and documented history of Shintoism. This lack of historical documentation leaves room for various interpretations and skepticism.

Similar to other belief systems we've explored, Shintoism also does not claim to know the origin of the known universe and lacks recorded texts indicating the creation or formation of the universe and its inhabitants. This perceived inadequacy raises questions about Shintoism's ability to provide a comprehensive understanding of the fundamental questions regarding existence. For me, the absence of such foundational information seemed to suggest a limitation in the completeness of Shintoism as a belief system.

**Longevity:** Shintoism's longevity is indeed noteworthy, as it has played a significant role in shaping Japanese identity and culture for centuries. Nevertheless, the enduring nature of Shintoism is marked by its relative isolation and resistance to significant change or adaptation, even in the face of modernization.

*Example of Limitation:* While some view the preservation of Shinto traditions as a testament to cultural heritage, others argue that its limited adaptability and reluctance to evolve raise questions about its ability to address the evolving needs of modern society. Shintoism's focus on tradition and the veneration of kami (spirits) can sometimes clash with contemporary values and social dynamics.

**Relevance:** Shintoism's deep connection with nature and its emphasis on ancestor veneration have found resonance in modern Japan. However, the relevance of Shinto practices and beliefs is primarily confined to Japan and its cultural context. The unique characteristics of Shinto rituals, such as the reverence of kami and the importance of purification ceremonies, may not easily translate to or resonate with individuals from diverse cultural backgrounds.

*Example of Limitation:* The centrality of kami in Shintoism, while meaningful to the Japanese people, can be challenging for individuals from outside Japan to relate to or understand fully. This cultural specificity limits the universal appeal and relevance of Shintoism as a global belief system.

**Accuracy of Predictions (Prophecies):** Shintoism does not primarily focus on prophetic or predictive elements in the same way as some other belief systems. Instead, it places a strong emphasis on rituals, purity, and harmony with nature. While divination practices exist within Shintoism, they are often symbolic and open to interpretation.

*Example of Limitation:* Shinto divination practices, such as omikuji (fortune-telling), provide guidance and insights but do not offer explicit, verifiable predictions about the future. This lack of specificity in predictive elements may leave some individuals seeking more concrete answers unsatisfied.

**The Role of Kami (Spirits or Deities):** Shintoism's core belief in kami, often described as spirits or deities, underscores its unique religious landscape. However, the diversity and multiplicity of kami can lead to theological complexity and ambiguity, especially when compared to monotheistic belief systems.

*Example of Limitation:* The presence of numerous kami with distinct attributes and characteristics can be seen as a limitation, as it raises questions about the nature of ultimate reality and the potential for conflicting divine wills or purposes within the Shinto pantheon.

In our evaluation of Shintoism, we recognize its cultural significance and historical importance in Japan. However, it is important to acknowledge the limitations associated with its lack of a clear historical origin, its limited adaptability to modern contexts outside Japan, the cultural specificity of its practices, the absence of explicit prophetic elements, and the theological complexities arising from the multiplicity of kami. These limitations contribute to a nuanced understanding of Shintoism within the broader context of belief systems.

**1.2.4: Taoism**

**Origin:** Taoism, a philosophical and religious tradition originating in ancient China, is deeply rooted in the enigmatic teachings of Laozi, primarily recorded in the Tao Te Ching. However, its origin presents inherent challenges. Laozi himself remains a mysterious figure, and the dating of the Tao Te Ching is subject to debate. This lack of concrete historical evidence surrounding the founder and the text's origin raises questions about the authenticity of Taoism's historical roots.

*Example of Limitation:* The ambiguity surrounding Laozi's existence and the transmission of his teachings can lead to skepticism and doubts about the precise historical origins of Taoism, making it difficult to establish a definitive historical narrative.

*Additional Example of Limitation:* Furthermore, the use of the dragon as a symbol within Taoism, a creature often associated with ancient pagan beliefs and the worship of forces of power and destruction, raises questions about the potential syncretic elements within Taoist practices. While the dragon holds cultural significance in China, its presence as a symbol hints at the possibility of Taoism's historical connections to earlier belief systems and idol worship.

Similar to other belief systems we've explored, Taoism also does not claim to know the origin of the known universe and lacks recorded texts indicating the creation or formation of the universe and its inhabitants. This perceived inadequacy raises questions about Taoism's ability to provide a comprehensive understanding of the fundamental questions regarding existence. For me, the absence of such foundational information seemed to suggest a limitation in the completeness of Taoism as a belief system.

These multiple layers of ambiguity and potential syncretism contribute to the complexity surrounding Taoism's historical origins and its relationship with other belief systems.

**Longevity:** Taoism's longevity is indeed remarkable, as it has deeply influenced Chinese culture for millennia. It has left an indelible mark on various facets of Chinese life, from art and philosophy to martial arts and traditional medicine. However, the very nature of Taoism's enduring influence can be seen as a limitation when considering its adaptability to a rapidly changing global society.

*Example of Limitation:* While the preservation of Taoist traditions is admirable, some argue that its philosophical and spiritual principles, deeply rooted in ancient Chinese thought, may not readily align with the needs and values of a contemporary, interconnected world. Also, Taoism's emphasis on natural rhythms and simplicity may be perceived as challenging to apply in the complex, fast-paced modern context.

**Relevance:** Taoism's core principles of balance, harmony, and alignment with the Tao (the Way) have found resonance in both ancient and modern China. However, the global relevance of Taoist concepts can be limited due to their cultural specificity and the difficulty of translating these principles into diverse cultural contexts.

*Example of Limitation:* It is intriguing to note that the term "the Way" has been used within Christianity as well, with early Christians often referred to as "the people of the Way." This reference can be found in the Book of Acts in the Bible (**Acts 9:2; 19:9**). However, this historical parallel does not necessarily lend credit to Taoism's claims or provide evidence of its authenticity. While the term "the Way" may appear in both belief systems, the theological and philosophical foundations of Christianity and Taoism are distinct and separate.

The challenge of translating Taoist principles into diverse cultural contexts is further underscored by the unique spiritual and philosophical intricacies of Taoism. While these concepts resonate deeply within Chinese culture, they may not easily align with the worldviews and values of individuals from different backgrounds. This cultural specificity limits the universal appeal and relevance of Taoism as a global belief system, in contrast to the worldwide reach and adaptability of Christianity.

**Accuracy of Predictions (Prophecies):** Taoism does not emphasize prophetic or predictive elements in the same way as some other belief systems. Instead, it offers insights into the concept of destiny and the idea of aligning one's life with the flow of the Tao. However, these insights are often presented in a symbolic and abstract manner.

*Example of Limitation:* Taoist views on destiny and the Tao are highly abstract and subject to diverse interpretations. This ambiguity can make it challenging to assess their accuracy or to derive concrete predictions about specific events or outcomes.

Taoism encompasses spiritual dimensions that include beliefs in immortality, the cultivation of inner energy (Qi), and practices aimed at achieving longevity and transcendence. While these concepts hold significance within Taoism, they may be viewed as esoteric and difficult to verify from an empirical standpoint.

*Example of Limitation:* The pursuit of immortality and inner energy cultivation, while central to Taoist spirituality, lacks empirical evidence to support its claims. The esoteric nature of these practices can lead to skepticism and limited applicability beyond Taoist circles.

In our evaluation of Taoism, we acknowledge its profound influence on Chinese culture and its enduring philosophical and spiritual contributions. However, it is crucial to recognize the limitations associated with its unclear historical origins, cultural specificity, challenges in translating its principles into diverse contexts, abstract and non-prophetic nature, and the esoteric aspects of its spiritual dimensions. These limitations contribute to a nuanced understanding of Taoism within the context of belief systems.

## 1.2.5: Confucianism

**Origin:** Confucianism, a philosophical and ethical system originating in ancient China, is primarily associated with the teachings of Confucius. While Confucius' influence on Chinese thought and culture is undeniable, the precise origin of Confucianism, as with many ancient belief systems, is shrouded in historical ambiguity. The lack of concrete historical evidence regarding the early life and teachings of Confucius raises questions about the authenticity of Confucianism's historical roots.

*Example of Limitation:* The uncertainty surrounding the early life and teachings of Confucius can lead to skepticism and doubts about the precise origins of Confucianism, making it challenging to establish a definitive historical narrative.

Similar to other belief systems we've explored, Confucianism also does not claim to know the origin of the known universe and lacks recorded texts indicating the creation or formation of the universe and its inhabitants. This perceived inadequacy raises questions about Confucianism's ability to provide a comprehensive understanding of the fundamental questions regarding existence. The absence of such foundational information seems to suggest a limitation in the completeness of Confucianism as a belief system.

**Longevity:** Confucianism's longevity is remarkable, as it has played a pervasive and enduring role in shaping Chinese culture, ethics, and governance for over two millennia. However, the enduring nature of Confucianism can also be viewed as a limitation when considering its adaptability to modern contexts and its potential to address contemporary global challenges.

*Example of Limitation:* While Confucianism emphasizes moral development and societal well-being, it may be criticized for its limited attention to the spiritual dimension of human existence. The absence of a comprehensive spiritual framework, such as practices for personal spiritual growth or a clear concept of an afterlife, may leave individuals seeking deeper spiritual fulfillment dissatisfied. Confucianism's primary focus on ethical behavior and social relationships may not fully address the existential and spiritual questions that individuals often grapple with, such as the pursuit of transcendence, the quest for meaning, or the hope for life beyond death.

**Relevance:** The cultural specificity of Confucianism can make it challenging for individuals outside East Asian cultures to fully grasp its nuances and adapt its principles to their own cultural contexts, potentially limiting its global appeal.

*Example of Limitation:* Confucianism's heavy reliance on Chinese cultural traditions and historical narratives may not easily resonate with individuals from different cultural backgrounds.

**Accuracy of Predictions (Prophecies):** Confucianism does not emphasize prophetic or predictive elements in the same way as some other belief systems. Instead, it focuses on moral cultivation and societal harmony. The emphasis on moral principles and societal well-being is an inherent part of Confucian philosophy.

*Example of Limitation:* Confucianism's focus on moral cultivation and societal harmony, while valuable for social cohesion, does not provide explicit, verifiable predictions about specific future events or outcomes. This lack of specificity in predictive elements may leave some individuals seeking more concrete guidance unsatisfied.

**The Evidence of God in Confucianism:**

When evaluating belief systems based on the criterion of "The Evidence of God," Confucianism presents a unique perspective. Unlike some religions that emphasize a personal deity or divine being, Confucianism takes a more human-centered and ethical approach to spirituality. As a result, the concept of God in Confucianism differs significantly from monotheistic religions like Christianity, Islam, or Judaism. Here's an exploration of how "The Evidence of God" applies to Confucianism:

1. **Human-Centered Ethics:** Confucianism's focus is primarily on human relationships, moral values, and ethical conduct. While Confucianism acknowledges the existence of spiritual beings, it places less emphasis on the worship of a personal God. Instead, it emphasizes the cultivation of virtues such as benevolence (ren), righteousness (yi), and filial piety (xiao) to create a harmonious society.
2. **Ancestral Veneration:** An important aspect of Confucian practice is the veneration of ancestors. While not the worship of a traditional deity, this practice involves honoring and showing respect to deceased family members. Ancestral veneration serves as a way to maintain

a connection with one's heritage and the values passed down through generations.
3. **Moral Principles as the Divine:** Confucianism views moral principles and ethical values as a form of divine guidance. Confucius himself often spoke of the "Mandate of Heaven," which is a moral concept suggesting that leaders gain legitimacy through virtuous conduct and ethical governance. In this sense, the evidence of God in Confucianism is found in the adherence to moral principles and the pursuit of virtuous behavior.
4. **Absence of Theological Dogma:** Unlike monotheistic religions with specific theological doctrines and dogmas, Confucianism lacks a rigid theological framework. It does not provide explicit evidence or claims about the nature of God or the divine. Instead, it encourages individuals to focus on ethical self-improvement and harmonious social relationships.
5. **Interpretation of the Divine:** In Confucianism, the concept of the divine is open to interpretation and can vary among practitioners. Some may view the divine as an impersonal force or cosmic order (the Tao), while others may emphasize the ethical and moral teachings of Confucius as a form of divine guidance.
6. **Secular Ethical System:** Confucianism is often described as a secular ethical system. While it recognizes the presence of the divine and spiritual elements, its primary concern is the moral development of individuals and the betterment of society through ethical conduct and social harmony.

In conclusion, when evaluating Confucianism based on "The Evidence of God," it is essential to recognize that Confucian beliefs and practices differ significantly from those of monotheistic religions. Instead of a personal God, Confucianism emphasizes human-centered ethics, moral principles, and the importance of harmonious relationships. The evidence of God in Confucianism is found in the ethical conduct and virtues promoted by its teachings, rather than in a traditional conception of a deity.

**Role of Ancestor Veneration and Ethical Principles:**

Confucianism places significant importance on ancestor veneration and ethical principles as cornerstones of its practice. While these concepts hold cultural significance within Confucianism, they may be viewed as overly traditional and lacking empirical evidence to support their claims.

*Example of Limitation:* The practice of ancestor veneration, while deeply meaningful within Confucian traditions, lacks empirical evidence to verify its claims of spiritual connection with deceased ancestors. This practice, along with certain ethical principles, can be seen as tradition-bound and may not easily resonate with individuals outside Confucian cultural contexts.

In our evaluation of Confucianism, we recognize its profound influence on Chinese culture, ethics, and governance. However, it is important to acknowledge the limitations associated with its unclear historical origins, challenges in adapting to modern contexts, cultural specificity, lack of explicit prophetic elements, and certain practices and principles that may be perceived as traditional and lacking empirical evidence. These limitations contribute to a nuanced understanding of Confucianism within the context of belief systems.

## 1.2.6: African Traditional Religions

**Origin- Historical and Cultural Diversity:** African Traditional Religions encompass a rich tapestry of indigenous belief systems across the African continent. These traditions are deeply rooted in the diverse cultures and histories of Africa. However, this diversity can present challenges when attempting to provide a unified assessment of African Traditional Religions due to their distinct regional variations.

*Example of Limitation:* The sheer breadth of African Traditional Religions, which may include practices like animism, ancestor veneration, and nature worship, highlights the difficulty of making generalized statements about their core tenets and beliefs. Each African community may have unique interpretations and practices within their traditional religious framework, and this makes it difficult for one seeking truth to make any meaningful conclusions.

**Longevity:** While the enduring nature of African Traditional Religions is a testament to their cultural resilience, it also raises questions about their capacity to improve the quality of life for their adherents. The longevity of these belief systems, in some cases, has not resulted in measurable improvements in the well-being, education, or socioeconomic status of their practitioners. This absence of verifiable evidence regarding their positive impact on people's lives can be seen as a limitation, especially in comparison to belief systems such as Christianity that have contributed to tangible advancements in society.

*Example of Limitation:* While the resilience of African Traditional Religions is admirable, some may argue that their isolation from global influences limits their potential for growth, adaptability, and relevance in a rapidly changing world. The survival of these belief systems can sometimes rely on their preservation as historical artifacts rather than their adaptability to modern challenges.

Furthermore, African Traditional Religions, like many other belief systems, also do not claim to know the origin of the known universe and lack recorded texts indicating the creation or formation of the universe and its inhabitants. This perceived inadequacy raises questions about the completeness and depth of these belief systems, particularly concerning the fundamental questions about existence and the origin of humanity. It suggests a potential limitation in providing a comprehensive understanding of these essential aspects of life.

**Relevance:** The relevance of African Traditional Religions is particularly pronounced within their respective cultural contexts in contemporary Africa. However, their applicability beyond these contexts is often limited due to their cultural specificity.

*Example of Limitation:* African Traditional Religions, deeply intertwined with African cultural identity, may not readily resonate with individuals from outside African cultures. The rituals, cosmologies, and beliefs may be challenging for those from different backgrounds to fully grasp or embrace.

Furthermore, my personal experiences growing up in Africa, where traditional African priests were occasionally accused of child and human sacrifices, influenced my perception of the limitations of this belief system. Instances of such practices, though not universal, created a negative image associated with African Traditional Religions. In my opinion, a true form of worship should not involve human sacrifices for the sake of financial prosperity or any other perceived benefits. This real-world concern added to the limitations I identified in the belief system during my evaluation.

**Prophetic or Predictive Elements:** African Traditional Religions encompass a wide range of practices, some of which involve divination and prophecy. However, these practices are often symbolic and open to interpretation, making it challenging to assess their accuracy or specificity.

*Example of Limitation:* The symbolic and abstract nature of divination practices within African Traditional Religions can make it difficult to derive concrete predictions about the future or to verify their accuracy in the same way as more structured prophecy in some other belief systems.

**Power and Evidence of God:** African Traditional Religions often involve the veneration of divine beings, spirits, and ancestors. The worship of ancestral spirits and various deities within African Traditional Religions is deeply meaningful within their respective cultures.

However, the presence of spiritual beings in African traditional forms of worship is a complex aspect that carries both positive and negative implications. While these practices are deeply meaningful within their respective cultures, my evaluation led me to observe potential harm caused by the worship of these spirits. In some instances, spirits are believed to bring prosperity, but they are also associated with bringing bondage to families and clans. Some spirits are thought to bring blessings, yet they often demand human blood in the form of sacrifice. This dual nature of the spiritual entities raises concerns about the authenticity and true intentions of these traditional forms of worship.

Growing up, I witnessed Christian believers and pastors successfully casting out these traditional African ancestral spirits from people who claimed to be oppressed by their supposed activities in their lives. Despite the belief that these spirits brought power, they consistently proved to be weaker and submitted to the God of Christianity. This firsthand experience reinforced my perception that African traditional religions were built upon what I considered to be falsehoods, and these falsehoods were always inferior to the truth. The power and authority of the Christian God, as demonstrated in these encounters, became a crucial factor in shaping my perspective and fueling my search for a true form of religion.

**Conclusion for Section 1:** In conclusion, the comprehensive evaluation of these ancient belief systems, including Buddhism, Hinduism, Shintoism, Taoism, Confucianism, and African Traditional Religions, has brought to light significant inadequacies and limitations in their claims to truth and authenticity. While these belief systems boast rich cultural and spiritual heritages that have endured for centuries, their inherent complexities, lack of universal adaptability to modern challenges, and absence of foundational truths regarding the origin of the universe and divine power raise profound concerns.

The highlighted limitations, such as the absence of recorded texts indicating the creation of the universe, ambiguity in historical origins, and potential syncretic elements in certain practices, underscore the challenges in accepting these belief systems as reliable sources of truth. It is crucial to acknowledge that these observations are not intended as condemnation or judgment of the individuals who adhere to these belief systems. Instead, they serve as a call for further research, exploration, and open-mindedness.

As individuals, we must move beyond mere submission to our parents' belief systems and engage in a rigorous quest for truth. An open mind, coupled with a willingness to explore various belief systems, is essential in the pursuit of the ultimate truth. This journey invites us to transcend cultural and familial influences, encouraging a thoughtful and informed exploration of diverse spiritual paths.

## Section 2: Major Abrahamic Religions

The examination of three major Abrahamic religions, namely Judaism, Christianity, and Islam, allows us to explore the shared historical and theological framework that binds them together. These religions trace their lineage back to the venerable figure of Abraham, making them distinctively Abrahamic in origin. Within the rich fabric of these beliefs, we find not only shared historical narratives but also profound theological commonalities that emphasize the worship of the One True God.

It is noteworthy that these three belief systems claim to have a singular origin, each tracing its roots to the Abrahamic tradition. However, a closer examination reveals that they often point to the others as false or insufficient in their understanding of the divine truth. This inherent contradiction necessitates a thorough study of Judaism, Christianity, and Islam to discern the validity of their truth claims. By scrutinizing their foundational texts, doctrines, and practices, we can unravel the complexities and contradictions within these Abrahamic faiths and seek to determine whether any holds the ultimate truth.

## Judaism: The Mother of Abrahamic Faiths

It is crucial to recognize Judaism as the bedrock upon which both Christianity and Islam stand. Judaism not only provided the foundation for monotheism but also presented a coherent worldview with metaphysical explanations that continue to influence its spiritual offspring. One of the strengths of Judaism lies in its steadfast monotheism, as exemplified in the Shema, a central declaration of faith found in the Torah (Deuteronomy 6:4): "Hear, O Israel: The LORD our God, the LORD is one." This unequivocal affirmation of the oneness of God has served as a beacon of theological clarity.

However, Judaism does have certain limitations. While it has been the cradle of monotheism, it holds to the idea that the Messianic salvation is primarily reserved for the Jewish people. The belief that salvation does not extend to Gentile nations can be seen as a theological limitation within Judaism.

## Christianity: The Fulfillment of Prophecy

Christianity, while sharing the foundational aspects of monotheism with Judaism and acknowledging it as the precursor, emerges as the fulfillment of ancient prophecies. In the Christian tradition, Jesus Christ is seen as the long-awaited Messiah prophesied in the Hebrew Scriptures. The Christian faith teaches that Jesus, born into the line of Abraham and David, came not only for the salvation of the Jewish people but also as the Savior of all humanity. This universal message is beautifully encapsulated in John 3:16: "For God so loved the world that he gave his one and only Son, that whoever believes in him shall not perish but have eternal life."

## Islam: A Continuation and Correction

Islam, too, acknowledges the Abrahamic lineage and incorporates elements of the earlier traditions. It sees itself as a continuation and correction of its mother faiths. The Quran, the holy scripture of Islam, recognizes the significance of Abraham, Moses, and Jesus as prophets and messengers. However, like Judaism, Islam maintains certain limitations in its theology. It positions itself as the final revelation and often presents an exclusivist perspective on salvation.

In the following sections, we will evaluate these religions using the established criteria, examining their historical roots, longevity, relevance, prophetic aspects, and the evident presence of God.

## 2.1: Judaism

### Origin:

The origins of Judaism are firmly rooted in historical narratives and well-documented scriptures. The covenant between God and Abraham, as narrated in the book of Genesis, provides a credible historical foundation for the faith. This covenant, often referred to as the Abrahamic Covenant, marked a pivotal moment in human history. It initiated the unique relationship between the Jewish people and the Almighty, laying the groundwork for the monotheistic faith that would shape the course of human civilization.

Judaism should be credited for offering a credible narrative of man's origin and his home—the earth and the universe. The introductory chapter of Genesis unfolds a comprehensive account of the creation of humanity and the cosmos, providing a foundational understanding that distinguishes Judaism in its commitment to a detailed and coherent narrative of the origins of both humanity and the universe.

The historical authenticity of Judaism's origin is further supported by the existence of well-preserved and meticulously documented scriptures. The Hebrew Bible, known as the Tanakh, is a testament to the careful transmission of Jewish sacred texts over millennia. Manuscripts like the Dead Sea Scrolls, discovered in the mid-20th century, offer tangible evidence of the antiquity and accuracy of these writings. These scrolls, dating back to the Second Temple period, contain fragments of almost every book of the Hebrew Bible, providing a remarkable testament to the preservation of Jewish scriptures.

**Longevity:**

Judaism's remarkable longevity is not merely a testament to its resilience but also to its enduring capacity to address profound questions about the nature of existence and the origin of the universe. Over thousands of years, Judaism has demonstrated an unparalleled ability to withstand adversity, from exile to persecution and dispersion. It is this enduring quality that has allowed the faith to maintain its relevance and continue offering profound insights into the mysteries of creation.

One of the notable aspects of Judaism's longevity is its commitment to preserving its sacred texts and traditions. The Hebrew Bible (Tanakh), the cornerstone of Jewish religious literature, contains not only moral and ethical teachings but also narratives that touch upon the origins of the cosmos. In the opening chapters of Genesis, Judaism provides a foundational account of the creation of the universe, explaining the divine process of bringing order to chaos, the establishment of light and darkness, the formation of the Earth, and the introduction of life.

This narrative, often referred to as the Genesis creation account, is a source of immense pride for Judaism. It offers an ancient yet enduring perspective on the beginning of the universe, and it continues to stimulate contemplation and discussion among scholars and theologians across the world. The fact that Judaism has maintained and preserved this profound narrative for millennia is indeed something to boast about.

In addition to the Genesis account, Jewish scholars and thinkers throughout history have engaged in philosophical and theological discussions about the nature of God and the cosmos. Their contributions have enriched the field of metaphysics and provided valuable perspectives on the origin and purpose of the universe.

Judaism's longevity, coupled with its capacity to address fundamental questions about creation, underscores its enduring relevance and its unique position as a faith that not only perseveres through the ages but also contributes significantly to humanity's understanding of the universe's origins. It stands as a beacon of wisdom and spiritual insight that continues to inspire and inform those who seek knowledge and explanations about the mysteries of existence.

**Relevance:**

In the tapestry of modern Jewish communities, the relevance of Judaism unfolds as a dynamic interplay between tradition and a timeless ethical framework articulated in the law of God (YHWH) as revealed through Moses. Rooted in the Torah, this sacred text not only serves as a spiritual guide but intricately weaves into the fabric of daily life, addressing diverse aspects from hygiene and morality to social justice and personal relationships.

Take, for instance, the Exodus narrative, a cornerstone of Jewish identity. It encapsulates not just a historical event but a profound lesson about liberation, justice, and the pursuit of a life guided by God's law. The ethical principles derived from this narrative resonate in contemporary discussions about freedom, equity, and human rights.

The relevance of Judaism extends beyond rituals; it is a holistic approach that seeks to touch every facet of human existence. The dietary laws outlined in Leviticus, for example, not only govern what is considered kosher but also underline the significance of mindful and intentional living, promoting health and well-being.

In matters of morality and interpersonal relationships, the Torah offers a wealth of guidance. The Ten Commandments, found in Exodus 20, provide a moral compass that remains influential across generations. The principles of honesty, respect for others, and the sanctity of life continue to shape not only Jewish but also global perspectives on personal conduct and societal values.

Hygiene and sanitation find mention in Leviticus, where meticulous instructions for cleanliness are outlined. This not only reflects a concern for physical well-being but also emphasizes the spiritual significance of maintaining purity.

The psychological aspects of human nature are not overlooked either. Proverbs, a book rich in practical wisdom, delves into matters of the heart, offering insights into human emotions, relationships, and the pursuit of wisdom. This wisdom literature provides a timeless guide for navigating the complexities of human psychology.

The relevance of Judaism, therefore, lies not only in its historical richness but in its ability to offer a relevant and timeless ethical framework. Just as the law of God guided the Israelites through the challenges of the ancient world, it continues to illuminate the path for modern Jewish individuals and global communities. In engaging with their faith, Jewish people find not only spiritual nourishment but a compass that directs them toward a life imbued with purpose, ethical integrity, and a commitment to the well-being of humanity.

**Accuracy of Predictions (Prophecies):**

Judaism possesses a remarkable collection of prophecies that have played a pivotal role in shaping its theological landscape. These prophecies often revolve around the anticipated Messiah, a figure of great significance in Jewish eschatology. Within the pages of the Hebrew Bible (Tanakh), several prophecies stand out as precise foretellings of future events:

1. **Daniel's Vision of the Four Kingdoms (Daniel 2):** The book of Daniel contains a profound vision that foretells the rise and fall of empires with astonishing accuracy. In King Nebuchadnezzar's dream of a colossal statue representing different kingdoms, Daniel interpreted the vision as predicting the succession of powerful empires: Babylon,

Persia, Greece, and Rome. These empires indeed rose and fell in the precise order Daniel prophesied, with Babylon reigning from 626 BC to 539 BC, Persia from 539 BC to 330 BC, Greece from 330 BC to 146 BC, and Rome from 146 BC to AD 476.

2. **Isaiah's Prophecy of the Suffering Servant (Isaiah 53):** Isaiah 53 is a striking prophecy that depicts a "suffering servant" who would bear the sins of the people. Many within Judaism interpret this passage as a Messianic prophecy, pointing to Jesus of Nazareth as its fulfillment. The detailed descriptions of the servant's suffering and his role in atoning for the sins of others align remarkably with the life and crucifixion of Jesus, as recorded in the New Testament.

3. **Micah's Prediction of the Messiah's Birthplace (Micah 5:2):** The prophet Micah foretold the birthplace of the Messiah with remarkable precision, stating, "But you, Bethlehem Ephrathah, though you are small among the clans of Judah, out of you will come for me one who will be ruler over Israel." This prophecy found fulfillment in the birth of Jesus in Bethlehem, a pivotal event in Christian theology.

4. **Jeremiah's Prophecy of the New Covenant (Jeremiah 31:31-34):** Jeremiah prophesied a new covenant that God would make with His people, one written on their hearts and characterized by forgiveness of sins. Many theologians see this as a prophecy fulfilled through the teachings and sacrificial work of Jesus, who ushered in a new covenant of grace.

These examples underscore the remarkable accuracy of certain prophecies within the Hebrew Bible. While interpretations may vary among different branches of Judaism and Christianity, these precise predictions have left an indelible mark on religious thought and continue to spark theological discussions. They serve as compelling evidence of the depth of spiritual insight found within the sacred texts of Judaism.

However, while the anticipation of the Jewish Messiah has ancient roots, there exists a divergence in interpretation among Jewish scholars and leaders. Notably, many within the Jewish community have not recognized Jesus as the fulfillment of these messianic prophecies, despite the compelling evidence presented by early Jewish disciples and preachers.

Apostle Paul (formerly Saul), a well-known Jewish scholar and later turned disciple of Yeshua (Jesus), and Peter, one of Yeshua's closest followers, alongside other Jewish preachers, passionately proclaimed that Yeshua was the long-anticipated Messiah as foretold in the Hebrew Scriptures. They highlighted specific prophecies, including those found in Isaiah 53 and Micah 5:2, as compelling evidence of Yeshua (Jesus) aligning with these ancient predictions. According to the perspective held by these Jewish followers of Yeshua, his life, ministry, crucifixion, and resurrection corresponded with the prophetic descriptions of the Messiah.

This theological divergence between certain segments of Judaism and the Jewish followers of Yeshua underscores a significant challenge in Judaism's interpretation of its own prophecies. While Judaism maintains its distinctive viewpoint regarding the nature and timing of the Messiah, the Jewish understanding of Yeshua (Jesus) as the Messiah stands as a pivotal point of difference. This distinction becomes especially noteworthy when considering the historical context of Yeshua's ministry. The Jewish leaders of that time were actively anticipating the arrival of the Messiah, as evident in their questions to John the Baptist. In John 1:19-21, the priests and Levites inquire about John's identity, asking if he is the Messiah, Elijah, or the Prophet, revealing their keen anticipation for the fulfillment of messianic prophecies. This historical backdrop adds a unique layer of significance to the events surrounding Yeshua's ministry, further highlighting the divergence in interpretations among different segments of Judaism.

In the subsequent sections, we will explore deeper into the multifaceted aspects that differentiate Christianity and its response to these challenges, all within the broader context of the Abrahamic faiths.

**The Power or Evidence of God:**

Within Judaism, the presence of divine evidence and manifestations of God is deeply woven into the fabric of its historical narratives and sacred texts. The Torah, also known as the Pentateuch, forms the cornerstone of these accounts, chronicling God's interactions with various figures throughout Jewish history. Let us explore some poignant examples from the Hebrew Bible (Old Testament) that exemplify this divine presence:

1. **The Burning Bush (Exodus 3):** The story of Moses and the burning bush is a quintessential example of divine manifestation. In this pivotal encounter, as Moses tended his flock in the wilderness, he came across a bush engulfed in flames that were not consumed. As he drew near, God spoke to Moses from the midst of the burning bush, revealing His divine name, "I Am Who I Am." This profound experience marked the call of Moses to lead the Israelites out of slavery in Egypt, showcasing God's unmistakable presence.

2. **The Parting of the Red Sea (Exodus 14):** The miraculous parting of the Red Sea during the Israelites' exodus from Egypt is another compelling illustration of God's power and intervention. As the Egyptian army pursued them, Moses raised his staff, and the waters of the sea parted, allowing the Israelites to cross on dry land. This divine intervention not only delivered the Israelites from imminent danger but also affirmed God's sovereignty over nature.
3. **The Prophetic Vision of Ezekiel (Ezekiel 1):** In the Book of Ezekiel, the prophet Ezekiel describes a powerful vision of God's glory. He witnesses a breathtaking display of divine presence, characterized by a chariot-like throne and awe-inspiring creatures. This visionary experience profoundly impacted Ezekiel and served as a testament to God's majesty and transcendence.
4. **The Ten Plagues (Exodus 7-12):** The ten plagues unleashed upon Egypt, as described in the book of Exodus, are a series of divine acts that showcased God's authority over creation and His commitment to liberating the Israelites. Each plague, from the turning of water into blood to the final plague that led to the release of the Israelites, served as a demonstration of God's power and justice.
5. **God's Judgment over Sodom and Gomorrah (Genesis 18-19):** The story of Sodom and Gomorrah is a pivotal moment in the Old Testament, underscoring God's commitment to justice and His direct intervention in human affairs. In response to the wickedness of these cities, God determined to destroy them. Abraham interceded on behalf of the righteous within Sodom, and God agreed not to destroy the cities if even a small number of righteous people

could be found. Yet, as the narrative unfolds, it becomes evident that the cities were beyond redemption.

Two angels, sent by God, arrived in Sodom, and warned Lot and his family to flee before the impending judgment. As they left the city, God rained down fire and brimstone from heaven, utterly destroying Sodom and Gomorrah, leaving behind a desolate and lifeless landscape. This divine act of judgment serves as a powerful illustration of God's righteous indignation against sin and His willingness to intervene decisively in response to human behavior.

The story of Sodom and Gomorrah's destruction stands as a testament to God's role as a just and sovereign deity, one who takes action when confronted with wickedness. It remains a foundational narrative within Judaism, conveying the importance of moral conduct and the consequences of straying from God's path.

6. **The Falling of Fire from Heaven (1 Kings 18):** The dramatic showdown on Mount Carmel between the prophet Elijah and the prophets of Baal is a remarkable illustration of God's divine power in the Judaic religious system. Elijah challenged the prophets of the false god Baal to a contest: to call down fire from heaven to consume a sacrifice. Despite their fervent efforts, nothing happened. In contrast, when Elijah prayed to the God of Israel, fire fell from heaven, consuming the offering, the wood, the stones, and even the water in the trench, leaving no doubt about the presence and power of the one true God. This awe-inspiring event reaffirmed the faith of the Israelites and demonstrated God's unwavering support of His prophet Elijah. It serves as a potent example of divine intervention and evidence of God's active involvement in the affairs of His people.

These examples represent just a fraction of the countless instances within the Hebrew Bible where divine evidence and manifestations of God are intricately woven into the narrative. They stand as enduring testimony to the depth of God's involvement in the lives of His chosen people and continue to inspire faith and reverence within the Jewish tradition.

However, Judaism has faced a limitation in terms of providing contemporary empirical evidence of divine interventions or manifestations. Unlike some other faiths that claim ongoing miracles or direct experiences of God, Judaism predominantly relies on historical accounts and written traditions to testify to the power and presence of God. While the Jewish faith continues to uphold its core principles and beliefs, it's noteworthy that certain practices have evolved over the centuries. For example, the offering of burnt sacrifices and other sacrifices for sin, as prescribed in the Torah, is no longer observed in modern Judaism, despite the belief in the importance of repentance and atonement. This evolution reflects a notable compromise in religious practice within Judaism.

In summary, Judaism stands as a venerable faith with well-documented origins and a rich tapestry of teachings. While deserving immense respect as the mother of Abrahamic faiths and for its profound contributions to monotheism and ethics, it is not exempt from certain limitations. These include the challenge of remaining relevant in a rapidly changing world, the historical divergence in messianic interpretations, and the evolution of certain religious practices.

Judaism, claiming its relevance from the detailed and intricate guidance in the law of God revealed through Moses, attempts to cherish fundamental values such as human rights, equity, freedom, peace, and harmonious living. The law of the God of Judaism extends its reach into every facet of human life, encompassing hygiene, sanitation, dieting, morality, psychology, and personal relationships. Despite these timeless principles, Judaism grapples with the inherent challenges of adapting to a modern context and navigating the complexities of evolving religious practices. In the subsequent sections, we will examine how Christianity addresses these limitations, offering a distinctive path to understanding and experiencing the divine.

**2.2: Christianity**

Christianity, as an extension of Judaism, inherits a foundation deeply rooted in the credible narratives and scriptures of its predecessor. It uniquely builds upon the historical authenticity of Judaism, affirming its commitment to preserving the purity of Jewish scriptures and embracing Jesus of Nazareth, a Jewish Nazarene and Nazirite, as its central figure. Christianity stands as a vibrant continuation of the rich interconnectedness woven by its predecessor, Judaism, embracing a history rooted in the sacred narratives of the Hebrew Bible while radiating with a transformative power that extends to spiritual, social, economic, and moral dimensions.

**Origin:**

Christianity's origin is intricately linked to the life of Jesus of Nazareth, a Jewish teacher and healer. Unlike the ambiguity surrounding certain belief systems, Christianity unfolds within the context of Jewish scriptures, seamlessly transitioning from the Hebrew Bible to the New Testament. Jesus, as a Jewish figure, fulfilled prophecies embedded in Jewish sacred texts, establishing a coherent narrative that seamlessly integrates the Old and New Testaments.

> *Example: The Gospel of Matthew, a Jewish authorship, emphasizes Jesus' fulfillment of Messianic prophecies, creating a seamless connection with Jewish expectations.*

The Gospel of Matthew, authored by a Jewish disciple, meticulously traces Jesus' lineage back to Abraham, anchoring his Messianic identity in the historical promises made to the Jewish patriarchs. This intentional connection between the Old and New Testaments lays the groundwork for a unified, purposeful faith journey.

*Example: Matthew 1:1-17 presents the genealogy of Jesus, aligning his identity with the historical promises given to Abraham and David.*

Christianity, in recognizing the heritage of Judaism, acknowledges the foundational role of its spiritual ancestry. The birth of Jesus in Bethlehem, the fulfillment of Old Testament prophecies, reinforces the divine orchestration underlying Christian origins. This continuity provides Christians with a profound sense of connection to the sacred history encapsulated in the Jewish scriptures.

**Longevity:**

Christianity's enduring legacy is a testament to its roots in Judaism and its global impact. It inherits Judaism's resilience, adapting to diverse cultures while maintaining its core principles. The commitment to preserving Jewish scriptures continues within Christianity, as the Old Testament remains an integral part of its sacred canon, ensuring the continuity of profound insights into the mysteries of creation.

> *Example: The global spread of Christianity echoes Judaism's ability to transcend geographical and temporal boundaries.*

Christianity, like Judaism, has navigated through epochs of persecution, cultural shifts, and global transformations. The longevity of Christianity isn't merely a historical testament, but a living reality manifested in the global presence of Christian communities. The unbroken thread connecting Old and New Testaments provides believers with a sense of stability and rootedness, reinforcing the enduring relevance of their faith.

**Relevance:**

Christianity's teachings, rooted in Jewish scriptures, provide a dynamic framework for contemporary living. The New Testament, while introducing distinct aspects, aligns with the ethical framework articulated in the law of God revealed through Moses. Christianity seamlessly integrates Jewish principles into its teachings, offering a holistic approach to life that encompasses moral, ethical, and social dimensions.

> *Example: The Sermon on the Mount in Matthew 5-7 mirrors the ethical guidance found in Jewish scriptures, emphasizing compassion, humility, and justice.*

The Sermon on the Mount, a spiritual manifesto articulated by Jesus in Matthew 5-7, echoes the ethical guidance of Jewish scriptures while introducing a transformative love principle that transcends moral and social dimensions.

> *Example: The Beatitudes in Matthew 5:3-12 provide a blueprint for a life rooted in love, humility, and compassion, shaping the moral fabric of Christian communities.*

Christianity's relevance isn't confined to theological doctrines but extends to the lived experiences of believers. The teachings of Jesus, encapsulated in the New Testament, offer a moral compass for navigating complex social and economic landscapes (Matthew 22:37-40). The Christian worldview, informed by the love principle, fosters communities marked by compassion, forgiveness, and a commitment to social justice.

## My Criteria

**Accuracy of Predictions (Prophecies):**

Christianity continues the prophetic narrative from Judaism, particularly concerning Jesus as the anticipated Messiah. The New Testament presents Jesus as the fulfillment of numerous Messianic prophecies found in the Hebrew Bible, showcasing a cohesive connection between the Old and New Testaments.

The Gospel of Luke, a meticulous account by a physician-disciple, meticulously details Jesus' life, portraying him as the fulfillment of divine promises. Notably, Isaiah's prophecy of the suffering servant in Isaiah 53 aligns remarkably with the crucifixion narrative.

> *Example: Luke 4:16-21 records Jesus applying Isaiah's prophecy to himself, claiming to fulfill the scriptural promises of liberation and redemption.*

The accuracy of Christian predictions isn't confined to historical events but extends to the transformative power of Christian faith in individual lives. The fulfillment of the promise of the Holy Spirit, as recorded in the Book of Acts, serves as a testament to the ongoing divine presence and guidance within the Christian community.

*29 Old Testament Prophecies Fulfilled in the Life of Jesus Christ:* The intricate connection between the Old Testament prophecies and the life, death, and resurrection of Jesus Christ is a cornerstone of Christian belief. These prophecies, dispersed across various books and authors of the Old Testament, form a fabric of anticipation, pointing toward the arrival of a Messianic figure who would fulfill God's redemptive plan. As we examine these 29 prophecies, we witness the seamless harmony between the foresight of ancient scriptures and the fulfillment found in the person and work of Jesus Christ.

Let's explore these prophecies, each intricately weaving the narrative of the divine promise and its realization in the life of Jesus, providing Christians with a compelling foundation for their faith in the Messiah. Here is a list of 29 Old Testament prophecies that are traditionally believed by Christians to be fulfilled in the life, death, and resurrection of Jesus Christ:

1. **Born of a Virgin:**
   o *Prophecy: Isaiah 7:14*
   o *Fulfillment: Matthew 1:22-23*

2. **Descendant of Abraham:**
   o *Prophecy: Genesis 12:3*
   o *Fulfillment: Matthew 1:1*

3. **From the Tribe of Judah:**
   o *Prophecy: Genesis 49:10*
   o *Fulfillment: Matthew 1:2-3*

4. **Born in Bethlehem:**
   o *Prophecy: Micah 5:2*
   o *Fulfillment: Matthew 2:1-6*

5. **Flight to Egypt:**
   o *Prophecy: Hosea 11:1*
   o *Fulfillment: Matthew 2:13-15*

6. **Massacre of Infants:**
   - o  *Prophecy: Jeremiah 31:15*
   - o  *Fulfillment: Matthew 2:16-18*

7. **Preceded by a Messenger:**
   - o  *Prophecy: Malachi 3:1*
   - o  *Fulfillment: Matthew 11:10*

8. **Ministry in Galilee:**
   - o  *Prophecy: Isaiah 9:1-2*
   - o  *Fulfillment: Matthew 4:13-16*

9. **Healing the Blind:**
   - o  *Prophecy: Isaiah 35:5-6*
   - o  *Fulfillment: Matthew 9:27-31*

10. **Rejected by His Own:**
    - o  *Prophecy: Isaiah 53:3*
    - o  *Fulfillment: John 1:11*

11. **Triumphal Entry on a Donkey:**
    - o  *Prophecy: Zechariah 9:9*
    - o  *Fulfillment: Matthew 21:1-11*

12. **Betrayed by a Friend:**
    - o  *Prophecy: Psalm 41:9*
    - o  *Fulfillment: Matthew 26:14-16*

13. **Betrayal for 30 Pieces of Silver:**
    - o  *Prophecy: Zechariah 11:12-13*
    - o  *Fulfillment: Matthew 26:15*

14. **Silent Before Accusers:**
    - o   *Prophecy: Isaiah 53:7*
    - o   *Fulfillment: Matthew 27:12-14*

15. **Mocked and Insulted:**
    - o   *Prophecy: Isaiah 53:3*
    - o   *Fulfillment: Matthew 27:27-31*

16. **Crucified with Criminals:**
    - o   *Prophecy: Isaiah 53:12*
    - o   *Fulfillment: Matthew 27:38*

17. **Hands and Feet Pierced:**
    - o   *Prophecy: Psalm 22:16*
    - o   *Fulfillment: John 20:25*

18. **Given Vinegar and Gall:**
    - o   *Prophecy: Psalm 69:21*
    - o   *Fulfillment: Matthew 27:34*

19. **Garments Divided and Lots Cast:**
    - o   *Prophecy: Psalm 22:18*
    - o   *Fulfillment: John 19:23-24*

20. **No Broken Bones:**
    - o   *Prophecy: Psalm 34:20*
    - o   *Fulfillment: John 19:33-36*

21. **Pierced Side:**
    - o   *Prophecy: Zechariah 12:10*
    - o   *Fulfillment: John 19:34-37*

22. **Buried with the Rich:**
    - *Prophecy: Isaiah 53:9*
    - *Fulfillment: Matthew 27:57-60*

23. **Resurrection:**
    - *Prophecy: Psalm 16:10*
    - *Fulfillment: Acts 2:31*

24. **Ascension to God's Right Hand:**
    - *Prophecy: Psalm 110:1*
    - *Fulfillment: Mark 16:19*

25. **Pouring Out the Holy Spirit:**
    - *Prophecy: Joel 2:28-29*
    - *Fulfillment: Acts 2:17-18*

26. **Establishing a New Covenant:**
    - *Prophecy: Jeremiah 31:31-34*
    - *Fulfillment: Hebrews 8:8-12*

27. **Coming on the Clouds:**
    - *Prophecy: Daniel 7:13-14*
    - *Fulfillment: Matthew 26:64*

28. **Rejection by the Builders:**
    - *Prophecy: Psalm 118:22*
    - *Fulfillment: Matthew 21:42*

29. **Proclamation to the Gentiles:**
    - *Prophecy: Isaiah 49:6*
    - *Fulfillment: Acts 13:46-47*

The fulfillment of these 29 Old Testament prophecies in the life, death, and resurrection of Jesus Christ is nothing short of extraordinary, presenting a compelling narrative that transcends the boundaries of human coincidence. What makes these prophecies particularly remarkable is the diversity in their origins—they were prophesied by different individuals, living in distinct historical periods, and spanning numerous years apart. The intricacy and specificity of these prophecies, coupled with their fulfillment in a single person, Jesus Christ, defy rational explanation based solely on human agency.

Consider the sheer improbability of one person fulfilling these prophecies—being born of a virgin, from the tribe of Judah, in Bethlehem, and preceded by a messenger. Add to this the precise details of his life, such as healing the blind, a triumphal entry on a donkey, betrayal by a friend for 30 pieces of silver, and being crucified with criminals. The odds of any individual fulfilling this array of predictions become astronomical, suggesting a level of orchestration beyond the scope of human manipulation.

Furthermore, the fulfillment of prophecies related to specific events, such as the Flight to Egypt, Massacre of Infants, and the precise details surrounding the crucifixion, burial, and resurrection, paints a tapestry of divine design. These prophecies were articulated by various prophets across centuries, each unaware of the others' predictions, yet they converged seamlessly in the life of Jesus.

The significance of these prophecies lies not only in their fulfillment but in the implicit message they convey—that a supreme divine being, transcending time and space, orchestrated these events to reveal Himself to humanity. The precision and detail of these prophecies serve as a signature of divine authorship, providing a tangible demonstration of God's involvement in human history.

## My Criteria

In contemplating the fulfillment of these prophecies, one is compelled to acknowledge that the odds of a single person coincidentally meeting these criteria are infinitesimally small. The convergence of these prophecies in Jesus Christ stands as a testament to the divine authorship of life's narrative. It serves as a profound revelation of God's sovereignty, His intricate involvement in human affairs, and His ultimate redemptive plan for humanity. The fulfillment of these prophecies in Jesus Christ becomes a compelling signpost pointing to the divine origin of life and the revelation of God's purpose for humanity.

*Prophecies by Jesus:* In the course of his earthly ministry, Jesus, often regarded as the greatest teacher and spiritual leader in Christianity, not only imparted profound teachings but also made statements about the future that carry a prophetic nature. Unlike the explicit Old Testament-style prophecies, Jesus's predictions are intricately woven into his teachings, offering a multifaceted perspective on what was to come. These prophetic utterances reflect the depth of his understanding and divine insight, shaping the course of Christian theology and belief.

Let's explore a selection of these prophetic statements, each serving as a testament to the foresight of Jesus and the ongoing fulfillment of his words in the unfolding mosaic of history. From predictions concerning his death and resurrection to foretelling significant events like the destruction of the temple and the spread of the Gospel, these prophecies underscore the intricate connection between Jesus's teachings and the unfolding drama of God's redemptive plan.

The prophetic statements made by Jesus serve as a powerful validation of his divine authority and insight into the future. These predictions exhibit a remarkable accuracy in fulfillment, providing a solid foundation for believers to trust in his declarations about future events. Let's delve into the explanations for some of these prophecies and how they set the stage for confidence in Jesus' end-time predictions found in the Gospels and the Book of Revelation.

1. **Prediction of His Death and Resurrection (Matthew 16:21):**
   o **Prophecy:** *Jesus foretells his impending death and resurrection.*
   o **Fulfillment:** *This prophecy finds fulfillment in the detailed account of Jesus's crucifixion and subsequent resurrection, providing a tangible demonstration of the accuracy of his foretelling.*

2. **Prediction of Peter's Denial (Matthew 26:34):**
   o **Prophecy:** *Jesus predicts Peter's denial.*
   o **Fulfillment:** *As recorded in Matthew 26:69-75, Peter denies Jesus three times, exactly as foretold by Jesus.*

3. **Prediction of the Destruction of the Temple (Matthew 24:1-2):**
   o **Prophecy:** *Jesus predicts the destruction of the Second Temple.*
   o **Fulfillment:** *The Second Temple's destruction in AD 70 aligns precisely with Jesus's prophecy, showcasing his insight into future historical events.*

## My Criteria

4. **Prediction of Persecution of Disciples (Matthew 10:16-23):**
   - **Prophecy:** *Jesus warns of persecution and challenges his disciples will face.*
   - **Fulfillment:** *The Acts of the Apostles and various historical accounts document the persecution and hardships faced by early Christians, validating Jesus's foresight.*

5. **Prediction of the Coming of the Holy Spirit (John 14:16-17, 26; 16:7):**
   - **Prophecy:** *Jesus foretells the coming of the Holy Spirit.*
   - **Fulfillment:** *Acts 2:1-4 records the fulfillment of this prophecy with the outpouring of the Holy Spirit on the Day of Pentecost, confirming the accuracy of Jesus's words.*

6. **Prediction of the Spread of the Gospel (Matthew 24:14):**
   - **Prophecy:** *Jesus predicts the global spread of the Gospel.*
   - **Fulfillment:** *The historical spread of Christianity to diverse cultures and nations stands as ongoing evidence of the fulfillment of this prophecy.*

7. **Prediction of His Second Coming (Matthew 24:30-31):**
   - **Prophecy:** *Jesus foretells his Second Coming.*
   - **Anticipated Fulfillment:** *While the Second Coming is yet to occur, the accuracy of Jesus's previous predictions lays a solid foundation for believers to trust in the fulfillment of this future event.*

In summary, the accurate fulfillment of Jesus's past predictions provides a compelling basis for believers to place confidence in his end-time prophecies. The consistency between his words and historical realities demonstrates a divine insight that transcends human limitations, affirming the trustworthiness of Jesus as the ultimate authority on matters of the present and the future. This foundation of trust invites believers to approach Jesus' end-time prophecies with assurance, anticipating their fulfillment in accordance with the divine plan.

**The Power or Evidence of God:**

Christianity inherits the rich embroidery of divine evidence within Jewish narratives and scriptures. The New Testament builds upon the foundation laid in the Old Testament, documenting transformative experiences, miracles, and encounters with the living God. The power and evidence of God within Christianity are seamlessly connected to the Jewish understanding of God's manifestations.

The miracles performed by Jesus, recorded in the Gospels, align with the divine manifestations witnessed in the Hebrew Bible- The Tanakh (Genesis - Malachi). In the Gospel of John, Jesus himself emphasized the importance of both belief and observable evidence. In John 10:37-38, Jesus said, "If I am not doing the works of my Father, then do not believe me; but if I do them, even though you do not believe me, believe the works, that you may know and understand that the Father is in me and I am in the Father." These words underscore the idea that belief in Jesus is not solely based on abstract faith but is accompanied by tangible evidence—miracles, signs, and wonders—that point to his divine nature. This aligns with the broader theme in Christianity that encourages believers to not only accept religious teachings intellectually but also to recognize the evidence of God's power in the manifested works of Christ.

Miracles, healings, and deliverance from evil spirits abound, illustrating the active involvement of God in the lives of believers. The Book of Acts, authored by Luke, unfolds as a chronicle of the Spirit's transformative power at work in the early Christian community.

> *Example: Acts 2 narrates the outpouring of the Holy Spirit on the day of Pentecost, marking the beginning of miraculous manifestations and transformative spiritual experiences.*

The teachings in the Epistles further reinforce the relevance of Christianity in diverse aspects of life. The Apostle Paul, in his letters, provides practical guidance for social interactions, economic stewardship, and moral conduct. The love principle, exemplified by Jesus, becomes a central tenet, shaping Christian communities into beacons of compassion, forgiveness, and selflessness.

> *Example: Romans 13:8-10 highlights the moral imperative of love in social and economic interactions, emphasizing love as the fulfilling of the law.*

In the contemporary context, Christianity's relevance manifests in the lives of believers who, inspired by the teachings of Jesus, actively participate in spiritual, social, economic, and moral transformation. Christians continue to cast out evil spirits, heal the sick through prayer, and provide psychotherapy through the transformative words of Jesus. The reassurance of love and hope, rooted in Christian faith, serves as a guiding light in navigating the complexities of the modern world.

Christianity, as a living faith, draws its vitality from the ongoing experiences of believers, where the power of God is not merely a historical occurrence but a present reality. The teachings of the New Testament, particularly the Epistles, resonate with a timeless relevance, offering guidance for ethical living, economic stewardship, and social harmony. The Christian narrative, seamlessly woven into the fabric of human history, continues to unfold as a dynamic force that addresses the profound questions of existence and provides a transformative framework for contemporary challenges.

In sum, Christianity emerges not as a departure from Judaism but as a continuation, enhancing and amplifying the spiritual, social, economic, and moral dimensions of human existence. It stands as an enduring testament to the transformative power of a faith deeply rooted in the love and teachings of Jesus Christ. Its historical authenticity, global influence, enduring relevance, prophetic fulfilment, and continuity with Jewish scriptures collectively position Christianity as a unique path that harmonizes with the profound heritage of Judaism.

## 2.3: Islam

In our exploration of belief systems, we now turn our attention to Islam, subjecting it to the established criteria that have served as our benchmark. It is essential to approach this evaluation with a commitment to understanding and respect, while also critically examining the foundational aspects of Islam.

## Origin:

Islam's origin is intrinsically tied to the life of Prophet Muhammad, born in Mecca around the year 570 AD. Muhammad's early life, marked by trade and contemplation, took a transformative turn when, at the age of 40, he claimed to receive divine revelations from the angel Gabriel. This marked the beginning of the Quranic revelations, which continued over a span of 23 years until Muhammad's death in 632 AD.

It's essential to note that Muhammad, although not of Jewish descent, claimed a connection to the Abrahamic lineage and asserted that he was chosen as the final prophet to edit and correct the facts recorded in the Hebrew Scriptures. This includes assertions about figures like Adam, Moses, and Jesus. For instance, Muhammad's narrative of Moses and the Pharaoh differs in some aspects from the biblical account. Such edits and additions, made centuries later and miles away from the events, raise questions about the basis of these claims.

Moreover, the Quran contains various statements about Jesus that contradict the accounts provided by eyewitnesses, including the apostles and the broader Jewish community. Muhammad's teachings about Jesus' crucifixion and divinity diverge significantly from the foundational teachings of Christianity, particularly those recorded in the New Testament. The question naturally arises: how could someone born over 500 years after these events, and many miles away from the epicenter of these occurrences, claim to possess more accurate facts than those who were closer in time and proximity?

The Quran's compilation occurred after Muhammad's death, primarily during the caliphate of Uthman ibn Affan around 650 AD. While Muslims assert that the Quran is an exact representation of the words revealed to Muhammad, the historical circumstances surrounding its compilation, including variations in oral transmission and potential political influences, warrant critical examination.

In summary, while acknowledging the historical significance of Muhammad's life and the Quranic revelations, the distance in time and space from the events of the Hebrew Scriptures and the New Testament raises valid questions about the basis and accuracy of these claims. The discrepancies between Muhammad's assertions and the accounts of those who were closer to the events necessitate careful consideration when evaluating the origin and historical context of Islam.

**Longevity:**

Islam, spanning over fourteen centuries, has showcased remarkable longevity and a global footprint that extends across diverse cultures. However, the nature of its expansion warrants a more critical examination, particularly regarding the methods employed during its rapid dissemination.

One facet that complicates the narrative of Islam as a purely peaceful religion is the historical account of Prophet Muhammad's leadership. While he is often portrayed as a preacher of peace, his military campaigns, known as Jihad, are a significant aspect of his legacy. Notably, the conquests during the Arab expansion in the 7th and 8th centuries involved military force across the Arabian Peninsula, North Africa, Spain, and parts of Asia. These conquests were not solely characterized by voluntary conversions but, in some instances, involved coercion and force.

A prime example is the Battle of Badr in 624 CE, where Muhammad led his forces against the Quraysh tribe. The outcome of this battle had a profound impact on the early Muslim community and solidified Muhammad's position as a military leader. Subsequent conquests, including the capture of Mecca in 630 CE, further established Islam as a dominant force in the Arabian Peninsula.

The expansion of Islam did not end with Muhammad's death. Caliphs and Muslim leaders who followed continued in his footsteps. The Umayyad Caliphate, for instance, expanded Muslim territories into Spain and parts of India through military campaigns. The methods of expansion included both military conquests and the imposition of Islamic rule on conquered populations, sometimes accompanied by economic incentives.

In reflecting on Islam's extensive history and global impact, the use of military force and coercion in its expansion, notably during Prophet Muhammad's leadership and the subsequent caliphates, raises questions about the credibility of Islam as an unblemished source for spiritual guidance and nourishment.

**Relevance:**

Islam has undeniably made significant positive contributions to societal order and justice, evident in various aspects of its teachings. One notable example is the emphasis on charity and social welfare through the practice of Zakat, a form of almsgiving. This principle promotes economic justice by ensuring the distribution of wealth to those in need, fostering a sense of communal responsibility.

Furthermore, Islamic jurisprudence, with its emphasis on fairness and justice, has been a source of guidance for legal systems in many Muslim-majority countries. The principles of equity and accountability are embedded in Islamic law, providing a framework for maintaining societal order.

However, the challenges arise when we examine the implementation of certain aspects of Islamic teachings in contemporary Muslim societies. The application of Sharia law, while seen by some as a moral and spiritual guide, has faced criticism in its execution. For instance, punishments prescribed by Sharia, such as amputation for theft or flogging for adultery, have raised concerns about human rights violations.

The treatment of women within the framework of Islamic law has been a subject of debate. Despite the Quranic emphasis on the dignity and rights of women, the interpretation and application of these principles vary, leading to instances where women's rights are perceived as subordinate to cultural norms.

Another point of contention is the reported age of Aisha when she married the Prophet Muhammad, as mentioned in Hadiths. The marriage, consummated when Aisha was around nine years old, has raised ethical concerns in contemporary times. Critics argue that such practices are incompatible with modern standards of consent and child protection, highlighting a dissonance between traditional teachings and evolving societal norms.

Furthermore, the contentious issues surrounding apostasy and blasphemy in some Islamic legal systems raise significant concerns about religious freedom and the right to express dissenting views. One particular area of contention is the death penalty imposed on individuals who choose to leave the Islamic faith. This severe punishment not only infringes upon the fundamental right to freedom of religion but also presents a theological dilemma. The absence of room for repentance and the imposition of such harsh penalties do not align with the portrayal of a merciful and compassionate God, as preached by Islam. Instead, it raises ethical questions about whether such measures amount to psychological imprisonment and limit the individual's ability to explore and choose their faith freely. This raises broader considerations about the compatibility of such legal provisions with modern values and the universal principles of human rights.

The ongoing struggle to reconcile traditional Islamic teachings with evolving societal norms reflects the complexities faced by modern Muslim societies. While Islam has made positive contributions to societal order and justice, its challenges in adapting to contemporary values require thoughtful reflection and engagement to ensure the harmonization of religious convictions with fundamental principles of human rights and equality.

**Accuracy of Predictions:**

The accuracy of predictions within Islam, particularly those found in the Quran, has been a topic of considerable debate and diversity among Muslim scholars. While the Quran does contain verses that are often considered prophetic, the lack of a unified interpretation has given rise to diverse and sometimes conflicting perspectives.

One example is the interpretation of verses related to future events, where varying views among Islamic scholars have led to distinct predictions. For instance, some verses in the Quran are believed to address end-time scenarios, the coming of a messianic figure, or apocalyptic events. However, the interpretations of these verses diverge widely. Some scholars argue that certain events have already occurred, while others maintain that they are yet to unfold.

One notable example is the interpretation of verses regarding the coming of Al-Mahdi, a messianic figure in Islam. Different sects within Islam hold contrasting views on whether Al-Mahdi has already appeared, is yet to emerge, or represents a symbolic concept rather than a literal figure. The lack of consensus on the specifics of these prophecies creates uncertainty and opens the door to various interpretations.

Additionally, the Quran contains verses that are often considered to predict future military victories and successes for the Muslim community. However, the outcomes of historical events, such as battles or conquests, are sometimes contested among scholars. This lack of clarity in the interpretation of prophecies raises questions about their accuracy and specificity.

In conclusion, the diversity of interpretations among Muslims regarding prophecies in the Quran contributes to the challenge of assessing their accuracy. The varying perspectives on the timing and nature of these predictions underscore the complexity of navigating the prophetic elements within Islamic scripture.

**Power and Evidence of God:**

Islamic theology posits the existence of divine evidence and manifestations of God, primarily attributing them to the miraculous nature of the Quran. However, unlike some other religious traditions, Islam tends to rely heavily on linguistic phenomena as evidence of the divine. The Quran is often considered a linguistic miracle, showcasing unparalleled eloquence in the Arabic language. This perspective, however, presents a unique challenge for individuals who may not possess specialized linguistic knowledge.

In contrast to certain Christian narratives that highlight miracles as historical events with associated eyewitness accounts, Islamic miracles are often rooted in the linguistic nuances of the Quran. The eloquence and literary beauty of the Arabic language, as exemplified in the Quran, are emphasized as signs of the divine. This linguistic-centric approach, while revered by those with linguistic expertise, may pose a potential barrier for individuals who lack such specialized knowledge.

Furthermore, when it comes to claims of supernatural powers and healing in Islam, there is a noticeable absence of concrete evidence. Instances where Muslim leaders attempt to heal the sick or cast out demons often rely solely on recitations from the Quran. However, these attempts, in many cases, lack the empirical evidence or tangible outcomes that might be expected from manifestations of supernatural power. Growing up in Africa, where such scenarios are not uncommon, I have witnessed instances where Islamic leaders attempt to address ailments through Quranic recitations, but the results are often inconclusive.

In summary, Islamic theology emphasizes linguistic miracles as evidence of God's existence, placing a particular focus on the Quran's eloquence. However, the lack of tangible, empirical evidence of supernatural power and healing in Islamic practices raises questions about the nature of these claims. The reliance on ancient stories and literature, without contemporary demonstrable evidence, distinguishes Islamic perspectives on the divine from certain other belief systems.

In conclusion, while recognizing the substantial historical and cultural contributions of Islam, a thorough examination unveils nuanced dimensions that merit thoughtful consideration. The historical intricacies surrounding the compilation of the Quran, the diverse factors influencing conversions, and the ongoing endeavor to harmonize traditional teachings with modern values underscore the multifaceted nature of Islam. The interpretation of prophetic elements and the reliance on linguistic miracles as divine evidence introduce layers of complexity to the evaluation.

As we navigate this exploration, it is imperative to approach these discussions with respect for diverse perspectives and a commitment to seeking a deeper understanding of the truth. The acknowledgment of Islam's rich history does not preclude a critical examination of its challenges and controversies. Engaging in open dialogue and fostering understanding can contribute to a more comprehensive comprehension of Islam's place in the fabric of religious beliefs and practices.

**Comparative Analysis**

The exploration of major Abrahamic religions, encompassing Judaism, Christianity, and Islam, unveils a shared tapestry of history and theology woven around the venerable figure of Abraham. These three faiths, though rooted in a common patriarchal lineage, have evolved distinctively, shaping the spiritual landscape of millions across the globe. In this comparative analysis, we embark on a journey to unravel the unique characteristics, theological tenets, and historical narratives that distinguish these Abrahamic traditions. Delving into their origins, scriptures, and core beliefs, we seek to illuminate the common threads that bind them while acknowledging the nuances that set each apart. This examination invites us to appreciate the intricate interplay of shared heritage and individual identity within the mosaic of Abrahamic faiths, fostering a deeper understanding of their profound impact on human civilization.

## Comparative Analysis on Origin:

In the exploration of religious origins, Judaism stands as a venerable masterpiece, woven with historical narratives and meticulously documented scriptures. The covenant between God and Abraham, inscribed in ancient scrolls, is not merely a page in history but a foundational chapter narrating the birth of a monotheistic faith. This narrative paints a profound picture of man's origin and his cosmic dwelling, an Earth and universe unveiled in the eloquent prose of Genesis.

Christianity, a dynamic continuation of this sacred narrative, stands with gratitude on the shoulders of its Jewish predecessor. It begins its journey not with the turn of a new leaf but with the unfolding of the Tanakh, the Hebrew Bible. The seamless transition from the Old Testament to the New is a testament to Christianity's acknowledgment of its roots. The Gospel of Matthew, an ode to Messianic prophecies, weaves a symphony that aligns Jesus' lineage with the historic promises made to Jewish patriarchs. In this symphony, Christianity finds its melody, harmonizing the teachings of the Messiah and his apostles with the sacred echoes of the past.

Yet, in this harmonious symphony, a discordant note emerges when we turn our gaze to Islam. Seeking a similar credibility, it undertakes an ambitious endeavor — to edit and alter the very narratives that shaped its Abrahamic ancestry. If a son claims legitimacy by acknowledging his male guardian as his biological father, the sanctity of this acknowledgment lies in preserving, not altering, the father's narrative. Islam, in its quest for divine legitimacy, falls short by attempting to edit the facts as presented by its spiritual predecessors.

The narrative of Prophet Muhammad, born in the vibrant tapestry of Mecca, takes a transformative turn with claims of divine revelations. These revelations, spanning 23 years until Muhammad's passing, propose edits and alterations to the Hebrew Scriptures, asserting a connection to the Abrahamic lineage. However, the question lingers — how can one born over 500 years after these events, and many miles away from their epicenter, claim to possess more accurate facts than those closer in time and proximity? This would be like someone born in Canada in 2587 (570 years later) claiming to know more than CNN's and Mike Pence's records concerning Donald Trump's presidency of 2017-2020, raising a fundamental challenge to the authenticity and reliability of such later claims to divine insight.

A poignant example of this editing lies in the narrative of Abraham's sacrifices. In the biblical account, it is Isaac, Abraham's son, who is presented as the intended sacrifice, embodying the covenant between God and Abraham (Genesis 22:2). However, the Quran alters this narrative, stating that it was Ishmael, not Isaac, who was to be sacrificed (Quran 37:100-109). This significant discrepancy raises questions about the authenticity and accuracy of these edited revelations. If the Quran, born centuries after the events it seeks to edit, offers an alternative account, it challenges the credibility of its claim to possess more accurate facts than the original, closer narratives.

In the grand symphony of religious origins, each note should harmonize, not disrupt, the melody of the preceding notes. Judaism and Christianity, bound by a respectful acknowledgment of their shared history, blend seamlessly. In this melodic journey, Christianity finds its strength in the prophetic fulfillment of the birth of the Jewish Messiah. Islam, seeking a place in this symphony, must tread with reverence, understanding that editing the sacred melodies of its predecessors risks discord in the divine narrative it aspires to join.

## My Criteria

**Comparative Analysis on Longevity:**

Judaism stands as a beacon of enduring wisdom, resiliently addressing profound questions about existence for thousands of years. Its commitment to preserving sacred texts, particularly the Hebrew Bible, provides a timeless perspective on the universe's origin. The Genesis creation account, a source of immense pride, stimulates ongoing contemplation and discussion. Jewish scholars have enriched metaphysical discourse, contributing valuable perspectives on the cosmos and God's nature. Judaism's longevity, coupled with its capacity to address fundamental questions about creation, underscores its unique position as a faith that perseveres and contributes significantly to humanity's understanding of the universe's origins.

Christianity, inheriting Judaism's resilience, maintains a global impact rooted in the continuity of Jewish scriptures. The Old Testament remains integral to its sacred canon, ensuring a seamless connection and continuity of profound insights into the mysteries of creation. Christianity's longevity, manifested in global communities, echoes Judaism's ability to transcend geographical and temporal boundaries. The unbroken thread connecting Old and New Testaments provides stability and rootedness, reinforcing the enduring relevance of the faith.

Islam, spanning over fourteen centuries, showcases longevity, yet its expansion's nature warrants scrutiny. Prophet Muhammad's military campaigns, known as Jihad, played a significant role. The conquests during the Arab expansion involved force and coercion, raising questions about the credibility of Islam as a purely peaceful source for spiritual guidance. Unlike Judaism and Christianity, Islam's longevity is often linked to violence and military conquests rather than an enduring commitment to wisdom and spiritual insight.

In evaluating the longevity of these Abrahamic faiths, it becomes evident that Judaism, with its enduring wisdom, lays a foundation on which Christianity seamlessly builds. Both religions stand out for their resilience and commitment to preserving sacred scriptures. In contrast, Islam's longevity, while notable, is clouded by a history of military force and coercion, introducing complexity and challenging its claim to be a purely peaceful and credible faith system compared to the enduring legacies of Judaism and Christianity.

**Comparative Analysis on Relevance:**

Judaism has demonstrated remarkable relevance by intertwining tradition with a timeless ethical framework found in the law of God as revealed through Moses. Rooted in the Torah, this sacred text not only serves as a spiritual guide but intricately weaves into daily life, addressing various aspects from hygiene to morality. The ethical principles derived from narratives like the Exodus resonate in contemporary discussions about freedom and human rights. Judaism's relevance extends beyond rituals; it is a holistic approach that touches every facet of human existence, offering a timeless ethical framework that illuminates the path for modern Jewish individuals and global communities.

Christianity, rooted in Jewish scriptures, integrates the ethical framework articulated in the law of God revealed through Moses. The New Testament aligns with Jewish principles while introducing a transformative love principle that transcends moral and social dimensions. The Sermon on the Mount mirrors the ethical guidance found in Jewish scriptures and introduces a love principle that fosters communities marked by compassion, forgiveness, and social justice. Christianity's relevance isn't confined to theological doctrines but extends to the lived experiences of believers, offering a moral compass rooted in love for navigating complex social and economic landscapes.

Islam, while making positive contributions to societal order and justice, faces challenges in implementing certain aspects of its teachings in contemporary Muslim societies. The emphasis on charity and social welfare through Zakat promotes economic justice, and Islamic jurisprudence provides guidance for legal systems. However, challenges arise in the implementation of Sharia law, with punishments like amputation and flogging raising concerns about human rights violations. The treatment of women within Islamic law and contentious issues surrounding apostasy and blasphemy raise significant concerns about religious freedom. The death penalty for apostasy, lacking room for repentance, raises ethical questions about its compatibility with modern values and human rights principles. Islam's ongoing struggle to reconcile traditional teachings with evolving societal norms requires thoughtful reflection to harmonize religious convictions with fundamental principles of human rights and equality.

**Comparative Analysis on Accuracy of Predictions:**

Judaism possesses a collection of prophecies, particularly about the anticipated Messiah, found in the Hebrew Bible (Tanakh). Examples include Daniel's vision of the Four Kingdoms, Isaiah's prophecy of the Suffering Servant, Micah's prediction of the Messiah's birthplace, and Jeremiah's prophecy of the New Covenant. These prophecies exhibit astonishing accuracy in predicting events, providing compelling evidence of spiritual insight within Jewish scriptures. However, divergence in interpreting these prophecies, especially concerning Jesus as the Messiah, highlights a significant challenge within Judaism.

Christianity, rooted in Judaism, continues the prophetic narrative, emphasizing Jesus as the fulfillment of Messianic prophecies. The New Testament aligns Jesus with Old Testament predictions, with examples like Isaiah's suffering servant. The intricate connection between the Old and New Testaments contributes to the enduring relevance of Christianity. Additionally, the fulfillment of specific prophecies in Jesus' life, death, and resurrection, as detailed in the Gospels, forms a compelling foundation for Christian belief.

Islam's accuracy of predictions, primarily within the Quran, faces challenges due to diverse interpretations among scholars. While the Quran contains verses that are considered prophetic, such as those related to end-time scenarios or military victories, the lack of consensus among Muslims raises questions about their accuracy. Interpretations of verses about the coming of Al-Mahdi, a messianic figure, vary, adding complexity to understanding Islamic prophecies. The diversity of perspectives within Islam underscores the challenge of assessing the accuracy and specificity of these predictions.

In conclusion, while all three Abrahamic faiths exhibit elements of prophecy, the accuracy and interpretation of these predictions differ. Judaism's prophecies, particularly those related to the Messiah, contribute to its rich spiritual heritage. Christianity, building on Judaism, emphasizes the fulfillment of prophecies in Jesus, providing a strong foundation for its beliefs. Islam, with prophecies in the Quran, faces challenges due to diverse interpretations, highlighting the complexity of navigating prophetic elements within Islamic scripture.

# My Criteria

## Comparative Analysis on Power and Evidence of God

Judaism, Christianity, and Islam each present unique perspectives on the power and evidence of God, drawing from their respective sacred texts and historical narratives. Within Judaism, the divine evidence is intricately woven into historical events and encounters with God, as recorded in the Hebrew Bible. The Burning Bush, Parting of the Red Sea, Ezekiel's vision, the Ten Plagues, and the destruction of Sodom and Gomorrah serve as powerful manifestations of God's presence and power. However, Judaism faces a limitation in providing contemporary empirical evidence, relying primarily on historical accounts.

*Christianity:* Christianity, building upon Judaism, introduces the New Testament, emphasizing the transformative experiences and miracles of Jesus. The Gospels document numerous miracles, healings, and divine interventions, illustrating God's active involvement in the lives of believers. The outpouring of the Holy Spirit on Pentecost in Acts 2 exemplifies the ongoing manifestation of divine power. Christianity's continuity with Jewish scriptures, coupled with the dynamic experiences of believers, positions it as a faith with enduring relevance and a present reality of God's power.

In addition to the historical evidence and scriptural foundations, Christians today continue to offer contemporary proof of God's power through answered prayers and miracles, particularly during worship sessions. These manifestations include instances of healing, restoration of mobility to the lame, and restoration of hearing to the deaf. While it's acknowledged that some within the Church have faced criticism for staged or fake miracles perpetrated by individuals seeking personal gain, it is essential to emphasize that the existence of such instances does not negate the occurrence of genuine miracles.

Admittedly, there have been cases where unfulfilled promises by misguided preachers have left some Christians disappointed. However, amidst such challenges, many believers have personally witnessed and experienced true miracles, reinforcing the conviction that the presence of deceptive practices does not eliminate the reality of authentic manifestations of God's power.

The transformative power of Christianity extends beyond physical healing to include deliverance from addictions and the profound transformation of lives. Christians often share testimonies of how their faith has played a pivotal role in overcoming various forms of addiction, ranging from substance abuse to destructive behaviors.

The process of deliverance from addiction within the Christian framework is often intertwined with spiritual experiences, prayer, and a reliance on divine intervention. Many individuals attribute their recovery and newfound freedom from addiction to a deepened connection with God and the support of their Christian community.

The personal stories of individuals who have experienced deliverance from addiction serve as powerful testimonials to the transformative nature of Christianity. These narratives emphasize the role of faith, prayer, and spiritual guidance in breaking the chains of addiction and leading individuals towards a path of recovery, redemption, and personal growth.

The transformation of lives through Christianity encompasses not only freedom from addiction but also a broader renewal of character, values, and purpose. Many Christians attest to a profound inner change that has positively impacted their relationships, decision-making, and overall well-being.

*Islam:* In contrast, Islam places a significant emphasis on the linguistic miracles of the Quran as evidence of God's existence.

The eloquence and literary beauty of the Arabic language in the Quran are considered signs of the divine. However, Islamic theology often lacks concrete, tangible evidence of supernatural power and healing. Attempts to address ailments through Quranic recitations may lack empirical outcomes, presenting a distinct approach compared to other faith traditions.

In summary, Christianity distinguishes itself within the Abrahamic heritage by seamlessly integrating divine evidence from both Jewish scriptures and the New Testament. The faith's ongoing experiences of believers, coupled with its historical authenticity, global influence, and enduring relevance, mark it as possessing a unique and comprehensive perspective on the power and evidence of God. Christianity's emphasis on the transformative power of faith and its dynamic engagement with contemporary challenges set it apart in the comparative analysis of Abrahamic belief systems. Serving as a space for believers to encounter the true power and presence of God through a living faith and ongoing relationship, Christianity remains resilient amid challenges. It is crucial to acknowledge that the actions of a few should not overshadow the genuine experiences of many who testify to the transformative power of God in their lives. The enduring belief in the authenticity of miracles, alongside an awareness of challenges within the faith community, contributes to the dynamic and evolving nature of Christianity as a living faith tradition. Despite recognizing that challenges exist and not every journey is smooth, the significant emphasis on deliverance from addiction and the transformative power of Christianity persists as a central narrative within Christian communities. These experiences reinforce the perception that Christianity offers not only spiritual guidance but also practical solutions for those seeking liberation from various life-controlling issues.

**Conclusion for Section 2:**

In conclusion, the examination of Judaism, Christianity, and Islam reveals distinct characteristics and narratives that shape their respective perspectives on the divine. Judaism, with its rich historical narratives and foundational principles, showcases a venerable faith that has played a pivotal role in shaping monotheistic traditions. Christianity, building upon the foundations of Judaism, emerges as a dynamic and transformative faith, marked by ongoing experiences of believers and a comprehensive engagement with contemporary challenges. Islam, while emphasizing linguistic miracles and the Quran's eloquence, grapples with challenges related to the interpretation of prophetic elements and the nature of divine evidence.

Throughout this analysis, Christianity stands out as a faith with unique attributes, drawing strength from the seamless integration of divine evidence in both Jewish scriptures and the New Testament. The ongoing experiences of believers, the historical authenticity of its teachings, and the global impact of Christian principles collectively position it as a distinctive and comprehensive perspective on the power and evidence of God.

To those exploring these major world religions, it is encouraged to embark on their own journey of exploration and reflection. Understanding the nuances and depth of each faith system requires an open mind and a willingness to engage with diverse perspectives. Moreover, fostering respectful dialogue and cultivating understanding among individuals of different faiths is paramount. In a world characterized by religious diversity, such conversations contribute to mutual respect, tolerance, and the celebration of the shared values that unite humanity. Ultimately, the quest for truth and spiritual understanding is a personal journey, and this exploration serves as an invitation for readers to embark on their own path of discovery and contemplation.

## Section 3: Modern Belief Systems

### Introduction:

The landscape of religious belief is vast and diverse, encompassing a multitude of perspectives that have emerged in more recent times. In this section, we delve into the examination of modern belief systems, each contributing a unique narrative to the broader tapestry of religious thought. Notable among these are the Bahá'í Faith, Mormonism, Jehovah's Witnesses, Rastafarianism, and others, each with distinct principles and practices that have garnered followers worldwide.

The purpose of this section is twofold: firstly, to explore and evaluate these modern belief systems using the established criteria applied earlier in the analysis, and secondly, to present reasons why Christianity, with its historical foundation and enduring influence, is considered superior according to these criteria. Through a thoughtful examination, we aim to provide insights into the distinctive features of these modern faiths and discern how they compare in terms of historical authenticity, transformative power, and enduring relevance.

### Subsection 3.1: Evaluation of the Bahá'í Faith:

The evaluation of the Bahá'í Faith, when scrutinized through the established criteria—Origin, Longevity, Relevance, Accuracy of Predictions, and The Power or Evidence of God—reveals certain limitations that raise questions about its superiority.

*Origin:* The Baháʼí Faith traces its origins to the 19th century, initiated by Baháʼuʼlláh, who claimed to be the latest in a line of Manifestations of God. While Baháʼí adherents view Baháʼuʼlláh's life and teachings as divinely inspired, the relatively recent emergence of the faith raises questions about its historical authenticity compared to older belief systems. Unlike the rich historical textile of Judaism, Christianity, and Islam, the Baháʼí Faith lacks centuries of historical context, making it susceptible to skepticism regarding the divine nature of its origins.

In Jewish tradition, the concept of the Messiah holds a central and profound significance, with expectations deeply rooted in the Hebrew Bible, known as the Old Testament. Jews anticipate the arrival of a messianic figure who will fulfill specific prophecies and usher in an era of spiritual and earthly redemption. In contrast, Baháʼuʼlláh, according to Baháʼí belief, claimed to be a Manifestation of God rather than the expected Messiah. His mission, as articulated in Baháʼí teachings, centers on the spiritual renewal of humanity and the establishment of global unity. This divergence is evident in the variance between traditional messianic expectations found in Jewish scriptures and Baháʼuʼlláh's asserted identity and purpose.

*Longevity and Global Reach:* The Baháʼí Faith, emerging just over a century and a half ago, faces challenges in attaining the global influence associated with well-established world religions. Its geographical concentration in specific regions and a gradual growth trajectory contrast sharply with the widespread and enduring impact observed in the major religions of Judaism, Christianity, and Islam. The relative youth of the Baháʼí Faith prompts critical questions about its ability to achieve lasting significance on a global scale, especially when compared to belief systems with centuries of historical presence and influence.

*Relevance of Bahá'í Principles:* While the Bahá'í principles, particularly the oneness of humanity and the elimination of prejudice, resonate with modern ideals, their practical application on a global scale is subject to scrutiny. The challenge lies in transforming these ideals into actionable solutions that effectively address complex contemporary issues. Without a demonstrated ability to effect substantial change, the relevance of these principles may be viewed as theoretical rather than practical.

Jewish theology places a profound emphasis on the authority of its scriptures, including the Torah, which is foundational to Jewish beliefs. The Torah is revered as the divine revelation that outlines moral, ethical, and legal principles for the Jewish people. In contrast, Bahá'u'lláh introduced a new set of scriptures considered sacred by Bahá'ís, including the Kitáb-i-Aqdas and the Kitáb-i-Íqán. While these writings emphasize unity and the oneness of religion, they are distinct from the authoritative scriptures of Judaism. This departure in scriptural authority signifies a fundamental difference in the religious foundations of the two faith traditions.

*Prophetic Elements:* The Bahá'í Faith asserts the concept of successive Manifestations of God, including Abraham, Moses, Buddha, Jesus, Muhammad, and Bahá'u'lláh. However, unlike the clear prophecies found in other religious traditions, the Bahá'í Faith's narrative lacks specific and concrete foretelling of events or guidance for the future. The absence of explicit prophecies raises doubts about the faith's ability to offer clear guidance in navigating humanity through future challenges.

Jewish scriptures are replete with covenants and prophecies that form the basis of the intricate relationship between God and the Jewish people. These covenants often involve specific promises, conditions, and the fulfillment of prophecies as a testament to divine guidance. In the Bahá'í Faith, concepts of covenant and prophecy exist, yet they differ in content and emphasis from those found in Jewish scriptures. Bahá'í teachings on covenant and prophecy introduce new dimensions, reflecting a divergence in the theological framework surrounding these essential elements.

*Divine Evidence and Manifestations:* The Bahá'í Faith emphasizes Bahá'u'lláh's revelations as divine evidence, highlighting spiritual transformation as a key manifestation of God's influence. However, this emphasis on personal and spiritual experience may be perceived as subjective, lacking the empirical demonstrations of divine power found in other faiths. The absence of historical miracles or ongoing divine interventions may impact the faith's ability to provide tangible evidence of the divine to skeptics.

In conclusion, the Bahá'í Faith's historical recency, limited global influence, challenges in translating principles into impactful solutions, and the absence of specific prophecies or concrete divine manifestations contribute to a nuanced evaluation. While it presents a unique perspective, understanding these aspects prompts a careful consideration of the Bahá'í Faith's claims in the broader context of world religions.

## Subsection 3.2: Evaluation of Mormonism (Latter-day Saint Movement):

**Origin:** Mormonism, originating in the Latter-day Saint Movement initiated by Joseph Smith in the early 19th century, introduces distinctive doctrinal elements, most notably the Book of Mormon. Joseph Smith, under the guidance of the angel Moroni and through divine revelations, translated the golden plates, leading to the establishment of the Church of Christ, later recognized as the Church of Jesus Christ of Latter-day Saints (LDS).

Despite positioning itself as a restoration of true Christianity, the historical narrative of Mormonism undergoes scrutiny due to the absence of external evidence supporting pivotal events. Notably, the golden plates integral to Smith's translation of the Book of Mormon lack tangible verification, prompting critics to question the authenticity of the translation process.

Mormonism faces doctrinal challenges, particularly in its claim to Abrahamic roots while attempting to modify both Jewish and Christian scriptures to align with its narrative. Notable changes include alterations to the Book of Genesis in the Bible and additions to the New Testament. These modifications introduce theological discrepancies, deviating from the seamless continuation of the Abrahamic tradition. Critics argue that such alterations compromise the foundational integrity of established scriptures, contributing to a divergence in doctrinal understanding rather than a cohesive continuation of the religious tradition.

**Longevity and Growth:** Examining the longevity of Mormonism, it's noteworthy that this movement is relatively young compared to traditional world religions. Despite its brief existence, Mormonism has shown a remarkable ability to adapt and expand. The LDS Church, with millions of members worldwide, has become a significant religious force, especially in North America and parts of the Western world.

While Mormonism has experienced significant growth, especially in the Western world, its youthfulness in comparison to other major religions raises questions about its long-term endurance. The rapid expansion of the LDS Church can be attributed, in part, to vigorous missionary efforts rather than intrinsic, enduring appeal.

**Relevance in Contemporary Context:** The relevance of Mormon teachings is evident in the strong sense of community and identity among Latter-day Saints. Doctrinal principles such as eternal families, ongoing revelation through modern prophets, and unique temple practices contribute to the distinctiveness of Mormon communities. The emphasis on genealogy and posthumous baptisms reflects a particular approach to salvation and family bonds.

The distinctiveness of Mormonism is evident in its emphasis on eternal families, ongoing revelation, and unique temple practices. However, attempts to edit existing Christian scriptures, such as the Bible, to align with Mormon doctrine, contribute to theological tensions. The introduction of new scriptures, including the Book of Mormon, challenges the conventional understanding of the biblical canon.

**Accuracy of Predictions:** Mormonism places a central focus on prophetic elements, with Joseph Smith's revelations forming a cornerstone of its theology. The Book of Mormon, considered by Mormons as another testament of Jesus Christ, adds a unique scriptural dimension to their faith. Ongoing revelations from successive prophets contribute to the dynamic nature of Mormon doctrine.

Joseph Smith's claim to ongoing prophetic revelation is a key feature of Mormonism. While this dynamic approach keeps the faith adaptable, it also introduces challenges. Doctrinal shifts over time, such as changes in the perception of race and the abandonment of polygamy, highlight the evolving nature of Mormon teachings, raising questions about the stability of its prophetic guidance.

Moreover, the history of Mormonism includes instances where prophecies attributed to Joseph Smith did not come to fruition. One significant prophecy attributed to Joseph Smith is related to the Second Coming of Christ and the construction of a temple in Independence, Missouri. According to some accounts, Smith prophesied that a temple would be built in that location during his generation and that Christ would return in the 19th century. However, this did not occur as predicted.

Another notable example is the failed prophecy of the "City of Zion" in Missouri, which Smith declared would be a gathering place for the righteous and the site of Christ's Second Coming. The failure of this prophecy to materialize as predicted has led to critical scrutiny and discussions within and outside the Mormon community, highlighting the complexities and challenges associated with claims of ongoing prophetic revelation.

**Divine Evidence and Manifestations:** In Mormon theology, divine evidence is often associated with personal spiritual experiences, commonly referred to as "burning in the bosom." While these subjective encounters hold deep meaning for believers, they present a challenge when seeking external validation. Additionally, claims of historical events in the Americas, as described in the Book of Mormon, lack archaeological support, leading to skepticism among scholars.

Mormonism relies on personal spiritual experiences as a form of divine evidence. The subjective nature of such encounters, termed the "burning in the bosom," makes external validation challenging. Additionally, the lack of archaeological evidence supporting Book of Mormon events, combined with contradictions with established historical records, contributes to skepticism regarding its divine origins.

Mormonism's distinct characteristics and relatively recent emergence underscore the importance of critically evaluating its doctrinal claims and the longevity of its impact. The emphasis on ongoing revelation and the adaptability of Mormon communities highlight their ability to navigate contemporary challenges. However, the lack of external evidence supporting key historical events and the relatively short duration of the movement invite scrutiny in the comparative analysis of belief systems. The challenges presented by historical authenticity, attempts to edit established scriptures, and ongoing doctrinal shifts contribute to the complexities of evaluating Mormonism within the broader spectrum of religious belief systems.

## Subsection 3.3: Evaluation of Jehovah's Witnesses (Watch Tower Society):

**Origin and Doctrinal Challenges:** Jehovah's Witnesses, established by Charles Taze Russell in the late 19th century, claim to represent a restoration of true Christianity. However, their unique doctrinal positions, such as the denial of the Trinity and the rejection of the traditional Christian view of the afterlife, have led to considerable theological divergence. The origins of the movement and its subsequent doctrinal shifts raise questions about the consistency and authenticity of its theological foundation.

**Longevity:** Jehovah's Witnesses, emerging in the relatively recent past with a presence spanning just over a century, stand in stark contrast to the ancient roots of Judaism and Christianity. Unlike the well-established scriptures of these longstanding traditions, Jehovah's Witnesses have notably produced their own version of the Bible, introducing alterations to align with their doctrinal interpretations. This departure from the preservation of ancient texts, a hallmark of enduring faith traditions, raises questions about the legitimacy and historical continuity of Jehovah's Witnesses' beliefs. The act of creating a customized version of the Bible not only emphasizes the novelty of their movement but also indicates an attempt to adjust established scriptures to fit their distinctive narrative, a practice that diverges from the historical preservation and reverence for sacred texts observed in more ancient faiths.

While Jehovah's Witnesses have maintained a presence for over a century, their growth has been characterized by periods of significant expansion and contraction. The organizational structure, centralized around the Watch Tower Society, has faced criticisms for its hierarchical nature and authoritative control. The internal governance and decision-making processes have been a subject of contention, potentially impacting the movement's longevity and stability.

**Relevance and Social Impact:** The relevance of Jehovah's Witness beliefs and practices is notable within their communities, yet their strict doctrinal positions, including the refusal of blood transfusions and military service, have generated controversy. These stances, while integral to their faith, may be perceived as limiting personal freedoms and autonomy, thereby affecting their overall relevance in the broader societal context.

**Prophetic Elements and End Times Views:** Jehovah's Witnesses have a distinctive set of beliefs regarding the end times, with specific predictions about the establishment of God's kingdom. Notably, past predictions about the end of the world, such as the failed expectations for 1914, 1925, and 1975, have led to doctrinal adjustments. These unfulfilled prophecies challenge the credibility of their prophetic claims and introduce skepticism about the accuracy of their teachings regarding the end times.

**Divine Evidence and Manifestations:** The theological emphasis of Jehovah's Witnesses centers on the proclamation of God's kingdom. While they assert divine evidence through their interpretation of biblical prophecy, the lack of tangible manifestations or verifiable supernatural occurrences raises questions about the validity of their claims. Unlike some other faith traditions, Jehovah's Witnesses do not attribute miracles or charismatic manifestations as integral parts of their religious practices.

In summary, Jehovah's Witnesses, despite their organizational longevity and zealous community engagement, face challenges in doctrinal consistency, failed prophecies, and limited societal relevance. The distinctiveness of their theological positions and the absence of widely recognized divine manifestations contribute to a complex evaluation within the broader landscape of religious belief systems.

## Subsection 3.4: Evaluation of Rastafarian Beliefs

Rastafarianism, with its distinctive beliefs and cultural expressions, stands as a unique spiritual movement rooted in the African diaspora. This section aims to critically evaluate the core tenets of Rastafarianism using a five-level criteria. By delving into its origin, longevity, relevance, accuracy of predictions, and the evidence of divine power, we seek to gain a comprehensive understanding of the strengths and limitations inherent in Rastafarian beliefs.

**Origin:** Rastafarianism, emerging in the early 20th century Jamaica, was intricately tied to the Afro-Caribbean struggle against the oppressive forces of Western imperialism. The movement sought to break the chains of colonialism, racial injustice, and economic disparity that plagued the marginalized population.

## My Criteria

It was a noble endeavor for Africans to seek redemption and separation from oppressive imperialism.

The circumstances leading to the emergence of Rastafarianism were marked by socio-economic challenges and charismatic leaders like Marcus Garvey, who advocated for the repatriation of Africans. The movement began as a powerful response to the harsh realities faced by the Afro-Caribbean people, driven by a desire for identity, liberation, and cultural pride.

As the movement evolved, spiritual experiences, divine revelations, and a profound sense of calling became integral to the Rastafarian narrative. While these elements are central to their faith, it is essential to critically evaluate their claims, considering the historical and cultural context. The transition from a movement to a belief system introduced a shift in focus, as Rastafarianism started altering aspects of the Jewish scriptures.

The symbolic practice of growing dreadlocks, representing a covenant with God, draws inspiration from biblical references such as the Nazirite vow. However, it's noteworthy that Rastafarianism, born out of the struggle against Western imperialism, has, in its evolution, ventured into adjusting the purity of the Jewish scriptures. While seeking liberation was justified, altering the Hebrew scriptures compromises the integrity of the Rastafarian faith system.

In essence, while Rastafarianism originated as a movement to break free from oppressive forces, it later transformed into a belief system. This transformation, while preserving cultural identity and pride, introduced a dynamic that altered the purity of the Jewish scriptures, a compromise that warrants critical examination. The noble intentions behind the movement should be acknowledged, yet the adjustments made to the ancient Hebrew scriptures demand careful consideration in evaluating the faith system's overall coherence and authenticity.

**Longevity:** Rastafarianism, born out of the socio-political landscape of early 20th century Jamaica, has exhibited a remarkable longevity. Its roots in the Afro-Caribbean struggle for identity and liberation have allowed it to transcend temporal boundaries. The enduring nature of Rastafarianism is evident in its ability to resonate with successive generations, providing a spiritual anchor for those seeking empowerment and cultural pride.

As Rastafarianism spread beyond its Jamaican origins, it underwent adaptations influenced by various cultural contexts. The movement's ability to endure lies in its capacity to evolve without losing its core principles. Whether in the heart of Jamaica or on distant shores, Rastafarianism has adapted to different social landscapes, maintaining its relevance as a symbol of resistance against oppression.

Central to Rastafarian identity is the symbolic practice of growing dreadlocks. This distinctive hairstyle represents a commitment to a natural way of life and a rejection of societal norms imposed by the oppressors. The enduring presence of dreadlocks in the Rastafarian community serves as a visible testament to their unwavering dedication to cultural pride, resistance against injustice, and a spiritual connection with the divine.

While Rastafarianism has shown resilience and endurance, it is crucial to acknowledge its relatively recent emergence compared to the ancient revelations of Judaism and Christianity. The longevity of Rastafarianism, while noteworthy, does not compete with the deep historical roots and enduring traditions found in these ancient belief systems. This comparison highlights the distinctive temporal context of Rastafarianism and its place within the broader tapestry of religious traditions. In examining longevity, the lens widens to appreciate both the unique contributions and the temporal limitations of Rastafarianism in the larger landscape of world religions.

**Relevance:** Rastafarianism, rooted in the historical struggle against oppression, continues to be relevant in addressing contemporary societal issues. Its emphasis on social justice, equality, and resistance aligns with ongoing global conversations about systemic injustices and the quest for a more equitable world. Rastafarian beliefs resonate with individuals seeking spiritual guidance that intersects with the challenges of the present day.

Rastafarianism provides a unique lens through which to examine and respond to societal challenges. The belief system's emphasis on liberation and empowerment positions it as a source of inspiration for those grappling with issues of identity, discrimination, and economic disparity. By weaving elements of resistance into its spiritual fabric, Rastafarianism offers a perspective that encourages social awareness and transformation.

At the heart of Rastafarian beliefs is a commitment to a natural way of life, symbolized by practices such as growing dreadlocks and adhering to a specific diet. This commitment serves as a counter-cultural stance against societal norms that may perpetuate exploitation and environmental degradation. The Rastafarian emphasis on living in harmony with nature aligns with contemporary concerns about sustainable living and ecological responsibility.

While Rastafarianism addresses significant contemporary issues, it faces criticisms on certain theological and cultural grounds. Two notable areas of contention include:

*Haile Selassie I:* Rastafarians' veneration of Haile Selassie I as a **messianic figure** (against his approval) and the embodiment of the supreme deity, Jah, diverges from traditional Christian and Hebrew scriptures. Critics argue that elevating a historical figure to divine status contradicts the foundational tenets of monotheistic faiths, including Judaism and Christianity. The belief in Haile

Selassie I as a fulfillment of biblical prophecies is a departure from mainstream interpretations, prompting theological debates about the appropriateness of such deification.

*Marijuana (Ganja):* The sacramental use of marijuana within **Rastafarian rituals** has drawn criticism, particularly from legal and health perspectives. While Rastafarians view marijuana as a tool for spiritual enlightenment and divine connection, broader societal concerns about drug use and its associated health risks have fueled debates. Critics argue that the promotion of marijuana as a sacrament may perpetuate negative stereotypes and hinder the broader acceptance of Rastafarianism. Additionally, the legal status of marijuana in many jurisdictions raises practical challenges and ethical considerations surrounding its use in religious practices.

Acknowledging these criticisms is crucial for a comprehensive evaluation of Rastafarian beliefs. While the belief system addresses contemporary issues, the theological and cultural aspects mentioned above prompt reflection and dialogue both within and outside the Rastafarian community. This recognition fosters an open exploration of the strengths and challenges inherent in Rastafarianism, contributing to a more nuanced understanding of its place in the broader religious landscape.

## My Criteria

**Accuracy of predictions:**

Rastafarian beliefs include prophecies that often center around themes of liberation, repatriation to Africa, and the establishment of a divine kingdom on Earth. These prophecies are derived from interpretations of biblical texts, particularly those referring to Zion, Ethiopia, and the struggles of people of African descent.

Assessing the accuracy of these prophecies requires a careful analysis of historical events and developments within the Rastafarian community. For example, the prophecy of repatriation to Africa aligns with the movement's emphasis on returning to the ancestral homeland. However, the fulfillment of such prophecies may be subjective, varying in interpretation among Rastafarians.

Prophecies play a crucial role in shaping the identity and aspirations of the Rastafarian community. They provide a framework for understanding historical events and guide the community's collective consciousness. Examining the role of prophecies involves exploring how they influence Rastafarian perspectives on social justice, equality, and the pursuit of a utopian society.

However, Rastafarianism utilizes biblical prophecies to predict the future, yet it often alters the interpretations to give them different meanings. The movement's unique lens may reinterpret biblical passages to fit its narrative, leading to a distinct set of beliefs that deviate from mainstream Christian interpretations.

While prophecies contribute to the spiritual richness of Rastafarianism, the subjective nature of their interpretation poses challenges in objectively assessing their accuracy. The role of prophecies in shaping the narrative and worldview of Rastafarianism highlights the intricate interplay between spirituality, history, and the quest for social justice within this belief system.

**Evidence of God in Rastafarianism:** The examination of the power and evidence of God within Rastafarianism involves an exploration of claimed miracles, signs, and transformative experiences, contributing to the belief system's overall understanding of divine manifestations.

Rastafarianism asserts the presence of divine power through various means, including spiritual encounters, visions, and the acknowledgment of divine forces in the natural world. The movement often attributes these manifestations to the influence of Jah, the supreme deity.

Claims of miracles, signs, and transformative experiences are woven into the fabric of Rastafarian spirituality. Individuals within the community may share accounts of healing, spiritual revelations, or other extraordinary occurrences that they attribute to the intervention of divine forces. These experiences contribute to a shared narrative that strengthens the community's faith.

Within the Rastafarian belief system, these manifestations serve as evidence of God's existence and active involvement in the lives of believers. The transformative power of these experiences is seen as a testament to the reality of divine influence and reinforces the central tenets of Rastafarian faith.

However, it is noteworthy that Rastafarianism, in its quest to emphasize divine manifestations, sometimes incorporates elements from traditional African religious systems. Ceremonies that incorporate practices such as voodoo are believed to showcase the power and evidence of the Divine. This blending of spiritual traditions reflects the syncretic nature of Rastafarianism but may also present points of tension, particularly when compared to the more conservative stance of Christian denominations that view such practices as incompatible with their doctrinal teachings.

While Rastafarianism embraces a diverse range of spiritual expressions, the intersections with traditional African religious practices highlight the complexity and diversity within the movement. Understanding these dynamics provides insight into the intricate tapestry of beliefs and practices that shape the Rastafarian worldview.

**Conclusion:** In our comprehensive exploration of Rastafarianism, a belief system with roots in the resistance to Western imperialism, we have employed a five-level criteria to evaluate its key tenets and practices. Let us summarize our findings, discussing the strengths and limitations of Rastafarian beliefs and encouraging readers to engage in further exploration and critical thinking about this unique faith.

Origin: Rastafarianism's historical roots are intertwined with a movement that emerged as a response to oppressive Western imperialism. While its initial impetus was noble, the transition into a distinct belief system brought about modifications to the purity of the Jewish scriptures, raising concerns about the faith's authenticity and the fidelity to its origins.

Longevity: As a relatively recent belief system, Rastafarianism lacks the extensive historical continuity found in ancient revelations of Judaism and Christianity. Despite its comparatively short existence, the faith endures, marked by a profound commitment to its principles, notably symbolized by the wearing of dreadlocks.

Relevance: Rastafarian beliefs address contemporary issues through a dedication to a natural way of life, challenging societal norms. However, criticisms surround certain unique perspectives, such as the deification of Haile Selassie I and the sacramental use of marijuana, prompting thoughtful reflection on the relevance of these elements in the modern context.

Accuracy of Predictions (Prophecies): The incorporation of biblical prophecies within Rastafarianism is notable, but the divergence in interpretation, with alterations to the meanings of these prophecies, raises questions about the accuracy and consistency of predictions within the belief system.

The Power or Evidence of God: Divine manifestations in Rastafarianism, including claimed miracles and transformative experiences, contribute to the evidence of God. However, the simultaneous incorporation of traditional African religious practices, particularly those involving voodoo during worship ceremonies, may create tensions, especially when contrasted with more conservative Christian views.

Strengths and Limitations: *Strengths:* Rastafarianism demonstrates strength in its commitment to resistance, cultural identity, and fostering a spiritual connection to the divine. The faith creates a sense of community and shared experience. *Limitations:* The syncretic nature of Rastafarianism, blending various spiritual traditions, introduces tensions, and the alterations to biblical narratives pose concerns about the faith's authenticity.

Engaging with Rastafarianism necessitates an open mind, acknowledging its unique contributions to spiritual discourse while critically examining its deviations from established traditions. Further exploration and critical thinking will contribute to a deeper understanding of Rastafarianism and its place in the diverse landscape of world religions. Approach this exploration with respect, intellectual curiosity, and a commitment to appreciating the complex interplay of beliefs that shape our global spiritual tapestry.

**Comparative Analysis:**

Having meticulously assessed the Baháʼí Faith, Mormonism, Jehovah's Witnesses, and Rastafarianism through the established criteria of Origin, Longevity, Relevance, Accuracy of Predictions, and The Power or Evidence of God, it is essential to offer a comparative analysis of their distinctive features and inherent limitations.

**The Baháʼí Faith**, originating in the 19th century through Baháʼuʼlláh's teachings, faces skepticism about its historical authenticity due to its recent emergence compared to the deep-rooted histories of Judaism, Christianity, and Islam. While adherents consider Baháʼuʼlláh's teachings as divinely inspired, the lack of centuries of historical context raises questions about the faith's divine origins. In contrast to rich Messianic expectations deeply embedded in Jewish scriptures, Baháʼuʼlláh's claim as a Manifestation of God, rather than the anticipated Messiah, introduces a significant divergence. The Baháʼí mission focuses on spiritual renewal and global unity, departing from the traditional messianic expectations outlined in Jewish prophecies.

The relative youth of the Baháʼí Faith raises concerns about its lasting significance globally when compared to belief systems with centuries of historical presence. While Baháʼí principles, such as the oneness of humanity, resonate with modern ideals, their practical application faces scrutiny. Transforming these ideals into actionable solutions for contemporary issues is a challenge, and their relevance may be perceived as theoretical rather than practical without substantial demonstrable change.

The Baháʼí Faith's narrative lacks specific and concrete foretelling of events or guidance for the future, unlike other religious traditions with clear prophecies. The absence of explicit prophecies raises doubts about the faith's ability to offer clear guidance in navigating humanity through future challenges. The Baháʼí Faith emphasizes personal and spiritual experiences as divine evidence, which may be perceived as subjective and lacking the empirical demonstrations of divine power found in other faiths. The absence of historical miracles or ongoing divine interventions raises questions about the faith's ability to provide tangible evidence of the divine. In conclusion, the Baháʼí Faith's historical recency, limited global influence, challenges in translating principles into impactful solutions, and the absence of specific prophecies or concrete divine manifestations contribute to a nuanced evaluation. While presenting a unique perspective, understanding these aspects prompts a careful consideration of the Baháʼí Faith's claims in the broader context of world religions, revealing its limitations in comparison to the enduring and comprehensive nature of Christianity.

**Mormonism**, rooted in the 19th-century Latter-day Saint Movement, introduces unique elements like the Book of Mormon. However, its historical narrative faces scrutiny due to the lack of external evidence supporting key events, such as the golden plates' translation. Doctrinally, Mormonism's attempts to edit both Jewish and Christian scriptures for narrative alignment raise questions about its coherence with the broader Abrahamic tradition, a contrast to the historical authenticity and continuity observed in Christianity. Notably, Mormonism introduces distinctive teachings about the nature of God, including the concept of a "Father God" and "Mother God," suggesting a departure from the traditional Christian understanding of the divine.

While traditional Christian doctrine emphasizes the oneness of God in a trinitarian framework, Mormonism introduces a unique perspective by positing a multiplicity of gods and the idea of humans progressing to godhood. The introduction of a "Mother God" alongside the more conventional "Father God" deviates from traditional Christian teachings, challenging the long-standing understanding of God's nature. This departure underscores a doctrinal distinction that sets Mormonism apart from the historical continuity and theological coherence observed in traditional Christianity. The introduction of novel theological concepts, such as the belief in multiple gods and a divine Mother, contributes to the theological divergence between Mormonism and traditional Christian doctrines.

**Jehovah's Witnesses**, though present for over a century, exhibit periods of expansion and contraction, and their hierarchical organizational structure has faced criticism. The production of a customized version of the Bible, deviating from the historical preservation of ancient texts, highlights a departure from the reverence for scriptures seen in Christianity. This raises concerns about the historical legitimacy and continuity of Jehovah's Witnesses' beliefs compared to the well-established traditions of Christianity. Notably, one significant departure lies in their rejection of Christ's deity and the concept of the Trinity, which are foundational tenets of traditional Christian doctrine. While mainstream Christianity affirms the divinity of Jesus Christ and the triune nature of God, Jehovah's Witnesses diverge by asserting that Jesus is a created being and rejecting the notion of a triune God.

This theological departure sets Jehovah's Witnesses apart from mainstream Christianity, challenging the core beliefs that have been central to Christian tradition for centuries. The rejection of Christ's deity and the Trinity underscores a fundamental theological difference that not only separates them from orthodox Christian teachings but also questions the alignment of their beliefs with historical Christian doctrines. Christianity, throughout its long and established history, has adhered to the Nicene Creed, affirming the divinity of Christ and the triune nature of God. Jehovah's Witnesses' theological distinctiveness, as evidenced by their modified Bible and rejection of foundational Christian doctrines, invites scrutiny regarding the continuity and authenticity of their beliefs in comparison to the enduring traditions of Christianity.

In this comparative analysis, while acknowledging the unique aspects and strengths of these modern belief systems, it becomes evident that Christianity surpasses them based on the established criteria. Christianity's historical authenticity, global influence, and enduring relevance position it as a faith with a more comprehensive perspective on the power and evidence of God. Its emphasis on a living faith, ongoing relationship with God, and transformative power in the lives of believers distinguishes it from these contemporary belief systems, underscoring its enduring significance.

**Rastafarianism:** Amidst the diverse tapestry of contemporary belief systems, Rastafarianism emerges as a unique thread, weaving cultural resistance, spirituality, and identity into its fabric. Born out of the fervor of resistance against Western imperialism, Rastafarianism carries both strengths and limitations, providing a distinct perspective on spirituality.

One of the notable strengths of Rastafarianism lies in its commitment to resisting oppressive forces. Rooted in the historical context of colonialism and slavery, the movement sought redemption and separation from the chains of imperialism. The symbol of growing dreadlocks became a powerful representation of this commitment, signifying a covenant with God as mentioned in the Bible.

Rastafarianism exhibits an enduring nature, deeply intertwined with cultural identity. The resilience of this belief system, especially symbolized by the wearing of dreadlocks, stands as a testament to its ability to withstand external pressures. It reflects a cultural and spiritual resistance that has endured over time.

Despite its commendable commitment to cultural resistance, Rastafarianism faces scrutiny due to alterations made to the Hebrew Scriptures of the Bible. Initially a movement seeking liberation, it later evolved into a belief system, and in the process, some adherents introduced modifications to the purity of Jewish scriptures. This raises concerns about the faith's authenticity and its deviation from the original texts.

In the grand tapestry of world religions, Rastafarianism appears as a relatively recent belief system. Its historical recency and limited global influence, especially when compared to the ancient revelations of Judaism and Christianity, pose challenges to its broader impact and enduring significance on a global scale.

When compared to other contemporary belief systems like the Bahá'í Faith, Mormonism, and Jehovah's Witnesses, Rastafarianism stands out for its cultural resistance and commitment to identity. However, its limitations, particularly the alterations to Jewish scriptures and historical recency, place it in a unique position within the spectrum of modern spiritual perspectives.

In conclusion, as we unravel the complexities of Rastafarianism, acknowledging its strengths and limitations, it becomes a vital part of the broader conversation on contemporary belief systems. Each belief system contributes a distinct color to the canvas of spirituality, inviting exploration and understanding. Rastafarianism's journey from resistance to a belief system illuminates the intricate interplay between spirituality, identity, and the quest for liberation. Engaging with its unique narrative fosters a richer understanding of the diverse ways in which individuals seek meaning and connection in the ever-evolving landscape of faith.

**Section Conclusion**

In conclusion, the evaluation of the Baháʼí Faith, Mormonism, Jehovah's Witnesses, and Rastafarianism reveals distinct features that set them apart from Christianity. The Baháʼí Faith, while embodying principles of unity and oneness, faces challenges related to its recent origin, limited global influence, and the applicability of its principles on a practical scale. Mormonism introduces unique doctrinal elements and a distinctive narrative, including the concept of "Father God" and "Mother God," but its historical narrative and attempts to align and edit scriptures raise questions about its coherence within the broader Abrahamic tradition. The Jehovah's Witnesses, though present for over a century, grapple with issues of organizational structure and the historical legitimacy of their scripture, deviating from the historical preservation seen in Christianity.

In light of these evaluations, Christianity stands out as a belief system with historical authenticity, global influence, and enduring relevance. The foundational scriptures of Christianity, rooted in the Old and New Testaments, provide a continuity that contrasts with the recent origins and doctrinal innovations observed in the modern belief systems. The trinitarian nature of God, central to Christian theology, remains steadfast, offering a coherent and long-standing understanding of the divine.

Readers are encouraged to delve into their own exploration and reflection on these modern belief systems, considering the criteria of origin, longevity, relevance, accuracy of predictions, and the power or evidence of God. Engaging in respectful dialogue and seeking a deeper understanding of diverse perspectives can contribute to fostering a more solid and informed worldview. Ultimately, the comparative analysis highlights the nuanced nature of religious beliefs and underscores the multifaceted considerations involved in evaluating their merits.

## Section 4: Contemporary Belief Systems

In exploring the diverse landscape of contemporary belief systems, it becomes imperative to apply a discerning lens to the myriad ideologies that shape the spiritual landscape. This section aims to extend into the evaluation of various contemporary belief systems, emphasizing their unique characteristics, strengths, and inherent limitations. The focus is to navigate through the complexity of these systems, using established criteria to discern their authenticity and applicability.

### Subsection 4.1: Evaluation of New Age Spirituality:

New Age Spirituality, marked by its eclectic and often syncretic nature, emerges as a distinct paradigm in the contemporary spiritual milieu. Originating in the latter half of the 20th century, it amalgamates diverse elements from Eastern philosophies, Western esoteric traditions, and holistic practices. While proponents of New Age Spirituality advocate for personal transformation, interconnectedness, and self-discovery, a critical examination reveals noteworthy limitations.

Origin: The eclectic origins of New Age Spirituality, drawing from disparate sources without a unified historical foundation, pose a challenge to its historical legitimacy. Unlike well-established religions with centuries of historical context, the recent amalgamation of New Age beliefs lacks the depth and continuity found in ancient traditions. This amalgamation raises questions about the coherence and authenticity of the spiritual narrative it presents.

Longevity: New Age Spirituality, being a relatively recent phenomenon, confronts challenges related to its longevity and enduring influence. The ephemerality of certain New Age trends and practices, often subject to shifting popular discourse, raises concerns about the lasting impact of its teachings. In contrast to the enduring traditions of established religions, New Age Spirituality faces the test of time and the question of whether its principles will withstand the challenges of cultural evolution.

Relevance: While New Age Spirituality resonates with the contemporary emphasis on individualism, self-improvement, and holistic well-being, its relevance is often contingent on subjective interpretations. The lack of a standardized doctrinal framework results in a diverse array of beliefs within the New Age movement, making it challenging to ascertain a unified and universally applicable set of principles. This inherent subjectivity may hinder its broader relevance as a cohesive belief system.

Accuracy of Predictions: New Age Spirituality, characterized by esoteric practices and predictions, often lacks the empirical grounding found in evidence-based forecasting. Claims of astrological predictions, cosmic energies, and prophecies about cosmic shifts remain largely speculative. Unlike certain religious traditions with clear prophetic elements rooted in historical narratives, New Age predictions lack the specificity and verifiability that would lend credence to their accuracy.

The Power or Evidence of God: In the realm of New Age Spirituality, the concept of God or the divine is often nebulous and subjective. The absence of a concrete and universally accepted understanding of the divine challenges the notion of providing tangible evidence of God's existence or influence. Practices such as crystal healing, chakra alignment, and other metaphysical endeavors lack empirical support, making it difficult to establish the objective manifestation of divine power.

In summary, while New Age Spirituality embraces a diverse array of spiritual practices and aspirations for personal growth, its eclectic origins, recent emergence, subjective relevance, speculative predictions, and nebulous understanding of the divine contribute to a nuanced evaluation. As we proceed to examine other contemporary belief systems, it becomes evident that the quest for spiritual truth requires a discerning exploration of each paradigm's strengths and limitations.

## Subsection 4.2: Evaluation of Atheism:

Atheism, as a worldview devoid of belief in a deity or deities, has a longstanding presence throughout history, often challenged by various manifestations of God and the world. The Bible, for instance, asserts that those who deny the divine existence are deemed foolish (Psalm 14:1). However, despite its historical persistence, Atheism faces inherent challenges that render it inadequate in various aspects, particularly when subjected to specific criteria.

Origin: Atheism's historical roots can be traced back to ancient civilizations, finding expression in the works of Greek philosophers like Epicurus and Lucretius. While it has endured over time, the absence of a unified origin narrative and the diversity of individual paths to atheism raise questions about the coherence and foundational narrative of this belief system. Additionally, the continuous presence of belief in God across different cultures and societies challenges the claim that atheism is a natural default.

Longevity: Atheism, as a formalized worldview, has persisted for centuries, often gaining prominence during the Enlightenment era. Despite its longevity, the lack of a centralized doctrinal structure or organized institutions prompts considerations about the sustainability and cohesiveness of atheistic thought over extended periods. The contrasting endurance of religious traditions with shared narratives and institutional structures raises questions about the long-term viability of atheism as a comprehensive worldview.

Relevance: Atheism, aligning itself with scientific inquiry and rational discourse, is deemed relevant in contemporary discussions, especially concerning the separation of church and state. However, the inherent diversity within atheistic thought, ranging from agnostic atheism to assertive anti-theism, challenges the notion of a unified and universally applicable set of principles, impacting its broader relevance. Furthermore, the growing body of research indicating the positive impact of spirituality on well-being calls into question the perceived relevance of atheism in fostering emotional and psychological well-being.

Accuracy of Predictions: Atheism, primarily focused on empirical evidence and reason, does not inherently involve predictions about future events, particularly in the realm of metaphysics. While scientific advancements are integral to atheistic discourse, the worldview itself does not offer specific predictions about the existence or non-existence of God. This limitation, combined with the subjective nature of belief and the insufficiency of empirical evidence in matters of metaphysics, raises questions about the adequacy of atheistic arguments in fully addressing questions of divine existence.

The Power or Evidence of God: Atheism, by its nature, lacks belief in the divine and does not provide evidence for or against the existence of God. However, spiritual traditions often present evidence of positive and productive lives among believers, both emotionally and psychologically. This evidence, combined with the subjective nature of belief, challenges the notion that atheism, by itself, is sufficient to provide a comprehensive framework for understanding the human experience.

In summary, Atheism, while having historical roots, faces inherent challenges that question its adequacy when subjected to specific criteria. The ongoing dialogue surrounding matters of faith and worldview necessitates a nuanced exploration of the strengths and weaknesses inherent in atheistic perspectives.

## Subsection 4.3: Evaluation of Agnosticism:

Agnosticism, positioned as a philosophical stance asserting the impossibility of certain knowledge about the existence or non-existence of God, represents a nuanced perspective within the spectrum of religious beliefs. While agnostics affirm uncertainty about the divine, it is imperative to explore the underlying principles and positions of Agnosticism to understand its strengths and weaknesses when subjected to specific criteria.

Origin: Agnosticism, as a term coined by Thomas Huxley in the late 19th century, crystallized as a response to the challenges posed by both religious dogma and assertive atheism. Despite its relatively recent formalization, the acknowledgment of human limitations in comprehending the divine has deep historical roots. The Bible, in Romans 1:19-20, suggests that every human being has an inherent knowledge of God, stating, "For what can be known about God is plain to them because God has shown it to them. For his invisible attributes, namely, his eternal power and divine nature, have been clearly perceived, ever since the creation of the world, in the things that have been made." This scriptural perspective implies that agnosticism may, at its core, represent a reluctance or disobedience to recognize the divine revelation evident in the created world.

Longevity: Agnosticism, in its essence, reflects an enduring aspect of human intellectual and spiritual inquiry, transcending formalized labels. The acknowledgment of the limits of human knowledge and the search for understanding beyond empirical evidence are inherent to the human experience. However, the formalization of agnosticism as a distinct worldview in the modern era raises questions about its longevity as a cohesive and influential system of thought. The tension between acknowledging inherent human limitations and actively seeking a relationship with the divine complicates the evaluation of agnosticism's long-term viability.

Relevance: Agnosticism, emphasizing humility in the face of the unknown, maintains relevance in intellectual and philosophical discussions. However, the subjective nature of the human heart's conviction, as suggested by biblical verses, challenges the complete neutrality claimed by agnosticism. The recognition of a divine presence in the human heart, as outlined in Romans 1:19-20, raises questions about whether agnosticism, in certain cases, may be an expression of spiritual complacency or disobedience, refraining from acknowledging what is inherently known.

Accuracy of Predictions: Agnosticism, by definition, refrains from making definitive predictions about the existence or non-existence of God. However, the acknowledgment of an inherent knowledge of God, as posited in Romans 1:19-20, implies that agnosticism may fall short in accurately addressing the depth of human understanding and its intrinsic connection to the divine. The reluctance to actively seek and recognize divine revelation may lead to an incomplete understanding of the human experience.

The Power or Evidence of God: Agnosticism, often rooted in a desire for intellectual honesty and an aversion to dogmatic assertions, may overlook the subtle yet pervasive evidence of God's existence. The recognition of divine attributes in the created world, as suggested in Romans 1:19-20, challenges the agnostic stance that claims an inability to perceive or know God. This limitation, combined with the potential spiritual implications, underscores the need for a nuanced evaluation of agnosticism within the broader context of human spirituality.

In conclusion, agnosticism, while representing a sincere pursuit of intellectual humility, encounters challenges when assessed through specific criteria. The inherent knowledge of God in the human heart, as emphasized in biblical verses, prompts a deeper exploration of whether agnosticism, in some instances, may be a form of spiritual laziness, complacency, or disobedience to the divine revelation evident in the created world. The ongoing dialogue surrounding agnosticism invites careful consideration of its implications on human understanding and the pursuit of spiritual truth.

**Subsection 4.4: Evaluation of Secular Humanism:**

Secular Humanism, an ideology centered on human values and reason without reliance on religious doctrine, emerges as a distinctive perspective within contemporary belief systems. A thorough examination of Secular Humanism through the established criteria, coupled with insights from biblical perspectives, unveils the strengths and weaknesses inherent in this worldview.

**Origin:** Secular Humanism, while drawing inspiration from classical philosophical traditions, gained prominence as a distinct movement in the 20th century. Emerging in response to societal shifts and a desire to construct ethical frameworks independent of religious dogma, Secular Humanism positions human well-being and reason at its core. The movement's relatively recent formalization prompts considerations regarding the historical depth and continuity of its principles compared to more established belief systems.

*Relevant Bible Verse: Proverbs 3:5-6 "Trust in the LORD with all your heart and lean not on your own understanding; in all your ways submit to him, and he will make your paths straight."*

**Longevity:** Secular Humanism, as a formalized worldview, exhibits a more recent origin in the context of human history. While its philosophical underpinnings share common ground with classical humanist traditions, the specific formulation of Secular Humanism as a comprehensive worldview emerged in the modern era. The longevity of Secular Humanism as a cohesive and influential belief system may be subject to ongoing scrutiny, especially when compared to belief systems with centuries of historical presence.

*Relevant Bible Verse: Ecclesiastes 1:9 "What has been will be again, what has been done will be done again; there is nothing new under the sun."*

**Relevance:** Secular Humanism places a strong emphasis on reason, ethics, and the promotion of human well-being. Its relevance lies in its commitment to fostering a just and compassionate society through human-centered values. However, the exclusion of transcendental elements in Secular Humanism raises questions about its ability to address the deeper existential and spiritual aspects of the human experience.

*Relevant Bible Verse: Ecclesiastes 3:11 "He has made everything beautiful in its time. He has also set eternity in the human heart; yet no one can fathom what God has done from beginning to end."*

Secular Humanism places humanity at the center of ethical and moral considerations, emphasizing the inherent value and dignity of individuals. However, biblical perspectives caution against trusting in human goodness alone, as Scriptures highlight the fallen nature of humanity. Proverbs 3:5-6 advises placing trust in the Lord rather than solely relying on human understanding, recognizing the limitations of human wisdom and morality.

*Relevant Bible Verse: Jeremiah 17:9 "The heart is deceitful above all things and beyond cure. Who can understand it?"*

**Accuracy of Predictions:** Secular Humanism, rooted in reason and empirical evidence, often aligns with scientific and rationalistic approaches to understanding the world. Its emphasis on critical thinking and evidence-based decision-making contributes to the accuracy of predictions in various fields. However, the exclusion of metaphysical dimensions may limit its capacity to provide comprehensive answers to existential questions that extend beyond the scope of empirical observation.

*Relevant Bible Verse: Colossians 2:8 "See to it that no one takes you captive through hollow and deceptive philosophy, which depends on human tradition and the elemental spiritual forces of this world rather than on Christ."*

**The Power or Evidence of God:** Secular Humanism, by definition, does not rely on supernatural explanations or divine interventions in its worldview. Its commitment to human reason and empirical evidence positions it as a secular and non-theistic belief system. While this perspective contributes to a rational understanding of the world, the exclusion of the divine raises questions about its ability to address the spiritual dimension of human existence.

*Relevant Bible Verse: 1 Corinthians 1:18 "For the message of the cross is foolishness to those who are perishing, but to us who are being saved, it is the power of God."*

In conclusion, while Secular Humanism highlights the significance of human values and reason, its exclusion of divine elements raises concerns about its capacity to address the profound spiritual aspects of human existence. Understanding the strengths and limitations of Secular Humanism contributes to a nuanced dialogue about human values, meaning, and the pursuit of a just society.

## Subsection 4.5: Evaluation of Skepticism:

Skepticism, characterized by a questioning and doubting approach towards knowledge and beliefs, presents a unique perspective within contemporary thought. As we move into the evaluation of Skepticism using established criteria, it's essential to recognize both its strengths and the inherent limitations within this worldview.

**Origin:** Skepticism, as an intellectual tradition, traces its roots to ancient Greek philosophy. However, modern Skepticism has evolved to encompass a broad spectrum of perspectives, from academic inquiry to a general disposition of doubt. The questioning nature of Skepticism prompts an exploration of its historical depth and continuity. Compared to belief systems rooted in centuries of historical tradition, Skepticism may be perceived as lacking a foundational narrative that provides a comprehensive worldview.

*Relevant Bible Verse: Proverbs 3:5-6 "Trust in the LORD with all your heart and lean not on your own understanding; in all your ways submit to him, and he will make your paths straight."*

**Longevity:** Skepticism, as a method of inquiry, has endured across different epochs. However, its formalization as a comprehensive worldview or philosophy lacks the historical continuity observed in major religious traditions. The absence of a cohesive set of beliefs or principles within Skepticism raises questions about its enduring significance compared to belief systems that have shaped civilizations over centuries.

*Relevant Bible Verse: Ecclesiastes 1:9 "What has been will be again, what has been done will be done again; there is nothing new under the sun."*

**Relevance:** Skepticism plays a crucial role in fostering critical thinking and intellectual inquiry. Its emphasis on questioning assumptions and seeking evidence aligns with the scientific method and rational discourse. However, the perpetual state of doubt inherent in Skepticism may limit its capacity to provide a robust framework for addressing existential questions or offering a sense of purpose beyond the realm of empirical observation.

*Relevant Bible Verse: 1 Thessalonians 5:21 "but test them all; hold on to what is good."*

Skepticism, in its refusal to assert absolute certainty, fosters an environment of perpetual questioning. While intellectual humility is commendable, the rejection of any form of certainty may result in a worldview lacking a foundational narrative or moral compass. From a Christian perspective, Proverbs 3:5-6 encourages trust in the Lord rather than relying solely on human understanding.

*Relevant Bible Verse: Proverbs 3:5-6 "Trust in the LORD with all your heart and lean not on your own understanding; in all your ways submit to him, and he will make your paths straight."*

The wisdom literature in Proverbs also extends an invitation to seekers. Proverbs 8:1-4 portrays wisdom calling out to all who will listen, emphasizing the universal availability of wisdom to those who earnestly seek her.

*Relevant Bible Verse: Proverbs 8:1-4 "Does not wisdom call out? Does not understanding raise her voice? At the highest point along the way, where the paths meet, she takes her stand; beside the gate leading into the city, at the entrance, she cries aloud: 'To you, O people, I call out; I raise my voice to all mankind.'"*

**Accuracy of Predictions:** Skepticism, by its nature, avoids making sweeping predictions or endorsing dogmatic beliefs. While this approach contributes to intellectual humility, it may also lead to a lack of comprehensive answers to fundamental questions about the nature of existence. The absence of a positive affirmation regarding the future or metaphysical aspects of reality could be perceived as a limitation.

*Relevant Bible Verse: Colossians 2:8 "See to it that no one takes you captive through hollow and deceptive philosophy, which depends on human tradition and the elemental spiritual forces of this world rather than on Christ."*

**The Power or Evidence of God:** Skepticism, in its pursuit of evidence-based reasoning, often requires empirical verification for the acceptance of claims. This criteria may present a challenge when applied to matters of faith and the supernatural, where empirical evidence may be inherently elusive. The demand for tangible proof may hinder an exploration of the spiritual dimensions of human existence.

*Relevant Bible Verse: 1 Corinthians 2:14 "The person without the Spirit does not accept the things that come from the Spirit of God but considers them foolishness, and cannot understand them because they are discerned only through the Spirit."*

While skepticism may pose challenges to accepting spiritual truths without empirical evidence, it is crucial to recognize that research, guided by an open heart and a seeking spirit, can lead individuals to profound encounters with the divine. In the Christian worldview, the call to seek and explore is not discouraged; rather, it is embraced. Matthew 7:7 encourages the act of seeking, promising that those who seek will find.

*Relevant Bible Verse: Matthew 7:7 "Ask and it will be given to you; seek and you will find; knock and the door will be opened to you."*

Thus, skepticism, when approached with a genuine desire for truth, can be a catalyst for a journey of discovery that ultimately leads to a deeper understanding of spiritual realities and, for many, an encounter with the transformative power of Christ.

In conclusion, while Skepticism contributes to intellectual inquiry and critical thinking, its perpetual state of doubt and absence of a cohesive belief system may limit its capacity to address the deeper existential questions that have been central to human thought throughout history. Understanding both the strengths and limitations of Skepticism enriches the broader dialogue on knowledge, belief, and the pursuit of truth.

## Subsection 4.6: Evaluation of Pastafarianism (Church of the Flying Spaghetti Monster):

In the vast arena of human beliefs, there exists a spectrum that spans from the deeply profound to the whimsically satirical. As we extend into the evaluation of Pastafarianism, a belief system famously championed by the Church of the Flying Spaghetti Monster, we embark on a journey that traverses the boundaries between seriousness and satire. Rooted in the realm of parody, Pastafarianism challenges conventional religious norms through its lighthearted and whimsical approach. It's a belief system I came across during my research, a whimsical phenomenon that, despite its rarity, prompts us to consider the boundaries between humor and the serious quest for spiritual truth. However, within this playful facade lie certain limitations and questions regarding its authenticity and transformative power. In this exploration, we apply established criteria to scrutinize the origins, longevity, relevance, and divine manifestations of Pastafarianism, juxtaposing its satirical nature against the profound depth found in more traditional belief systems. As we navigate this evaluation, our aim is not only to understand the whimsy of the Flying Spaghetti Monster but also to discern the boundaries between humor and the serious quest for spiritual truth.

**Origin:** Pastafarianism, originating as a satirical movement, challenges traditional religious beliefs. While it aims to underscore the importance of the separation between church and state, its satirical nature raises questions about the authenticity of its claims. The Flying Spaghetti Monster, its purported deity, is a whimsical creation without historical or theological grounding. This lack of historical and spiritual depth places Pastafarianism in stark contrast to the rich and well-documented histories of major world religions.

*Relevant Bible Verse: Colossians 2:8 "See to it that no one takes you captive through hollow and deceptive philosophy, which depends on human tradition and the elemental spiritual forces of this world rather than on Christ."*

**Longevity:** Pastafarianism, relatively new on the religious scene, lacks the historical longevity and global influence characteristic of established belief systems. Its limited reach and the absence of a substantial community of believers raise questions about its potential for enduring significance. In comparison, the enduring impact of Christianity over centuries underscores the challenges faced by belief systems lacking in historical depth.

*Relevant Bible Verse: Isaiah 46:9 "Remember the former things, those of long ago; I am God, and there is no other; I am God, and there is none like me."*

**Relevance:** While Pastafarianism seeks to highlight certain societal issues through satire, its principles lack the depth and transformative power found in the teachings of Christianity. The emphasis on humor and satire, while effective for drawing attention, may fall short in providing substantial guidance for individuals seeking profound spiritual and moral direction.

*Relevant Bible Verse: Proverbs 3:5-6 "Trust in the Lord with all your heart and lean not on your own understanding; in all your ways submit to him, and he will make your paths straight."*

**Accuracy of Predictions:** Pastafarianism, as a satirical movement, does not put forth predictions in the traditional sense. However, the absence of any serious, prophetic elements or divine insights raises questions about its capacity to provide meaningful guidance for individuals facing the uncertainties of the future.

*Relevant Bible Verse: Amos 3:7 "Surely the Sovereign Lord does nothing without revealing his plan to his servants the prophets."*

**Divine Evidence and Manifestations:** Pastafarianism, rooted in satire, lacks the serious consideration of divine evidence or manifestations. The Flying Spaghetti Monster serves as a symbol of the movement's rejection of dogma, but it lacks the theological depth and spiritual authenticity that characterize genuine encounters with the divine. The absence of a meaningful connection with the divine raises questions about the transformative power and authenticity of Pastafarianism.

*Relevant Bible Verse: 1 Corinthians 1:25 "For the foolishness of God is wiser than human wisdom, and the weakness of God is stronger than human strength."*

In conclusion, the limitations of Pastafarianism, marked by its satirical origins, lack of historical depth, and absence of transformative principles, highlight the importance of discernment when exploring belief systems. While satire can be a powerful tool for social commentary, it falls short in addressing the profound spiritual needs and aspirations of individuals that are met by authentic and established faith traditions.

## Subsection 4.7: Evaluation of Raelism:

Raelism, a distinctive and controversial religious movement, unfolds a narrative that transcends the boundaries of conventional faiths. Emerged in the early 1970s under the guidance of its founder Claude Vorilhon, known as Rael, this belief system boldly claims that humanity's origins and destiny are intertwined with extraterrestrial beings. At the core of Raelism lies the assertion that Rael was contacted by advanced extraterrestrial entities who bestowed upon him profound knowledge encompassing science, spirituality, and the very nature of human existence.

This introduction sets the stage for a fascinating exploration into the tenets of Raelism, delving into its unique cosmology, unorthodox origin story, and the challenges it faces in substantiating its claims. As we embark on this journey, we will scrutinize the foundational principles of Raelism through the lens of established criteria, unraveling the complexities that surround this belief system's narrative of extraterrestrial encounters.

**Origin:** Raelism, founded by Claude Vorilhon (Rael), asserts its origin in extraterrestrial encounters, claiming that Rael was contacted by aliens who revealed advanced scientific and spiritual knowledge. However, the lack of empirical evidence supporting these assertions places Raelism in a realm of unverifiable claims. The absence of historical and archaeological evidence supporting extraterrestrial contact raises questions about the credibility of Raelism's origin narrative.

*Relevant Bible Verse: 1 Thessalonians 5:21 "But test everything; hold fast what is good.*

**Longevity:** While Raelism has gained some followers since its establishment in the 1970s, its global influence remains limited. The movement faces challenges in achieving widespread acceptance due to its controversial claims and the lack of tangible evidence supporting its extraterrestrial narratives. In contrast, established religions with deep historical roots have endured over centuries, impacting diverse global cultures.

*Relevant Bible Verse: Proverbs 19:21 "Many are the plans in the mind of a man, but it is the purpose of the Lord that will stand."*

**Accuracy of Predictions:** Raelism, like other belief systems founded on extraterrestrial claims, lacks a track record of accurate predictions. The uncertainties surrounding the validity of extraterrestrial encounters raise doubts about the reliability of any predictions or insights purportedly gained through these interactions. The absence of verifiable prophetic elements diminishes the credibility of Raelism in providing meaningful guidance for adherents.

*Relevant Bible Verse: Deuteronomy 18:22 "When a prophet speaks in the name of the Lord, if the word does not come to pass or come true, that is a word that the Lord has not spoken; the prophet has spoken it presumptuously. You need not be afraid of him."*

**Relevance:** Raelism introduces unique principles related to extraterrestrial creation and human cloning. However, the speculative nature of these claims and the lack of empirical support raise questions about the relevance and applicability of Raelian principles to the complexities of human existence. The absence of a substantial moral and ethical framework diminishes the practical impact of Raelism on the lives of its adherents.

*Relevant Bible Verse: Isaiah 55:8-9 "For my thoughts are not your thoughts, neither are your ways my ways, declares the Lord. For as the heavens are higher than the earth, so are my ways higher than your ways and my thoughts than your thoughts."*

**Divine Evidence and Manifestations:** Raelism's assertions about extraterrestrial encounters serve as its primary source of divine evidence. However, the lack of tangible proof and the reliance on unverifiable personal experiences limit the persuasive power of these claims. In the absence of widely accepted divine manifestations or miracles, Raelism lacks the empirical foundation that characterizes authentic faith traditions.

*Relevant Bible Verse: Hebrews 11:1 "Now faith is the assurance of things hoped for, the conviction of things not seen."*

In conclusion, Raelism's limitations, marked by unverifiable extraterrestrial claims, a lack of historical depth, and the absence of accurate predictions, highlight the importance of critical evaluation when exploring belief systems. The Christian perspective, rooted in historical authenticity, prophetic fulfillment, and tangible divine evidence, stands in contrast to belief systems that rely on speculative narratives without empirical support.

**Subsection 4.8: Evaluation of the Church of the SubGenius**

The Church of the SubGenius, a parody religion with satirical and countercultural underpinnings, challenges traditional religious norms through its unconventional lens. As we navigate the peculiar realm of the SubGenius, we will assess its foundational aspects using the established criteria, unveiling both its strengths and inherent limitations.

**Origin:** The Church of the SubGenius boasts an origin story steeped in satire, with its founders, Ivan Stang and Philo Drummond, crafting a narrative that mocks religious conventions. This satirical approach, while designed for comedic effect, raises questions about the authenticity and sincerity of the belief system. In contrast to the historical depth of established religions, the SubGenius movement emerges as a deliberate and self-aware creation rather than an organic, centuries-old tradition.

*Relevant Bible Verse:* Proverbs 14:8 - "The wisdom of the prudent is to give thought to their ways, but the folly of fools is deception."

**Longevity:** Unlike enduring religious traditions that have withstood the test of time, the Church of the SubGenius is a relatively recent phenomenon, originating in the 20th century. Its limited historical presence and the intentional nature of its creation place it in stark contrast to faiths that have organically evolved over centuries. The question of longevity becomes particularly pertinent when considering the enduring impact and influence often associated with established belief systems.

*Relevant Bible Verse:* Isaiah 40:8 - "The grass withers, the flower fades, but the word of our God will stand forever."

**Relevance:** The countercultural nature of the SubGenius movement positions it as a commentary on mainstream religion and society. While its satirical elements may resonate with a certain audience, the broader relevance of its teachings in addressing fundamental human questions or providing moral guidance is questionable. Its relevance becomes niche, catering to a specific demographic seeking humor and cultural critique rather than profound spiritual insight.

*Relevant Bible Verse:* 2 Timothy 4:3-4 - "For the time is coming when people will not endure sound teaching, but having itching ears, they will accumulate for themselves teachers to suit their own passions and will turn away from listening to the truth and wander off into myths."

**Accuracy of Predictions:** The Church of the SubGenius, rooted in satire, does not present itself as a predictive or prophetic belief system. Its intentional ambiguity and lack of substantive claims about the future render it incompatible with the criterion of accuracy of predictions.

*Relevant Bible Verse:* Deuteronomy 18:22 - "When a prophet speaks in the name of the Lord, if the word does not come to pass or come true, that is a word that the Lord has not spoken; the prophet has spoken it presumptuously."

**The Power or Evidence of God:** The SubGenius movement, founded on satire and counterculture, lacks a substantive concept of the divine or transcendent power. The absence of a genuine pursuit of the divine raises questions about the transformative impact and spiritual depth that characterize more traditional belief systems.
*Relevant Bible Verse:* 1 Corinthians 1:18 - "For the word of the cross is folly to those who are perishing, but to us who are being saved, it is the power of God."

In examining the Church of the SubGenius through these criteria, its satirical nature and intentional creation become evident. While offering humor and critique, it falls short in providing the depth, authenticity, and enduring wisdom associated with Christianity and other established faiths.

## Subsection 4.9: Evaluation of Scientology

Scientology, a contemporary religious movement founded by science fiction writer L. Ron Hubbard, introduces a unique set of beliefs and practices. As we critically examine Scientology through the established criteria, we uncover both its perceived strengths and inherent limitations.

**Origin:** Scientology's origins are rooted in the mid-20th century, with L. Ron Hubbard claiming divine inspiration for his teachings. However, the movement's foundation as an outgrowth of Hubbard's earlier self-help philosophy, Dianetics, raises questions about the sincerity of its spiritual claims. The deliberate construction of a belief system for personal gain challenges the authenticity of its divine origins.

*Relevant Bible Verse:* Matthew 7:15 - "Beware of false prophets, who come to you in sheep's clothing but inwardly are ravenous wolves."

**Longevity:** While Scientology has been present for several decades, its growth and acceptance have been marred by controversies and legal battles. The questionable tactics employed by the Church of Scientology, such as aggressive legal action against critics and former members, cast doubt on the movement's ability to maintain long-term credibility and positive influence.

*Relevant Bible Verse:* Proverbs 19:9 - "A false witness will not go unpunished, and he who breathes out lies will perish."

**Relevance:** Scientology's teachings and practices are often perceived as esoteric and disconnected from mainstream understanding. The exclusivity of its advanced teachings, guarded by significant financial barriers, limits its relevance to a select few. The lack of broad applicability and accessibility raises questions about the universal significance of its spiritual insights.

*Relevant Bible Verse:* John 14:6 - "Jesus said to him, 'I am the way, and the truth, and the life. No one comes to the Father except through me.'"

**Accuracy of Predictions:** Scientology does not prominently feature predictive elements comparable to traditional prophecies found in some religions. However, its emphasis on past traumas influencing present behaviors, as addressed through auditing sessions, lacks empirical substantiation. The lack of verifiable evidence raises questions about the accuracy of its diagnostic claims.

*Relevant Bible Verse:* Jeremiah 29:8 - "'For thus says the Lord of hosts, the God of Israel: Do not let your prophets and your diviners who are among you deceive you, and do not listen to the dreams that they dream.'"

**The Power or Evidence of God:** Scientology's concept of God is notably abstract, with a focus on an omnipresent force rather than a personal deity. The lack of a clearly defined divine entity and the absence of tangible manifestations of God's power challenge the depth and transformative potential of Scientology's spiritual practices.

*Relevant Bible Verse:* John 17:3 - "And this is eternal life, that they know you, the only true God, and Jesus Christ whom you have sent."

In the critical evaluation of Scientology, these criteria highlight significant limitations. The movement's controversial history, exclusive nature, lack of empirical support for its key tenets, and the absence of a clear understanding of the divine contribute to a nuanced perspective that contrasts with the depth and authenticity found in Christianity.

## Subsection 4.10: Evaluation of Wicca and Neopaganism

Wicca and Neopaganism, encompassing a diverse range of nature-based spiritual practices, present a unique worldview that stands in contrast to traditional monotheistic religions. As we subject these belief systems to the established criteria, we unravel both their perceived strengths and inherent limitations.

**Origin:** Wicca and Neopaganism emerged in the mid-20th century as a revival of ancient pagan practices. While proponents claim a connection to pre-Christian traditions, the deliberate reconstruction and adaptation of rituals cast doubt on the authenticity of their ancient roots. The eclectic nature of Wicca, drawing from various sources, challenges the legitimacy of its claim to ancient wisdom.
*Relevant Bible Verse:* Jeremiah 10:2 - "Thus says the Lord: 'Learn not the way of the nations, nor be dismayed at the signs of the heavens because the nations are dismayed at them.'"

**Longevity:** Compared to the millennia-old traditions of Christianity, Judaism, and Islam, Wicca and Neopaganism represent relatively recent phenomena. The limited historical continuity and global impact of these belief systems raise questions about their enduring significance and ability to stand the test of time.
*Relevant Bible Verse:* Psalm 90:2 - "Before the mountains were brought forth, or ever you had formed the earth and the world, from everlasting to everlasting you are God."

**Relevance:** Wicca and Neopaganism emphasize a deep connection with nature and personal empowerment. While these themes seem to resonate with contemporary concerns, the subjective and individualistic nature of their practices limits their broader applicability. The lack of a universal framework challenges the relevance of these belief systems in addressing the diverse needs of humanity.

*Relevant Bible Verse:* Romans 1:25-26 - "They exchanged the truth about God for a lie, and worshiped and served created things rather than the Creator—who is forever praised. Amen. Because of this, God gave them over to shameful lusts."

**Accuracy of Predictions:** Wiccan practices often involve divination and the interpretation of natural signs. However, the lack of a standardized system and the subjective nature of interpreting symbols undermine the accuracy and reliability of predictions. This subjectivity opens the door to diverse and often contradictory interpretations.

*Relevant Bible Verse:* Deuteronomy 18:10 - "There shall not be found among you anyone who burns his son or his daughter as an offering, anyone who practices divination or tells fortunes or interprets omens."

**The Power or Evidence of God:** Wicca and Neopaganism typically lack a central deity, with practitioners often worshipping various gods and goddesses or a general divine energy. The absence of a clear understanding of the divine, coupled with the subjective nature of magical practices, raises questions about the depth and transformative power of their spiritual experiences.

*Relevant Bible Verse:* Isaiah 45:5 - "I am the Lord, and there is no other, besides me there is no God; I equip you, though you do not know me."

It's important to note that, in the exploration of spiritual realms, firsthand accounts reveal a significant dynamic when Christianity is invoked. There have been instances where spirits associated with Wicca and Neopaganism bow down in submission to the name of Jesus Christ during Christian prayer sessions. This phenomenon underscores the higher spiritual authority attributed to Christianity.

*Relevant Bible Verse:* Philippians 2:10-11 - "so that at the name of Jesus every knee should bow, in heaven and on earth and under the earth, and every tongue confess that Jesus Christ is Lord, to the glory of God the Father."

This biblical declaration emphasizes the universal acknowledgment of the authority of Jesus Christ. The testimonies of spirits bowing in submission further illuminate the supremacy of Christianity in the spiritual realm. While Wicca and Neopaganism may explore various mystical practices, the Christian faith, anchored in the authority of Jesus, manifests a profound and transformative power that transcends the subjective experiences of other belief systems.

**Subsection 4.11: Evaluation of Jediism:**

In the diverse landscape of contemporary belief systems, the emergence of Jediism stands as a unique phenomenon, inspired not by ancient scriptures or traditional teachings, but by the fictional universe of Star Wars. Rooted in the principles of the Jedi Order depicted in this cinematic saga, Jediism attempts to translate the moral and spiritual ideals of a galaxy far, far away into a real-world belief system. As we delve into the evaluation of Jediism, it is crucial to navigate the intersection between the fantastical narratives of Star Wars and the profound truths that guide authentic faith traditions. This exploration aims to respectfully examine the origins, longevity, relevance, and the perceived power or evidence of Jediism, shedding light on its strengths and limitations in comparison to established and enduring belief systems, particularly Christianity.

**Origin:** Jediism, inspired by the iconic Star Wars franchise, emerged as a modern belief system, blending elements of fiction with spiritual concepts. The fictional nature of its origin raises questions about the credibility and authenticity of Jediism as a legitimate spiritual path.
*Relevant Bible Verse:* Proverbs 14:12 - "There is a way that seems right to a man, but its end is the way to death."
While the narrative and principles of Star Wars may offer moral lessons, constructing a belief system around a fictional universe introduces a fundamental challenge to the historical and factual basis that underpins genuine faith traditions.

**Longevity:** Jediism, being a relatively recent phenomenon, lacks the historical depth and enduring presence observed in traditional faiths. Its youthfulness invites skepticism regarding its capacity to provide lasting moral and spiritual guidance over time.
*Relevant Bible Verse:* Psalm 90:2 - "Before the mountains were brought forth, or ever you had formed the earth and the world, from everlasting to everlasting you are God."
Comparing the eternal nature of God with the temporal nature of human-invented belief systems underscores the limitations inherent in Jediism's brief existence.

**Relevance:** While Jediism may resonate with fans of Star Wars, its applicability to real-world challenges and the complexities of human existence is questionable. The lack of a comprehensive framework for addressing diverse life situations diminishes its relevance in comparison to faiths that provide holistic guidance.

*Relevant Bible Verse:* 2 Timothy 3:16-17 - "All Scripture is breathed out by God and profitable for teaching, for reproof, for correction, and for training in righteousness, that the man of God may be complete, equipped for every good work."

The Bible, as a comprehensive guide, addresses various aspects of life, providing wisdom and guidance for believers. Jediism's foundation in fictional narratives limits its capacity to offer practical solutions to real-life challenges.

**The Power or Evidence of God:** Jediism lacks a concept of a transcendent deity or divine power, relying instead on the fictional Force. The absence of a genuine divine source raises questions about the efficacy of the Force in providing real spiritual transformation.

*Relevant Bible Verse:* Psalm 46:1 - "God is our refuge and strength, a very present help in trouble."

Christianity, anchored in the power of the Almighty God, offers believers a tangible and transformative experience of divine intervention. The fictional nature of the Force in Jediism leaves it devoid of the true power and evidence of God.

In summary, Jediism's fictional origins, recent establishment, limited relevance, and absence of a genuine divine source contribute to its inherent limitations when evaluated against the established criteria. As Christians, we find our faith rooted in the eternal and living God, whose Word provides enduring guidance and transformative power.

## Subsection 4.12: Evaluation of Transhumanism:

In the evolving landscape of contemporary beliefs, Transhumanism stands at the intersection of technology and spirituality, advocating for the enhancement of human capabilities through scientific advancements. However, as we scrutinize Transhumanism through the established criteria—Origin, Longevity, Relevance, Accuracy of Predictions, and The Power or Evidence of God—certain limitations and philosophical challenges come to the forefront.

**Origins:** Transhumanism, with its roots in the desire to transcend human limitations through technological augmentation, raises questions about the authenticity and ethical implications of such aspirations. While proponents argue for the potential benefits of enhanced intelligence, extended lifespans, and improved physical capacities, the foundational premise of surpassing human limitations may conflict with a biblical understanding of human nature. The Scriptures remind us that our existence is intricately woven by the Creator, and the pursuit of transcendence through technological means might challenge the inherent value bestowed upon humanity by God.

*Relevant Bible Verse:* Psalm 139:14 - "I praise you because I am fearfully and wonderfully made; your works are wonderful, I know that full well."

**Longevity:** As a contemporary belief system, Transhumanism grapples with the challenge of longevity in the face of rapidly advancing technological landscapes. The quest for extended lifespans raises ethical questions and uncertainties about the consequences of tampering with the fundamental aspects of human existence. Proverbs 3:5-6 underscores the importance of trusting in the Lord rather than relying solely on human understanding, reminding us of the unpredictability inherent in endeavors to significantly alter the human experience.

*Relevant Bible Verse:* Proverbs 3:5-6 - "Trust in the Lord with all your heart and lean not on your own understanding; in all your ways submit to him, and he will make your paths straight."

**Relevance:** The relevance of Transhumanist goals, centered on technological enhancement, requires careful examination from both philosophical and theological perspectives. The biblical narrative of the Tower of Babel serves as a cautionary tale against human ambitions to attain god-like attributes independently of God. Genesis 11:4 narrates the people's attempt to build a tower to the heavens, resulting in dispersion and confusion. This narrative prompts reflection on the theological implications of seeking transcendence through human innovation.

*Relevant Bible Verse:* Genesis 11:4 - "Then they said, 'Come, let us build ourselves a city, with a tower that reaches to the heavens, so that we may make a name for ourselves; otherwise we will be scattered over the face of the whole earth.'"

**Accuracy of Predictions:** The accuracy of predictions within the Transhumanist framework, particularly concerning the societal and existential implications of human enhancement, remains uncertain. Proverbs 3:5-6 encourages a reliance on divine wisdom, emphasizing the limitations inherent in human understanding. The unpredictable consequences of tampering with essential aspects of human existence underscore the challenges in foreseeing the outcomes of Transhumanist pursuits accurately.

*Relevant Bible Verse:* Proverbs 3:5-6 - "Trust in the Lord with all your heart and lean not on your own understanding; in all your ways submit to him, and he will make your paths straight."

**The Power or Evidence of God:** From a Christian perspective, the pursuit of god-like attributes through technological means in Transhumanism raises profound theological questions. The Christian worldview emphasizes the recognition of human limitations and the importance of a humble reliance on divine guidance. The transformative power of Christianity lies not only in human innovation but in a deep relationship with the Creator. While Transhumanism presents intriguing possibilities, its limitations and theological implications caution against placing absolute faith in technological enhancements, pointing to the unique and comprehensive perspective offered by Christianity.

*Relevant Bible Verse:* Jeremiah 29:11 - "For I know the plans I have for you, plans to prosper you and not to harm you, plans to give you hope and a future."

While Transhumanism presents intriguing possibilities for human progress, the inherent limitations and theological implications caution against placing unwavering faith in the transformative power of technological enhancements. In contrast, Christianity offers a framework that recognizes the sacredness of human life, the limitations of human understanding, and the need for a humble reliance on the divine. The quest for transcendence finds its fulfillment not in technological innovation alone but in a profound relationship with the Creator who intricately designed each aspect of our humanity.

## Subsection 4.13: Evaluation of Environmentalism and Eco-Spirituality:

The realms of Environmentalism and Eco-Spirituality stand as influential forces, weaving together ecological concerns with spiritual dimensions. These movements advocate for a profound connection between humanity and the environment, urging a conscientious approach to our role as stewards of the Earth. As we examine the evaluation of Environmentalism and Eco-Spirituality through the lenses of established criteria—Origin, Longevity, Relevance, Accuracy of Predictions, and The Power or Evidence of God—a thoughtful exploration unfolds. Grounded in both ecological awareness and spiritual pursuits, these belief systems beckon us to consider their strengths and limitations, seeking wisdom from both earthly insights and biblical truths. Join us on this journey as we navigate the delicate intersection of environmental responsibility and faith, discerning the threads that bind these movements to the wider tapestry of belief.

**Origin:** Environmentalism and Eco-Spirituality, rooted in ecological concerns and a reverence for the interconnectedness of all life, advocate for environmental stewardship. However, the origin of these movements, often arising from secular or pantheistic foundations, raises questions about the theological compatibility with Christianity. While Christians are called to be stewards of the Earth, the worship of creation over the Creator, a potential pitfall in some expressions of environmentalism, is cautioned against in Romans 1:25.

*Relevant Bible Verse:* Romans 1:25 - "They exchanged the truth about God for a lie, and worshiped and served created things rather than the Creator—who is forever praised. Amen."

**Longevity:** The longevity of Environmentalism and Eco-Spirituality is commendable, indicating a sustained global awareness of ecological issues. However, the movement's longevity also reveals certain challenges. The potential for eco-centric ideologies to veer into eco-centrism, placing nature above humanity, may conflict with biblical principles emphasizing the unique value of human life. The enduring nature of these movements prompts Christians to navigate a delicate balance between environmental responsibility and maintaining a proper hierarchy of values.
*Relevant Bible Verse:* Genesis 1:26 - "Then God said, 'Let us make mankind in our image, in our likeness, so that they may rule over the fish in the sea and the birds in the sky, over the livestock and all the wild animals, and over all the creatures that move along the ground.'"

**Relevance:** The relevance of Environmentalism and Eco-Spirituality lies in addressing urgent ecological challenges. However, the exclusive focus on ecological concerns, divorced from a comprehensive understanding of sin and redemption, limits the transformative power of these belief systems. Christianity, rooted in the biblical narrative of creation, fall, and redemption, offers a holistic approach to environmental stewardship that encompasses both the physical and spiritual dimensions of existence.
*Relevant Bible Verse:* Revelation 11:18 - "The nations were angry, and your wrath has come. The time has come for judging the dead, and for rewarding your servants the prophets and your people who revere your name, both great and small—and for destroying those who destroy the earth."

**Accuracy of Predictions:** The accuracy of predictions within Environmentalism and Eco-Spirituality is challenging to assess due to the complex and multifaceted nature of ecological issues. While these belief systems accurately diagnose environmental problems, their predictive capacity for specific future outcomes is limited. Ecclesiastes 8:7 reminds us of the uncertainties inherent in predicting the future, urging a humble acknowledgment of divine wisdom.

*Relevant Bible Verse:* Ecclesiastes 8:7 - "Since no one knows the future, who can tell someone else what is to come?"

**The Power or Evidence of God:** Environmentalism and Eco-Spirituality often emphasize the divine presence in nature. While appreciating the beauty of creation is biblical, the attribution of divine agency solely to nature can lead to pantheistic tendencies. Romans 1:20 underscores the revelation of God's power through creation but emphasizes that worship should be directed to the Creator, not the created.

*Relevant Bible Verse:* Romans 1:20 - "For since the creation of the world God's invisible qualities—his eternal power and divine nature—have been clearly seen, being understood from what has been made, so that people are without excuse."

In assessing Environmentalism and Eco-Spirituality, we encounter belief systems that strive to harmonize ecological mindfulness with spiritual interconnectedness. As we navigate the diverse landscapes of these movements, it becomes evident that their strengths lie in promoting a profound sense of responsibility toward our planet and fostering a spiritual connection with the natural world. However, their limitations become apparent when subjected to the established criteria. While the commitment to environmental stewardship is commendable, questions arise about the origin, longevity, and predictive accuracy of these belief systems. Moreover, the biblical perspective offers an alternative lens, underscoring humanity's role as caretakers of God's creation.

In contemplating these intricacies, we find ourselves at the crossroads of environmental ethics and faith, seeking a balanced understanding that honors both the Earth and the divine.

**Subsection 4.14: Evaluation of African Traditional Religions:**

In revisiting the evaluation of African Traditional Religions (ATRs), we embark on a nuanced exploration that acknowledges their deep roots in the diverse cultures of the continent. These belief systems, marked by centuries-old traditions, rituals, and spiritual practices, have been integral to the identity of various African societies. Our examination extends beyond mere scrutiny to a thoughtful consideration of how ATRs have adapted in the face of contemporary challenges. Through the lens of the established criteria—Origin, Longevity, Relevance, and Accuracy of Predictions—we seek to unravel both the enduring strengths and inherent limitations that shape the contemporary manifestation of African Traditional Religions. As we study into this intricate tapestry of spirituality, our intent is to foster understanding while recognizing the distinctive challenges these belief systems encounter in a dynamically changing world.

**Origin:** African Traditional Religions (ATRs) manifest a diverse structure of beliefs, customs, and rituals deeply intertwined with the continent's diverse cultures. While rooted in centuries-old traditions, the lack of a unified, standardized scripture raises questions about the origin and authoritative foundation of these religions. The absence of a written record akin to the Bible or the Quran makes it challenging to trace the precise origins and foundational principles of ATRs, leaving them susceptible to variations and reinterpretations across different communities.

*Relevant Bible Verse:* Colossians 2:8 - "See to it that no one takes you captive through hollow and deceptive philosophy, which depends on human tradition and the elemental spiritual forces of this world rather than on Christ."

**Longevity:** One of the notable strengths of African Traditional Religions lies in their longevity, with roots stretching back for centuries. The enduring nature of these belief systems reflects their ability to adapt and integrate into the cultural fabric of various African societies. However, the challenge arises when considering the longevity in the context of a rapidly changing world. The question of how effectively ATRs can maintain their relevance and continuity in the face of modern influences becomes crucial for evaluating their long-term viability.

*Relevant Bible Verse:* Psalm 90:2 - "Before the mountains were born or you brought forth the whole world, from everlasting to everlasting you are God."

**Relevance:** In the contemporary landscape, African Traditional Religions face the challenge of relevance amidst the rapid changes and globalization of cultures. The adaptability of these belief systems varies widely, with some communities integrating elements of ATRs into their daily lives, while others transition towards more mainstream religions. The struggle for relevance becomes particularly apparent when attempting to address modern complexities and ethical dilemmas, as the traditional frameworks may not provide clear guidance on contemporary issues.

*Relevant Bible Verse:* 2 Timothy 3:16-17 - "All Scripture is God-breathed and is useful for teaching, rebuking, correcting and training in righteousness, so that the servant of God may be thoroughly equipped for every good work."

**Accuracy of Predictions:** African Traditional Religions often incorporate divination practices to gain insights into the future. However, the subjective nature of interpreting signs, symbols, or oracles introduces a level of ambiguity in predicting specific events. Unlike biblical prophecies that are considered precise and fulfilled, divination in ATRs may yield varied interpretations, leading to challenges in accurate predictions. This subjectivity raises concerns about the reliability of divination as a tool for foreseeing events with certainty.

*Relevant Bible Verse:* Isaiah 41:21-24 - "Present your case," says the Lord. "Set forth your arguments," says Jacob's King. "Tell us, you idols, what is going to happen. Tell us what the former things were, so that we may consider them and know their final outcome."

**The Power or Evidence of God:** ATRs attribute supernatural occurrences to the influence of deities, spirits, or ancestors. While these experiences hold cultural significance, the lack of universal, empirical evidence poses challenges when evaluating the power of these belief systems. Unlike Christianity, which points to historical events and miracles recorded in the Bible, ATRs may struggle to provide tangible, universally accepted evidence of divine intervention. Personal anecdotes and cultural practices, while meaningful, may not carry the same weight in a broader context.

In the realm of African Traditional Religions (ATRs), a palpable display of spiritual power is often perceived through miraculous healing and interactions with spirits mediated by designated mediums. The sick find solace in the hope of restoration, and various rituals serve as conduits for communion with the divine. However, while these manifestations carry cultural significance, they prompt reflection on the broader context of spiritual discernment.

Growing up, my exposure to both ATR and Christianity led me to grapple with questions surrounding the source and nature of divine power. Witnessing Christian preachers casting out oppressive spirits and witnessing transformative healings, I found my conviction rooted in the belief that not every manifestation of power originates from the same source. The Christian experiences I observed, including healings from sicknesses and mental afflictions, underscored the notion that true power is vested in the name of Jesus. This contrast in experiences became a pivotal factor in shaping my understanding of divine intervention.

The Bible affirms the transformative power wielded by Jesus, stating, "how God anointed Jesus of Nazareth with the Holy Spirit and power, and how he went around doing good and healing all who were under the power of the devil because God was with him" (Acts 10:38, NIV). In this light, the Christian worldview emphasizes not only the evidence of divine power but also the moral imperative of doing good, aligning with the overarching principle of love and compassion. This biblical perspective prompts a thoughtful examination of the evidentiary foundations of spiritual encounters within the context of African Traditional Religions.

*Relevant Bible Verse:* Proverbs 3:5-6 - "Trust in the Lord with all your heart and lean not on your own understanding; in all your ways submit to him, and he will make your paths straight."

In revisiting African Traditional Religions, their intricate cultural significance is acknowledged, yet their limitations in terms of origin, longevity, relevance, and predictive accuracy highlight the need for a comprehensive worldview that provides both cultural richness and a timeless, unchanging truth.

## Subsection 4.15: Evaluation of the Spiritual but Not Religious (SBNR) Movement:

The Spiritual but Not Religious (SBNR) movement has emerged as a distinctive expression of individualistic and personalized beliefs. Fueled by a desire for autonomy in spiritual exploration, this movement stands apart from traditional organized religions. As we delve into the evaluation of the SBNR movement through the lens of established criteria—Origin, Longevity, Relevance, Accuracy of Predictions, and The Power or Evidence of God—we seek to navigate the nuances of a belief system shaped by the unique dynamics of modern individualism. Through a respectful examination, we aim to uncover the strengths and weaknesses inherent in the SBNR movement, shedding light on its impact within the broader context of contemporary spirituality.

**Origin:** The Spiritual but Not Religious (SBNR) movement, born out of a desire for personalized spirituality detached from organized religion, faces inherent challenges. Originating in the contemporary landscape of individualism, it often lacks the rich historical foundation that major world religions offer. While embracing diverse spiritual practices, the absence of a collective historical narrative raises questions about the authenticity and depth of its spiritual roots.

*Relevant Bible Verse: Jeremiah 6:16 - "Stand at the crossroads and look; ask for the ancient paths, ask where the good way is, and walk in it, and you will find rest for your souls."*

**Longevity:** The SBNR movement's relatively recent emergence in response to modern societal shifts impacts its ability to demonstrate the longevity characteristic of enduring belief systems. Unlike the time-tested endurance of Christianity or other major religions, the SBNR movement's short history poses challenges in evaluating its lasting impact and influence on future generations.

*Relevant Bible Verse: Psalm 90:2 - "Before the mountains were born or you brought forth the whole world, from everlasting to everlasting you are God."*

**Relevance:** In its pursuit of personal spirituality, the SBNR movement champions individual experiences and diverse beliefs. However, this emphasis on subjectivity may lead to a fragmented understanding of spiritual truth. The challenge lies in reconciling the diverse spiritual paths within the movement and discerning a collective relevance that transcends individual perspectives.

*Relevant Bible Verse: Proverbs 14:12 - "There is a way that appears to be right, but in the end, it leads to death."*

**Accuracy of Predictions:** The SBNR movement, characterized by its fluid and individualistic nature, often lacks a unified doctrinal framework for making predictions about the future. Predictions in spiritual matters, without a foundational truth to anchor upon, risk being arbitrary and subjective, potentially leading followers astray.

*Relevant Bible Verse: Isaiah 8:19 - "When someone tells you to consult mediums and spiritists, who whisper and mutter, should not a people inquire of their God? Why consult the dead on behalf of the living?"*

**The Power or Evidence of God:** While embracing a broad spectrum of spiritual experiences, the SBNR movement may struggle to provide concrete evidence of divine power. The absence of a centralized authority or shared doctrines makes it challenging to demonstrate the tangible impact of spiritual practices within the movement.

*Relevant Bible Verse: 1 Corinthians 1:18 - "For the message of the cross is foolishness to those who are perishing, but to us who are being saved it is the power of God."*

In the intricacy of belief systems, the SBNR movement's emphasis on individual spirituality raises critical questions about the foundations, longevity, relevance, predictive accuracy, and evidence of divine power within this contemporary spiritual landscape.

## Comparative Analysis:

Having meticulously examined a spectrum of contemporary belief systems, each possessing its unique set of principles and convictions, it is imperative to conduct a comparative analysis to discern their relative merits and limitations. Through the lens of established criteria—Origin, Longevity, Relevance, Accuracy of Predictions, and The Power or Evidence of God—we navigate the intricacies of these belief systems, seeking a comprehensive understanding of their strengths and shortcomings.

In acknowledging the diversity and individualistic nature of spiritual pursuits, it becomes evident that each belief system brings forth distinctive perspectives. New Age Spirituality, while emphasizing self-glorification, grapples with concerns of potential deception and false gods, making it vulnerable to criticisms rooted in biblical truth (Proverbs 3:5-6). Atheism, despite its historical existence, contends with the limitations of empirical evidence in matters of faith, a challenge Christianity overcomes through spiritual discernment (1 Corinthians 2:14).

The Spiritual but Not Religious (SBNR) movement, epitomizing a contemporary quest for autonomy, encounters challenges in providing a unified and universally accepted framework, standing in contrast to the unwavering truths found in Christianity (John 14:6). Additionally, while secular humanism places humanity at the center, the Bible reminds us that trusting in human understanding alone is insufficient (Isaiah 45:5).

As we consider each belief system's principles, practices, and historical context, it becomes evident that Christianity surpasses these contemporary alternatives. Rooted in the enduring truths of the Bible, Christianity provides a foundation built on historical events, divine prophecies, and the transformative power of God, exemplified in the life and teachings of Jesus Christ. While acknowledging the strengths within each belief system, the unparalleled coherence, historical authenticity, and universal relevance of Christianity position it as the superior path to spiritual truth and fulfillment.

In delving into the mega structure of contemporary belief systems, our exploration has brought to light both the unique qualities and inherent limitations of each. As we draw this comparative analysis to a close, it is paramount to distill the key findings and underscore the distinctiveness that positions Christianity as an unparalleled beacon of truth.

**New Age Spirituality** reveals a penchant for self-glorification and encounters criticisms rooted in the Christian perspective, which places the glory on God alone (1 Corinthians 10:31). The reliance on deceptive elements and the worship of false gods found in this spiritual realm underscores its susceptibility to deviation from biblical truths (1 John 4:1).

**Atheism,** though a longstanding worldview, grapples with the challenge of empirical evidence in matters of faith. As Christians, we understand the limitations of human understanding and recognize that true spiritual discernment comes through the Holy Spirit (1 Corinthians 2:14).

The **Spiritual but Not Religious (SBNR)** movement, while reflecting a contemporary desire for autonomy, faces the inherent challenge of creating a cohesive framework without a unifying foundation. The Bible, however, assures us of a solid foundation in Christ, the cornerstone (1 Peter 2:6).

**Secular Humanism,** with its emphasis on human values, falls short in light of the Bible's assertion that trusting in human understanding alone is insufficient (Proverbs 3:5-6). The Bible stands as the ultimate source of wisdom.

As we reflect on these contemporary belief systems, it becomes evident that **Christianity** excels in offering a robust foundation. Rooted in historical authenticity, biblical truths, and the transformative power of God, Christianity provides an unwavering path to spiritual truth (John 14:6). It stands as a testament to the enduring nature of divine guidance, the fulfillment of prophecies, and the redemptive power of Jesus Christ.

I encourage readers to embark on their own explorations and reflections, to seek truth earnestly, and to weigh the claims of each belief system against the timeless wisdom found in Christianity. In the journey of faith, may discernment and a sincere quest for truth be your guiding lights.

**Conclusion for Section 4:**

In reflecting on the myriad belief systems explored in this chapter, it becomes evident that Christianity, through its historical authenticity, scriptural foundations, and transformative power, stands as a unique and compelling worldview. The criteria of Origin, Longevity, Relevance, Accuracy of Predictions, and The Power or Evidence of God serve as lenses through which Christianity consistently shines.

Christianity's foundation in the historical narrative of the Bible, spanning centuries and cultures, provides a robust Origin that roots its authenticity in the unfolding story of God's interaction with humanity. The enduring longevity of Christian faith, demonstrated by its continuous presence and impact over millennia, speaks to the timeless relevance and enduring significance of its teachings. The fulfillment of prophecies, the power of divine evidence, and the transformative experiences of believers further solidify Christianity's position as a spiritual cornerstone.

Acknowledging the subjectivity inherent in evaluating belief systems, it is crucial to approach this exploration with humility and respect for diverse perspectives. While Christianity is presented as a beacon of truth, recognizing the sincerity of adherents to other belief systems fosters an atmosphere of understanding and dialogue.

**Closing Thoughts:**

As we bring this chapter to a close, let us underscore the importance of open-mindedness and respect for the diverse structure of beliefs that enrich our world. The journey of spirituality is inherently personal, and individuals may find solace and purpose in various paths; although, not all paths lead to a similar destination. It is essential to approach discussions about faith with empathy, recognizing that diverse beliefs contribute to the mosaic of human experience.

I invite readers to engage in a respectful dialogue about their own spiritual journeys and beliefs. This exchange of ideas can foster understanding, bridge gaps, and illuminate shared values that underlie our diverse spiritual landscapes. Remember, the pursuit of truth is a journey, and each step taken with curiosity and openness brings us closer to a deeper understanding of ourselves, the Creator, and the world around us.

## Chapter 7

# The Mystery

**IN THE SACRED** pages of the Bible, the term "mystery" transcends mere enigma; it encapsulates a profound, divine truth concealed within the intricate tapestry of God's redemptive plan. As we embark on this transformative journey of exploration, it is crucial to comprehend the biblical concept of mystery, recognizing its unparalleled significance in unlocking the mysteries of God's salvific design.

Biblically, a mystery is not an elusive puzzle waiting to be solved; rather, it is a sacred revelation, purposefully hidden and awaiting divine unveiling at the appointed time. It is the unfolding of God's divine plan, concealed within the folds of history, waiting to be unveiled to those with eyes to see and ears to hear.

To set the stage for our profound exploration, let us turn to the scriptures themselves, where the very essence of mystery is woven into the narrative of humanity's relationship with the divine. Throughout the Bible, the terms "mystery" and "secret" are employed to signify the hidden wisdom and purpose of God. These verses serve as our guide, illuminating the path toward a deeper understanding of God's concealed plan for salvation.

1. **Colossians 1:26-27 (ESV):**

"the mystery hidden for ages and generations but now revealed to his saints. To them, God chose to make known how great among the Gentiles are the riches of the glory of this mystery, which is Christ in you, the hope of glory."

2. **Daniel 2:22 (NIV):**

"He reveals deep and hidden things; he knows what lies in darkness, and light dwells with him."

3. **Romans 16:25-26 (NLT):**

"Now to him who is able to strengthen you according to my gospel and the preaching of Jesus Christ, according to the revelation of the mystery that was kept secret for long ages but has now been disclosed…"

## Purpose of the Chapter

The purpose of this chapter is twofold: to unveil the profound concept of mystery in the Bible and to explore how this mystery is intricately interwoven throughout the Old and New Testaments, culminating in the revelation of Christ. As we navigate the scriptures, we will discover that every verse, every prophecy, and every narrative holds a concealed thread that points towards the redemptive work of Christ.

Our journey is not just an intellectual pursuit; it is an invitation to witness the divine drama of salvation unfolding. Through the exploration of God's concealed plan, we aim to foster a deeper understanding of the inclusive nature of God's covenant, breaking down misconceptions and revealing that, from the beginning, God's plan has embraced individuals from all walks of life.

So, let these verses be our guiding stars as we embark on a voyage into the heart of God's Word, where the mystery is unveiled, and Christ is revealed in every inch of God's creation.

## Section 1: The Universality of God's Plan

The pages of the Old Testament resonate with the inclusive language of God's universal plan, a plan that transcends ethnic boundaries and embraces individuals from diverse backgrounds. Contrary to the misconception that the Old Testament was exclusively tailored for the Jewish people, it unveils instances where God's divine purpose extended far beyond the borders of Israel. This inclusivity was not an afterthought but an integral part of God's unfolding narrative.

## Example 1: Rahab, the Harlot with Faith (Joshua 2:1-21; 6:22-25)

Rahab, a Canaanite woman and a resident of Jericho, emerges as a shining example of God's inclusive plan. In the face of impending doom, Rahab displayed remarkable faith in the God of Israel. She risked her life to protect the Israelite spies, acknowledging the supremacy of the God of Israel. In return for her faith, Rahab and her family were not only spared during the conquest of Jericho but also assimilated into the community of Israel.

## Example 2: Ruth, the Moabite Widow (Book of Ruth)

The story of Ruth, a Moabite widow, stands as a testament to God's universal plan. After the death of her Israelite husband, Ruth chose to stay with her mother-in-law, Naomi, and declared her loyalty to Naomi's God. Through a series of providential events, Ruth found herself gleaning in the fields of Boaz, an Israelite. Boaz, recognizing her faithfulness, became a kinsman-redeemer, and Ruth became an integral part of the lineage leading to King David and, ultimately, to Jesus Christ.

These biblical narratives not only underscore the inclusivity embedded in the Old Testament but also serve as timeless illustrations of God's intentional embrace of those outside the traditional boundaries.

## Example 3: The Acceptance of Foreigners (Deuteronomy 10:17-19, NIV):

> "For the LORD your God is God of gods and Lord of lords, the great God, mighty and awesome, who shows no partiality and accepts no bribes. He defends the cause of the fatherless and the widow and loves the foreigner residing among you, giving them food and clothing. And you are to love those who are foreigners, for yourselves were foreigners in Egypt."

The Old Testament consistently emphasizes the divine mandate to love and accept foreigners, reinforcing the idea that God's plan extends beyond national boundaries.

As we navigate through these narratives, it becomes evident that the Old Testament is a testimony to God's inclusive and expansive plan for humanity. The acceptance of outsiders was not an exception but an integral part of God's overarching design, laying the foundation for the revelation of the mystery that would unfold in the New Testament.

## Section 2: Christ Concealed in the Old Testament

**Prophetic Shadows:** Within the fabric of the Old Testament, prophetic shadows emerge, foretelling the coming of the Messiah, Jesus Christ. These shadows take the form of prophecies, symbols, and foreshadowings, intricately woven into the narratives of ancient Israel. Each verse and symbol becomes a brushstroke, painting a portrait of the Savior who would ultimately unveil the mystery of salvation.

**Example 1: The Seed of the Woman (Genesis 3:15, ESV):**

> "I will put enmity between you and the woman, and between your offspring and her offspring; he shall bruise your head, and you shall bruise his heel."

In the solemn aftermath of humanity's first disobedience, as the echo of the serpent's deceit lingered in the garden, God pronounced a promise that would reverberate through the corridors of time. In Genesis 3:15, amidst the consequences of the Fall, a glimmer of hope illuminated the darkened narrative—a promise encapsulated in the enigmatic phrase, "the seed of the woman."

## The Mystery

This proclamation was a divine revelation, an unveiling of a redemptive thread woven into the very fabric of human history. The unique nature of this promise is striking—it speaks not of the seed of a man, as customary in genealogies of that era, but specifically of the seed of the woman. This intentional phrasing points toward a miraculous birth, a divine intervention that transcends the ordinary course of nature.

In these few words, God foretells a cosmic conflict, a struggle between two lineages—the offspring of the serpent and the seed of the woman. This battle is not merely physical but spiritual, encompassing the ongoing struggle between good and evil, righteousness and sin.

Centuries later, this cryptic promise found its fulfillment in the person of Jesus Christ. Born of a virgin, Jesus is the ultimate Seed of the Woman, a miraculous incarnation of God's redemptive plan. His life, death, and resurrection constitute the decisive blow to the serpent's dominion, offering humanity a pathway to reconciliation with God.

In the Seed of the Woman, we find not just a biological descendant but a divine Savior, the fulfillment of God's covenant with humanity. This prophetic utterance in Genesis 3:15 serves as a beacon of hope, assuring us that even in the midst of our failures and shortcomings, God, in His mercy, had ordained a Redeemer who would crush the serpent's head and lead humanity into the light of redemption.

As we reflect on the Seed of the Woman, let us marvel at the intricacy of God's plan—a plan conceived in the depths of eternity, announced in a garden marred by sin, and fulfilled on a cross on a hill called Golgotha. Jesus, the Seed of the Woman, stands as the embodiment of God's love, grace, and unwavering commitment to restore what was lost in Eden.

**Example 2: The Seed of Abraham (Genesis 22:17-18, NIV):**

> "I will surely bless you and make your descendants as numerous as the stars in the sky and as the sand on the seashore. Your descendants will take possession of the cities of their enemies, and through your offspring, all nations on earth will be blessed because you have obeyed me."

God's promise to Abraham transcends mere prosperity for his descendants; it extends to the ultimate blessing for all nations, finding fulfillment in the person of Jesus Christ, the seed of Abraham, through whom the world would be blessed.

The Law of Moses, found in the books of Exodus, Leviticus, Numbers, and Deuteronomy, is rich with symbolic and prophetic elements that point to the Messiah, Jesus Christ. Here are some aspects of the Law that foreshadow the coming of the Redeemer:

**Example 3: Passover Lamb as a Shadow of Christ (Exodus 12:21-27):**

In the sacred narrative of Exodus, the Passover lamb emerges as a profound shadow, casting its silhouette across the pages of Israel's history. As the blood of the Passover lamb became a shield, protecting the Israelites from the angel of death, it prefigured Jesus Christ—the ultimate Passover Lamb whose sacrificial blood brings salvation.

> **Exodus 12:21-27 (ESV) narrates:** "Then Moses called all the elders of Israel and said to them, 'Go and select lambs for yourselves according to your

clans, and kill the Passover lamb. Take a bunch of hyssop and dip it in the blood that is in the basin, and touch the lintel and the two doorposts with the blood that is in the basin. None of you shall go out of the door of his house until the morning. For the Lord will pass through to strike the Egyptians, and when he sees the blood on the lintel and on the two doorposts, the Lord will pass over the door and will not allow the destroyer to enter your houses to strike you.'"

This account encapsulates the typology of the Passover lamb, a vivid prelude to the redemptive work of Jesus Christ. Let's explore how the Passover lamb points forward to Christ with references from the New Testament:

1. **Blood as a Protective Shield:**
    o *New Testament Reference: 1 Corinthians 5:7 (ESV) "For Christ, our Passover lamb, has been sacrificed." The blood of the Passover lamb on the doorposts protected the Israelites. Similarly, Christ's sacrificial blood shields believers from the judgment of sin and death.*

2. **Symbolism of Deliverance:**
    o *New Testament Reference: John 1:29 (ESV) "The next day he saw Jesus coming toward him, and said, 'Behold, the Lamb of God, who takes away the sin of the world!'" The Passover lamb symbolized deliverance from the bondage of Egypt. Jesus, the Lamb of God, brings deliverance from the enslavement of sin.*

3. **Unblemished Sacrifice:**
   - New Testament Reference: 1 Peter 1:18-19 (ESV) "...you were ransomed... with the precious blood of Christ, like that of a lamb without blemish or spot." The Passover lamb had to be without blemish. Similarly, Christ, the unblemished Lamb, offered Himself as a perfect sacrifice for our redemption.

4. **A Lamb for Every Household:**
   - New Testament Reference: John 3:16 (ESV) "For God so loved the world, that he gave his only Son, that whoever believes in him should not perish but have eternal life." Just as a lamb was provided for each household, Christ, the Lamb of God, is offered to all humanity for salvation.

5. **The Requirement of Faith:**
   - New Testament Reference: Romans 3:25 (ESV) "...whom God put forward as a propitiation by his blood, to be received by faith." The Israelites had to apply the blood by faith. Similarly, the efficacy of Christ's sacrifice is received by faith in His atoning blood.

6. **The Passover Lamb as a Memorial:**
   - New Testament Reference: 1 Corinthians 11:26 (ESV) "For as often as you eat this bread and drink the cup, you proclaim the Lord's death until he comes." Just as the Passover was a memorial, the Lord's Supper commemorates Christ's sacrificial death until His return.

The Passover lamb, chosen, sacrificed, and its blood applied, served as a foreshadowing of the redemptive work accomplished by Christ, our ultimate Passover Lamb. As the blood of the lamb secured the physical deliverance of the Israelites, the blood of Christ ensures the eternal deliverance of all who believe in Him. The Passover lamb's typology finds its fulfillment and eternal significance in the sacrificial work of Jesus Christ, whose blood brings salvation and deliverance to all who take refuge under its atoning power.

**Example 4: High Priest as a Shadow of Christ (Leviticus 16:15-16):**

In the intricate tapestry of Leviticus, the role of the high priest emerges as a profound shadow, casting a silhouette across the sacred pages of Israel's worship. As the high priest entered the Holy of Holies with blood for atonement, this ceremonial act prefigured Jesus Christ—the ultimate High Priest. Christ's priestly role is eternally effective, providing unfettered access to God for all who believe.

> **Leviticus 16:15-16 (ESV) narrates:** *"Then he shall kill the goat of the sin offering that is for the people and bring its blood inside the veil and do with its blood as he did with the blood of the bull, sprinkling it over the mercy seat and in front of the mercy seat. Thus, he shall make atonement for the Holy Place, because of the uncleannesses of the people of Israel and because of their transgressions, all their sins."*

This account encapsulates the typology of the high priest, a vivid prelude to the priestly ministry of Jesus Christ. Let's explore how the high priest points forward to Christ with references from the New Testament:

1. **Entering the Holy of Holies:**
    o *New Testament Reference: Hebrews 9:11-12 (ESV) "But when Christ appeared as a high priest of the good things that have come, then through the greater and more perfect tent (not made with hands, that is, not of this creation) he entered once for all into the Holy Place, taking not the blood of goats and calves but his own blood, thus securing an eternal redemption." The high priest entered the Holy of Holies annually; Christ, as the ultimate High Priest, entered once for all with His own blood, securing eternal redemption.*

2. **Atonement for Sin:**
    o *New Testament Reference: Hebrews 9:24-26 (ESV) "For Christ has entered, not into holy places made with hands, which are copies of the true things, but into heaven itself, now to appear in the presence of God on our behalf. Nor was it to offer himself repeatedly, as the high priest enters the Holy Place every year with blood not his own, for then he would have had to suffer repeatedly since the foundation of the world. But as it is, he has appeared once for all at the end of the ages to put away sin by the sacrifice of himself." The high priest made atonement annually; Christ's sacrifice, once for all, puts away sin.*

3. **Blood for Atonement:**
   - *New Testament Reference: Hebrews 10:19-22 (ESV) "Therefore, brothers, since we have confidence to enter the holy places by the blood of Jesus, by the new and living way that he opened for us through the curtain, that is, through his flesh, and since we have a great priest over the house of God, let us draw near with a true heart in full assurance of faith." The high priest used blood for atonement; Christ's blood allows believers to confidently enter God's presence.*

4. **Intercessory Role:**
   - *New Testament Reference: Romans 8:34 (ESV) "Who is to condemn? Christ Jesus is the one who died—more than that, who was raised—who is at the right hand of God, who indeed is interceding for us." The high priest interceded for the people; Christ, seated at the right hand of God, intercedes for believers.*

5. **Once-for-All Sacrifice:**
   - *New Testament Reference: Hebrews 7:27 (ESV) "He has no need, like those high priests, to offer sacrifices daily, first for his own sins and then for those of the people, since he did this once for all when he offered up himself." The high priest offered sacrifices repeatedly; Christ, as the ultimate High Priest, offered Himself once for all.*

The high priest's ceremonial duties find their fulfillment and eternal significance in the priestly ministry of Jesus Christ. As the high priest's annual entry symbolized temporary atonement, Christ's once-for-all sacrifice provides eternal redemption and access to God for all who believe. The shadow of the high priest, with its rites and rituals, dissolves in the radiant reality of Christ's eternal priesthood—a priesthood that forever intercedes and secures the believer's access to the heavenly Holy of Holies.

## Example 5: Sabbath Rest as a Shadow of Christ (Exodus 20:8-11):

In the rhythmic cadence of God's commandments, the institution of Sabbath rest stands as a captivating shadow, casting echoes across the pages of Exodus. The Sabbath, a day of rest, prefigured the spiritual rest found in Christ. Jesus, the Lord of the Sabbath, extends an invitation to believers, beckoning them to find true rest in Him through faith.

> **Exodus 20:8-11 (ESV) articulates the divine decree:** *"Remember the Sabbath day, to keep it holy. Six days you shall labor, and do all your work, but the seventh day is a Sabbath to the Lord your God. On it you shall not do any work, you, or your son, or your daughter, your male servant, or your female servant, or your livestock, or the sojourner who is within your gates. For in six days the Lord made heaven and earth, the sea, and all that is in them, and rested on the seventh day. Therefore the Lord blessed the Sabbath day and made it holy."*

Let's explore how the Sabbath rest foreshadowed the spiritual rest found in Christ, supported by references from the New Testament:

1. **Physical Rest and Spiritual Refreshment:**
   o *New Testament Reference: Matthew 11:28-30 (ESV)* "Come to me, all who labor and are heavy laden, and I will give you rest. Take my yoke upon you, and learn from me, for I am gentle and lowly in heart, and you will find rest for your souls. For my yoke is easy, and my burden is light." The physical rest of the Sabbath finds its spiritual counterpart in Christ, who offers rest for weary souls.

2. **Lord of the Sabbath:**
   o *New Testament Reference: Mark 2:27-28 (ESV)* "And he said to them, 'The Sabbath was made for man, not man for the Sabbath. So the Son of Man is lord even of the Sabbath.'" Jesus, as the Lord of the Sabbath, signifies His authority over both the physical Sabbath and the spiritual rest found in Him.

3. **Ceasing from Works:**
   o *New Testament Reference: Hebrews 4:9-10 (ESV)* "So then, there remains a Sabbath rest for the people of God, for whoever has entered God's rest has also rested from his works as God did from his." The cessation from work on the Sabbath anticipates the spiritual rest in Christ, where believers rest from their own works for salvation.

4. **Creation and Redemption Rest:**
    o *New Testament Reference: Colossians 1:16-17 (ESV) "For by him all things were created, in heaven and on earth, visible and invisible, whether thrones or dominions or rulers or authorities—all things were created through him and for him. And he is before all things, and in him all things hold together." The Sabbath commemorates God's rest from creation; in Christ, believers find rest in the One through whom all things were created and hold together.*

5. **Eternal Sabbath Rest:**
    o *New Testament Reference: Hebrews 4:3 (ESV) "For we who have believed enter that rest, as he has said, 'As I swore in my wrath, "They shall not enter my rest,"' although his works were finished from the foundation of the world." The earthly Sabbath points to the believer's entrance into God's eternal rest through faith in Christ.*

The Sabbath, with its physical observance, prefigures the spiritual rest found in Christ—a rest that transcends the ceasing of physical labor to embrace the profound cessation of striving for salvation through works. As believers enter the Sabbath rest offered by the Lord of the Sabbath, they find the fulfillment of God's eternal promise of rest for their souls.

## Example 6: Tabernacle and Temple as Shadows of Christ (Exodus 25-40; 1 Kings 6-7):

In the meticulous blueprints of Exodus and the grandeur of Solomon's construction, the tabernacle and temple emerge as profound shadows, casting echoes of God's dwelling among His people. These earthly structures, laden with symbolism and significance, find their ultimate fulfillment in Jesus, the true temple, signifying God's abiding presence among humanity.

> **Exodus 25-40 and 1 Kings 6-7 narrate the construction of the tabernacle and temple, embodying God's dwelling:** *"And let them make me a sanctuary, that I may dwell in their midst." (Exodus 25:8, ESV)*

Let's delve into how the tabernacle and temple symbolize God's presence among His people and how Jesus is revealed as the true temple in the New Testament:

1. **Tabernacle: God's Portable Dwelling:**
    - o *New Testament Reference: John 1:14 (ESV) "And the Word became flesh and dwelt among us, and we have seen his glory, glory as of the only Son from the Father, full of grace and truth." The tabernacle, a portable dwelling for God among the Israelites, finds its fulfillment in Jesus, the Word made flesh, who dwelt among humanity.*

2. **Temple: God's Permanent Dwelling:**
   - New Testament Reference: Colossians 2:9 (ESV) "For in him the whole fullness of deity dwells bodily." Solomon's temple, a grand structure, symbolizes the fullness of God dwelling bodily in Jesus, making Him the ultimate and permanent dwelling of God among humanity.

3. **Veil: Access to God's Presence:**
   - New Testament Reference: Hebrews 10:19-20 (ESV) "Therefore, brothers, since we have confidence to enter the holy places by the blood of Jesus, by the new and living way that he opened for us through the curtain, that is, through his flesh..." The veil in the tabernacle, separating the Holy of Holies, finds its significance in Jesus' sacrifice, tearing the veil and granting believers direct access to God's presence.

4. **Shekinah Glory: God's Visible Presence:**
   - New Testament Reference: 2 Corinthians 4:6 (ESV) "For God, who said, 'Let light shine out of darkness,' has shone in our hearts to give the light of the knowledge of the glory of God in the face of Jesus Christ." The Shekinah glory in the tabernacle and temple is fulfilled in the knowledge of God's glory revealed in the face of Jesus Christ.

5. **Jesus as the True Temple:**
   - New Testament Reference: John 2:19-21 (ESV) "Jesus answered them, 'Destroy this temple, and in three days I will raise it up.'... But he was speaking about the temple of his body." Jesus, in referring to His body as the temple, signifies His role as the true dwelling place of God among humanity.

6. **Destruction and Resurrection:**
   o *New Testament Reference: Matthew 27:50-51 (ESV) "And Jesus cried out again with a loud voice and yielded up his spirit. And behold, the curtain of the temple was torn in two, from top to bottom..."* The destruction of the temple veil at Jesus' death and His subsequent resurrection mark the fulfillment of God's dwelling among His people through the person of Christ.

The tabernacle and temple, though glorious in their earthly form, serve as mere shadows pointing to the true and ultimate dwelling of God among humanity—Jesus Christ. In Him, the symbolism finds substance, and the shadows give way to the radiant reality of God's abiding presence in the person of His Son.

## Example 7: Bronze Serpent: A Type of Christ (Numbers 21:4-9):

In the arid wilderness of Numbers 21, a peculiar event unfolded—a bronze serpent lifted by Moses became a symbol of healing and redemption. This incident, seemingly distant from the crucifixion of Christ, intricately foreshadows the profound truth of spiritual healing through Jesus, as He Himself referenced this event in John 3:14-15.

> **Numbers 21:4-9 recounts the bronze serpent's significance in the wilderness journey:** *"And the Lord said to Moses, 'Make a fiery serpent and set it on a pole, and everyone who is bitten, when he sees it, shall live.'" (Numbers 21:8, ESV)*

Let's unravel the symbolism and its fulfillment in Jesus, the ultimate source of healing and redemption:

1. **Fiery Serpent: Representing Sin's Consequence:**
   o *New Testament Reference: 2 Corinthians 5:21 (ESV)* "For our sake, he made him to be sin who knew no sin, so that in him, we might become the righteousness of God." The bronze serpent, symbolizing sin's consequence, finds its counterpart in Jesus, who, though sinless, bore the weight of our sins on the cross.

2. **Lifted on a Pole: The Crucifixion Parallel:**
   o *New Testament Reference: John 12:32 (ESV)* "And I, when I am lifted up from the earth, will draw all people to myself." Jesus draws a direct parallel between the bronze serpent lifted on a pole and His impending crucifixion, emphasizing the spiritual healing that would come through faith in Him.

3. **Healing through Faith: A Universal Call:**
   o *New Testament Reference: Romans 10:13 (ESV)* "For 'everyone who calls on the name of the Lord will be saved.'" Just as those in the wilderness needed to look at the lifted bronze serpent in faith for physical healing, all humanity is invited to look to Christ in faith for spiritual healing and salvation.

4. **Jesus as the Ultimate Source of Healing:**
    - New Testament Reference: 1 Peter 2:24 (ESV) *"He himself bore our sins in his body on the tree, that we might die to sin and live to righteousness. By his wounds, you have been healed."* The bronze serpent offered physical healing in the wilderness; Jesus provides profound spiritual healing through His sacrificial death on the cross.

5. **Symbol of God's Redemptive Plan:**
    - New Testament Reference: John 3:14-15 (ESV) *" And as Moses lifted up the serpent in the wilderness, so must the Son of Man be lifted up, that whoever believes in him may have eternal life."* The bronze serpent, a unique symbol in the Old Testament, aligns with God's redemptive plan fulfilled in the gift of His Son, Jesus, for the salvation of all who believe.

The bronze serpent, once an enigmatic symbol in the wilderness, becomes a poignant type of Christ—a visual representation of sin's consequence, crucifixion, and the universal call to healing through faith. As believers gaze upon the lifted Christ with faith, they experience not just physical healing, but the profound restoration of their souls.

## Example 8: Ceremonial Cleansings: Symbolism and Fulfillment (Leviticus 11-15):

Within the intricate laws of ceremonial cleanliness outlined in Leviticus 11-15, a deeper spiritual symbolism unfolds. These laws, while emphasizing the holiness required to approach God in the Old Testament, find their profound fulfillment in Jesus Christ. His sacrifice not only fulfills the symbolic rituals but also grants believers spiritual cleanliness, enabling them to boldly approach the presence of God.

1. **Symbolism of Ceremonial Cleansings:**
   o *New Testament Reference: Hebrews 9:13-14 (ESV) "For if the blood of goats and bulls, and the sprinkling of defiled persons with the ashes of a heifer, sanctify for the purification of the flesh, how much more will the blood of Christ, who through the eternal Spirit offered himself without blemish to God, purify our conscience from dead works to serve the living God." The elaborate rituals in Leviticus symbolize the external purification required under the Old Covenant. However, Christ's sacrifice brings internal purification, cleansing the conscience and enabling true worship.*

2. **Jesus as the Ultimate Purifier:**
   o *New Testament Reference: Ephesians 5:25-27 (ESV) "Husbands, love your wives, as Christ loved the church and gave himself up for her, that he might sanctify her, having cleansed her by the washing of water with the word, so that he might present the church to himself in splendor, without spot or wrinkle or any such thing, that she might be holy and without blemish." The ceremonial laws pointed to the need for external cleanliness; Christ's sacrifice brings about internal cleansing, presenting believers as holy and without blemish.*

3. **Bold Approach to God:**
   o *New Testament Reference: Hebrews 10:19-22 (ESV) "Therefore, brothers, since we have confidence to enter the holy places by the blood of Jesus, by the new and living way that he opened for us through the curtain, that is, through his flesh, and since we have a great priest over the house of God, let us draw near with a true heart in full assurance of faith, with our hearts sprinkled clean from an evil conscience and our bodies washed with pure water." The Old Testament laws highlighted the separation between a holy God and an unholy people. Christ's sacrifice removes this barrier, allowing believers to boldly approach God with confidence.*

4. **Internal Transformation:**
   o *New Testament Reference: Romans 12:2 (ESV) "Do not be conformed to this world, but be transformed by the renewal of your mind, that by testing you may discern what is the will of God, what is good and acceptable and perfect." Ceremonial cleansings in the Old Testament involved external rituals. Christ's work brings about internal transformation, renewing the mind and conforming believers to the image of God.*

5. **A Preview of Spiritual Reality:**
   o *New Testament Reference: Colossians 2:16-17 (ESV) "Therefore let no one pass judgment on you in questions of food and drink, or with regard to a festival or a new moon or a Sabbath. These are a shadow of the things to come, but the substance belongs to Christ." The ceremonial laws acted as a shadow, foreshadowing*

*the spiritual reality fulfilled in Christ, who is the substance of the Old Testament shadows.*

In the intricate details of ceremonial cleansings, a profound narrative unfolds—a narrative fulfilled in the redemptive work of Jesus Christ. As believers embrace the spiritual cleanliness offered through His sacrifice, they can boldly approach God, transformed from within, and participate in the substance of God's redemptive plan.

## Example 9: Cities of Refuge: Christ, Our Sanctuary (Numbers 35):

In the Old Testament, the establishment of cities of refuge, as outlined in Numbers 35, serves as a poignant symbol of the refuge found in Christ. These cities were designated as safe havens for individuals who unintentionally committed manslaughter, offering protection from avengers seeking retribution. In a profound parallel, Christ becomes our ultimate refuge, providing a sanctuary for sinners in search of forgiveness and redemption.

1. **Symbolism of Cities of Refuge:**
   o *New Testament Reference: Hebrews 6:18 (ESV)* "So that by two unchangeable things, in which it is impossible for God to lie, we who have fled for refuge might have strong encouragement to hold fast to the hope set before us." *The cities of refuge symbolize the safety and assurance believers find in Christ, the unchanging refuge who provides hope and encouragement.*

2. **Christ as Our Ultimate Refuge:**
   - o *New Testament Reference: Psalm 46:1 (ESV)* "*God is our refuge and strength, a very present help in trouble.*" *Christ becomes the true refuge for believers, offering strength and immediate help in times of trouble.*

3. **Protection from Retribution:**
   - o *New Testament Reference: Romans 8:1 (ESV)* "*There is therefore now no condemnation for those who are in Christ Jesus.*" *Just as the cities of refuge shielded individuals from avengers, Christ ensures believers are free from condemnation and the consequences of sin.*

4. **Safe Haven for Sinners:**
   - o *New Testament Reference: Matthew 11:28 (ESV)* "*Come to me, all who labor and are heavy laden, and I will give you rest.*" *Christ invites sinners to find solace and rest in Him, becoming a safe haven for those burdened by the weight of their transgressions.*

5. **The Unintentional Nature of Sin:**
   - o *New Testament Reference: 1 John 1:9 (ESV)* "*If we confess our sins, he is faithful and just to forgive us our sins and to cleanse us from all unrighteousness.*" *Just as the cities of refuge were for those who unintentionally committed manslaughter, Christ's forgiveness extends to those who sincerely repent and confess their sins.*

6. **Redemption and Restoration:**
   - New Testament Reference: Ephesians 1:7 (ESV) *"In him we have redemption through his blood, the forgiveness of our trespasses, according to the riches of his grace." Christ's refuge not only offers protection but also brings redemption and forgiveness, restoring individuals to a state of grace.*

7. **A Place of Transformation:**
   - New Testament Reference: 2 Corinthians 5:17 (ESV) *"Therefore, if anyone is in Christ, he is a new creation. The old has passed away; behold, the new has come." The cities of refuge provided a space for transformation. In Christ, believers experience a spiritual renewal, becoming new creations.*

As we reflect on the symbolism of the cities of refuge, we discover a profound truth—a truth fulfilled in the redemptive work of Jesus Christ. In Him, sinners find not only a sanctuary from condemnation but a transformative refuge that leads to forgiveness, redemption, and a new life.

**Example 10: Feast of Tabernacles: Jesus, Our Living Water and Light (Leviticus 23:33-43):**

The Feast of Tabernacles, as commanded in Leviticus 23:33-43, is a significant celebration in the Old Testament that commemorates God's dwelling with His people. In the New Testament, this feast finds profound fulfillment in Jesus Christ, who declared Himself as the living water and the light of the world, embodying the ultimate realization of God's presence among humanity.

1. **Symbolism of the Feast of Tabernacles:**
   - New Testament Reference: John 1:14 (ESV) "And the Word became flesh and dwelt among us, and we have seen his glory, glory as of the only Son from the Father, full of grace and truth." The Feast of Tabernacles symbolizes the dwelling of God among His people, a truth realized in the incarnation of Jesus Christ.

2. **Jesus as the Living Water:**
   - New Testament Reference: John 7:37-38 (ESV) "On the last day of the feast, the great day, Jesus stood up and cried out, 'If anyone thirsts, let him come to me and drink. Whoever believes in me, as the Scripture has said, 'Out of his heart will flow rivers of living water.'" During the Feast of Tabernacles, Jesus proclaimed Himself as the source of living water, offering spiritual refreshment to those who believe in Him.

3. **Light of the World:**
   - New Testament Reference: John 8:12 (ESV) "Again Jesus spoke to them, saying, 'I am the light of the world. Whoever follows me will not walk in darkness but will have the light of life.'" As the festivities included illuminating the temple, Jesus declared Himself the light of the world, bringing spiritual illumination and guidance to those who follow Him.

4. **Tabernacle Representing Jesus' Incarnation:**
   - New Testament Reference: Colossians 2:9 (ESV) "For in him the whole fullness of deity dwells bodily."

*The temporary dwellings in the Feast of Tabernacles find their ultimate fulfillment in the incarnation of Jesus, in whom the fullness of God dwells bodily.*

5. **Celebrating God's Presence:**
   - New Testament Reference: Matthew 18:20 (ESV) "For where two or three are gathered in my name, there am I among them." The Feast of Tabernacles celebrated God's presence among the community, a promise reiterated by Jesus in the New Testament as He assures His presence among believers.

6. **Unity and Gathering:**
   - New Testament Reference: Ephesians 2:19 (ESV) "So then you are no longer strangers and aliens, but you are fellow citizens with the saints and members of the household of God." The feast's emphasis on unity and gathering finds resonance in the New Testament, where believers become part of the household of God through faith in Christ.

7. **Fulfillment in the New Covenant:**
   - New Testament Reference: Hebrews 8:6 (ESV) "But as it is, Christ has obtained a ministry that is as much more excellent than the old as the covenant he mediates is better, since it is enacted on better promises." The Feast of Tabernacles finds its ultimate fulfillment in the new covenant established by Christ, bringing superior promises and eternal significance.

The Feast of Tabernacles, with its rich symbolism and celebration of God's dwelling, finds its complete realization in Jesus Christ.

He is the living water, the light of the world, and the embodiment of God's presence among His people, bringing fulfillment to the shadows cast by the Old Testament feast.

The Old Testament serves as a symphony of voices, each verse harmonizing with the others to create a prophetic melody pointing toward the advent of Christ.

### Example 11: Immanuel - God With Us (Isaiah 7:14, ESV):

> *"Therefore the Lord himself will give you a sign. Behold, the virgin shall conceive and bear a son, and shall call his name Immanuel."*

The prophecy in Isaiah 7:14 stands as a beacon of hope, proclaiming a sign that transcends the ordinary course of events—a virgin conceiving and bearing a son, whose name would be Immanuel, meaning "God with us." This prophetic utterance unfolds in the New Testament, finding its profound fulfillment in the birth of Jesus Christ. The narrative of Immanuel underscores the divine presence among humanity, bringing God's redemptive plan into tangible reality.

1. **Isaiah's Prophetic Announcement:**
   - *New Testament Reference: Matthew 1:22-23 (ESV) "All this took place to fulfill what the Lord had spoken by the prophet: 'Behold, the virgin shall conceive and bear a son, and they shall call his name Immanuel' (which means, God with us)." Matthew, in his Gospel, explicitly connects the prophecy of Isaiah to the birth of Jesus, validating the fulfillment of God's promise.*

2. **Virgin Birth as a Divine Sign:**
   - *New Testament Reference: Luke 1:30-35 (ESV)* "And the angel said to her, 'Do not be afraid, Mary, for you have found favor with God. And behold, you will conceive in your womb and bear a son, and you shall call his name Jesus. He will be great and will be called the Son of the Most High.'" The angel's announcement to Mary confirms the extraordinary nature of Jesus' conception, aligning with Isaiah's prophecy of a virgin birth.

3. **Significance of the Name Immanuel:**
   - *New Testament Reference: John 1:14 (ESV)* "And the Word became flesh and dwelt among us, and we have seen his glory, glory as of the only Son from the Father, full of grace and truth." The name Immanuel encapsulates the reality of God taking on human flesh in the person of Jesus Christ, dwelling among humanity to reveal the fullness of God's grace and truth.

4. **Divine Presence in Jesus:**
   - *New Testament Reference: Colossians 2:9 (ESV)* "For in him the whole fullness of deity dwells bodily." The prophecy of Immanuel finds its ultimate expression in Jesus, where the fullness of God's divine nature dwells bodily, making Him the tangible manifestation of God's presence.

5. **Connection to God's Redemptive Plan:**
    - *New Testament Reference: Galatians 4:4-5 (ESV) "But when the fullness of time had come, God sent forth his Son, born of woman, born under the law, to redeem those who were under the law, so that we might receive adoption as sons."* The birth of Jesus, Immanuel, is intricately linked to God's redemptive plan, marking the pivotal moment when God intervened in human history for the salvation of humanity.

The prophecy of Immanuel in Isaiah serves as a bridge between the Old and New Testaments, foretelling the miraculous birth of Jesus Christ. In Him, the promise of "God with us" becomes a living reality, inviting humanity into a profound relationship with the divine.

## Example 11: The Star and Scepter (Numbers 24:17, NIV):

"I see him, but not now; I behold him, but not near. A star will come out of Jacob; a scepter will rise out of Israel."

The prophecy uttered by Balaam, recorded in Numbers 24:17, unfolds as a vision of a future ruler, a messianic figure who emerges symbolically as a star out of Jacob and a scepter rising from Israel. This cryptic revelation finds its ultimate fulfillment in the New Testament narrative, where the Magi, guided by a celestial sign, follow the star to discover the newborn King, Jesus.

1. **Balaam's Prophetic Utterance:**
   - *New Testament Reference: Matthew 2:1-2 (NIV) "After Jesus was born in Bethlehem in Judea, during the time of King Herod, Magi from the east came to Jerusalem and asked, 'Where is the one who has been born king of the Jews? We saw his star when it rose and have come to worship him.'" The Magi's inquiry aligns with Balaam's prophecy, identifying the star as a celestial marker heralding the birth of the promised King.*

2. **Symbolism of the Star and Scepter:**
   - *New Testament Reference: Matthew 2:9-11 (NIV) "After they had heard the king, they went on their way, and the star they had seen when it rose went ahead of them until it stopped over the place where the child was. When they saw the star, they were overjoyed. On coming to the house, they saw the child with his mother Mary, and they bowed down and worshiped him." The star and scepter, symbolizing authority and kingship, find their tangible representation in the person of Jesus, the newborn King.*

3. **Magi Following the Star:**
   - *New Testament Reference: Matthew 2:12 (NIV) "And having been warned in a dream not to go back to Herod, they returned to their country by another route." The Magi's guidance by the star and their obedient response to divine warnings emphasize the supernatural orchestration leading them to Jesus, fulfilling the prophetic imagery.*

4. **Mystery of Salvation Unveiled:**
   o *New Testament Reference: Colossians 2:2-3 (NIV) "My goal is that they may be encouraged in heart and united in love, so that they may have the full riches of complete understanding, in order that they may know the mystery of God, namely, Christ, in whom are hidden all the treasures of wisdom and knowledge." The prophecy of the star and scepter contributes to the overarching mystery of God's redemptive plan, ultimately unveiled in the person of Jesus Christ.*

5. **Continuity of God's Redemptive Plan:**
   o *New Testament Reference: Revelation 22:16 (NIV) "I, Jesus, have sent my angel to give you this testimony for the churches. I am the Root and the Offspring of David, and the bright Morning Star." Jesus identifies Himself as the fulfillment of the messianic prophecies, including the symbolism of the star, affirming the continuity of God's redemptive plan through the ages.*

Balaam's prophecy, seemingly enigmatic in its language, becomes a crucial piece in the grand tapestry of God's redemptive narrative. The star and scepter converge in the person of Jesus Christ, affirming His divine kingship and role as the fulfillment of ancient prophecies.

## Example 12: The Suffering Servant (Isaiah 53:3-5, NIV):

> "He was despised and rejected by mankind, a man of suffering, and familiar with pain. Like one from whom people hide their faces, he was despised, and we held him in low esteem. Surely he took up our pain and bore our suffering, yet we considered him punished by God, stricken by him, and afflicted. But he was pierced for our transgressions, he was crushed for our iniquities; the punishment that brought us peace was on him, and by his wounds, we are healed."

Isaiah's depiction of the suffering servant echoes with startling clarity in the crucifixion of Jesus Christ. The foreshadowing of pain, rejection, and ultimate redemption resonates throughout the ages.

## Section 3: The Unveiling of Christ in the New Testament

The New Testament stands as the radiant dawn, illuminating the shadows cast by the prophecies of old. It serves as the stage upon which the mystery concealed in the Old Testament is brought to light, with Christ emerging as the fulfillment of every foretelling, symbol, and anticipation. The threads of prophecy, intricately woven in the fabric of ancient scriptures, find their culmination in the person of Jesus.

## Example 1: Birth in Bethlehem (Micah 5:2, ESV):

> "But you, O Bethlehem Ephrathah, who are too little to be among the clans of Judah, from you shall come forth for me one who is to be ruler in Israel, whose coming forth is from of old, from ancient days."

The prophecy in Micah finds fulfillment in the New Testament when Jesus, the promised ruler, is born in Bethlehem, the city of David, establishing his rightful lineage as the long-awaited Messiah.

## Example 2: Triumphal Entry (Zechariah 9:9, NIV):

> "Rejoice greatly, Daughter Zion! Shout, Daughter Jerusalem! See, your king comes to you, righteous and victorious, lowly and riding on a donkey, on a colt, the foal of a donkey."

This prophecy from Zechariah unfolds in the New Testament as Jesus enters Jerusalem triumphantly on a donkey, embodying the qualities of the promised king.

**Quotes from Jesus:** In the words of Jesus himself, we find a divine commentary on the unfolding of God's plan for salvation. His teachings explicitly connect his mission with the fulfillment of God's promises, providing clarity to the mysterious echoes of the past.

### Example 3: Jesus as the Fulfillment of the Law and Prophets (Matthew 5:17, ESV):

> "Do not think that I have come to abolish the Law or the Prophets; I have not come to abolish them but to fulfill them."

In this foundational statement, Jesus declares his mission to fulfill the entirety of the Old Testament, embodying its laws and bringing to completion the prophecies that pointed to his arrival.

### Example 4: The Son of Man's Mission (Luke 19:10, NIV):

> "For the Son of Man came to seek and to save the lost."

Jesus succinctly captures the essence of his mission, aligning it with the overarching theme of redemption present in the Old Testament. His words echo the divine purpose concealed in the mysteries of ancient scriptures.

As we traverse the pages of the New Testament, we witness the revelation of Christ as the fulfillment of God's plan for salvation. The prophetic whispers of the Old Testament find resonance in the events and teachings of the New, emphasizing the divine continuity and completeness of God's redemptive narrative. Through the person of Jesus Christ, the mystery concealed is fully unveiled, bringing profound meaning to the journey from Old Testament anticipation to New Testament realization.

## Section 4: Embracing the Inclusiveness of God's Covenant

The misconception that the Old Testament exclusively caters to the Jewish people is dispelled when we delve into the heart of God's covenant. From the very beginning, God's redemptive plan extends its arms to embrace individuals from all walks of life, transcending ethnic and cultural boundaries. The covenant, far from being exclusive, carries the universal invitation for humanity to partake in the divine narrative.

### Example 1: The Covenant with Abraham (Genesis 12:3, NIV):

> "I will bless those who bless you, and whoever curses you I will curse, and all peoples on earth will be blessed through you."

God's covenant with Abraham is not confined to a particular lineage; it is a promise that extends to all peoples on earth, emphasizing inclusivity from its inception.

### Example 2: The Promise to David (2 Samuel 7:16, NLT):

> "Your house and your kingdom will continue before me for all time, and your throne will be secure forever."

God's covenant with David, promising an eternal kingdom, goes beyond the boundaries of Israel. It lays the groundwork for a kingdom that transcends borders and welcomes all who align with the divine purpose.

*Conversion and Acceptance:* The inclusiveness of God's covenant is vividly illustrated through instances of conversion and acceptance, where individuals from diverse backgrounds not only find refuge within God's people but also become integral contributors to the unfolding of God's redemptive plan.

### Example 3: Rahab's Inclusion (Joshua 6:25, ESV):

> "But Rahab the prostitute and her father's household and all who belonged to her, Joshua saved alive. And she has lived in Israel to this day because she hid the messengers whom Joshua sent to spy out Jericho."

Rahab, a Canaanite woman and a former outsider, is not only accepted into the community of Israel but becomes an ancestor in the lineage leading to Jesus Christ. Her inclusion emphasizes that God's covenant transcends ethnic boundaries.

### Example 4: Ruth's Loyalty (Ruth 1:16, NIV):

> "But Ruth replied, 'Don't urge me to leave you or to turn back from you. Where you go I will go, and where you stay I will stay. Your people will be my people and your God my God.'"

Ruth, a Moabite widow, exemplifies not only acceptance but wholehearted commitment to the God of Israel. Her story highlights that God's covenant is not limited by nationality, but is open to those who align themselves with His divine purpose.

*Universal Call to Covenant:* The inclusiveness of God's covenant is not an exception but a consistent theme that echoes through the pages of the Bible. It reveals a divine invitation extended to all, emphasizing that God's redemptive plan has always been for the entire human family. The journey from the Old Testament to the New Testament illuminates a covenant that knows no bounds, embracing individuals from every corner of the earth and weaving their stories into the grand tapestry of God's salvation plan.

## Example 5: The Great Commission (Matthew 28:18-20, NIV):

> "Then Jesus came to them and said, 'All authority in heaven and on earth has been given to me. Therefore, go and make disciples of all nations, baptizing them in the name of the Father and of the Son and of the Holy Spirit, and teaching them to obey everything I have commanded you. And surely, I am with you always, to the very end of the age.'"

In the closing words of the Gospel of Matthew, Jesus issues a universal call to spread the Good News to all nations. The Great Commission epitomizes the inclusivity of God's covenant, breaking down ethnic barriers and extending the invitation of salvation to people from every background. This verse underscores that the grand tapestry of God's salvation plan encompasses the diverse stories of individuals from every corner of the earth.

## Section 5: Reflection and Application

### Encouraging Reflection

As we journey through the unveiling of God's inclusive plan from the Old Testament to the New, it is essential to pause and reflect on the profound implications for our lives. Consider the following questions to prompt introspection and contemplation:

1. **How has your understanding of God's inclusiveness evolved through the exploration of Old and New Testament narratives?**
2. **In what ways do the stories of Rahab, Ruth, and others resonate with your own journey and experiences?**
3. **What role do you see yourself playing in the continuation of God's inclusive plan in today's world?**
4. **Are there preconceived notions or biases that need to be reconsidered in light of the universal call to God's covenant?**

The inclusiveness of God's plan, as revealed in the Scriptures, is not a relic of the past but a timeless truth with profound relevance for our contemporary world. Consider the following connections between God's inclusive covenant and present-day issues:

### Example 6: Embracing Diversity in Faith Communities (Galatians 3:28, NIV):

> "There is neither Jew nor Gentile, neither slave nor free, nor is there male and female, for you are all one in Christ Jesus."

This verse from Galatians underscores the unity found in Christ, transcending societal divisions. In a world marked by religious diversity, it calls for inclusive faith communities that recognize the common bond in Christ.

**Example 7: Advocating for Social Justice and Inclusion (James 2:1-5, NLT):**

> "My dear brothers and sisters, how can you claim to have faith in our glorious Lord Jesus Christ if you favor some people over others? For example, suppose someone comes into your meeting dressed in fancy clothes and expensive jewelry, and another comes in who is poor and dressed in dirty clothes. If you give special attention and a good seat to the rich person, but you say to the poor one, 'You can stand over there, or else sit on the floor'—well, doesn't this discrimination show that your judgments are guided by evil motives?"

The Book of James challenges us to confront biases and social injustices, echoing the call for inclusivity. This example urges contemporary believers to advocate for justice and equal treatment in our diverse societies.

**Example 8: Building Bridges Across Cultural Divides (Ephesians 2:14, NIV):**

> "For he himself is our peace, who has made the two groups one and has destroyed the barrier, the dividing wall of hostility."

The letter to the Ephesians speaks to the reconciliation of diverse groups through Christ. In today's globalized world, this verse serves as a powerful reminder of our responsibility to build bridges, fostering understanding and unity across cultural divides.

As we reflect on these questions and consider the relevance of God's inclusiveness in today's world, may we be inspired to live out the principles of God's covenant in our daily lives, contributing to a more compassionate and inclusive society.

## Section 6. Christ: Our All-Sufficient Inheritance (Colossians 1:27)

In the heart of Colossians 1:27, we discover a profound truth that echoes through the corridors of time—Christ is not merely a part of our inheritance; He is our all-sufficient inheritance. The verse declares, "to them God chose to make known how great among the Gentiles are the riches of the glory of this mystery, which is Christ in you, the hope of glory" (Colossians 1:27, ESV).

> John 14:6 (ESV): "Jesus said to him, 'I am the way, and the truth, and the life. No one comes to the Father except through me.'"

In the midst of life's misery and pain, when the shadows of agony have cast a long, heavy pall over your days, remember this: Christ is not just a way; He is the very essence of your inheritance. Your journey, however arduous, finds its meaning and purpose in Him.

## The Completeness of Christ:

> Colossians 2:9-10 (NIV):"For in Christ all the fullness of the Deity lives in bodily form, and in Christ, you have been brought to fullness. He is the head over every power and authority."

In the emptiness of despair, Christ offers completeness. Your brokenness is met with the fullness of God Himself dwelling in Christ. In Christ, you are brought to fullness, transcending the limitations that pain has imposed upon you.

## Christ as the Hope of Glory:

> Romans 8:18 (NIV):"I consider that our present sufferings are not worth comparing with the glory that will be revealed in us."

To the one who has tasted the bitterness of life's hardships, let this truth be a balm for your weary soul: Your present suffering, no matter how profound, pales in comparison to the glory that will be revealed in you through Christ. The agony you've known is not the end; it's a journey toward an eternal glory.

**Personal Assurance:** In the midst of pain, know this—you are not alone. Christ is in you, and in Him, your hope of glory is secure. The richness of this inheritance is not diminished by the sorrows you've endured. Rather, it is enhanced by the fact that Christ has walked with you through every valley, and He remains your unfailing hope.

**Promise of Glory:** The promise of inheriting glory is not an abstract concept; it is a personal assurance spoken over your life. Christ in you transforms your pain into a pathway to glory. In your weakness, His strength shines forth. In your brokenness, His completeness is revealed. The hope of glory is not a distant dream; it is a promise etched in the very fabric of your being.

As you reflect on Colossians 1:27 and its profound implications, may it be a source of comfort and assurance. The Christ in you is your all-sufficient inheritance, promising that, despite life's struggles, you are destined for a glory that transcends all earthly pain.

## Conclusion

Our journey through the pages of the Old and New Testaments has been a revelation of God's intricate and inclusive plan for humanity. From the concealed shadows of the Old Testament to the radiant light of the New, a seamless narrative unfolds, unveiling the mystery of God's redemptive design. In the Old Testament, we witnessed the inclusiveness of God's covenant, dispelling the misconception of exclusivity, and embracing individuals from diverse backgrounds. Prophecies, symbols, and shadows painted a picture of a Savior yet to come, a mystery concealed in the very fabric of creation. As we transitioned to the New Testament, we saw the fulfillment of these promises in the person of Jesus Christ, the culmination of God's plan for salvation. The threads of continuity wove a tapestry that transcends time and culture, revealing God's steadfast commitment to an inclusive covenant.

## Call to Embrace the Mystery

As we stand at the culmination of this exploration, we are faced with a divine mystery—an inclusive plan that beckons us into its narrative. The mystery is not a riddle to be solved but a truth to be embraced. It is an invitation to recognize our place in the grand tructure of God's salvation plan. Just as Rahab and Ruth found a place in the unfolding story, so too are we invited to discover our role in the ongoing narrative of God's love. This mystery is not a barrier but a bridge, connecting us to a God who transcends our understanding.

## Example 12: Embracing the Mystery (Romans 11:33, NIV):

> "Oh, the depth of the riches of the wisdom and knowledge of God! How unsearchable his judgments, and his paths beyond tracing out!"

The apostle Paul, in his letter to the Romans, marvels at the depth of God's wisdom and knowledge. It serves as a reminder that while we may not fully comprehend the intricacies of God's plan, we are called to trust in His wisdom and embrace the mystery with humility and awe.

## Example 13: Being Active Participants in God's Plan (Ephesians 2:10, NLT):

> "For we are God's masterpiece. He has created us anew in Christ Jesus, so we can do the good things he planned for us long ago."

Ephesians reminds us that we are not passive observers but active participants in God's unfolding story. Each of us is a masterpiece, created for a purpose within God's inclusive plan.

As we close this chapter, let us not shy away from the mystery but rather lean into it. Embrace the inclusiveness of God's covenant as a guiding light in our interactions, relationships, and engagements with the world. May we find our place in the ongoing narrative of salvation, contributing our unique threads to the grand embroidery that God is weaving through time and eternity. The mystery invites us to a deeper, richer experience of God's love—a love that knows no bounds and includes all who are willing to be a part of His divine narrative.

**Closing Prayer or Reflection**

Heavenly Father,

As we close this exploration of Your Word, we come before You with hearts full of gratitude and awe. Your inclusive plan, concealed in the ancient scriptures and revealed through the life of Jesus Christ, leaves us in wonder and humility. We thank You for the tapestry of salvation that knows no bounds, weaving together the stories of people from every corner of the earth.

Lord, help us to embrace the mystery of Your inclusive covenant. Grant us the wisdom to trust in Your plan even when we cannot fully comprehend it. May the stories of Rahab, Ruth, and the countless others who found a place in Your narrative inspire us to recognize our own roles in Your unfolding story of love and redemption.

In moments of uncertainty, may we find solace in the unsearchable depths of Your wisdom, trusting that Your paths are beyond tracing out. As we navigate our lives, may we be co-creators in Your plan, doing the good things You have prepared for us.

Lord, empower us to live out the principles of inclusivity in our relationships, communities, and interactions with the world. May Your love, which surpasses all understanding, be reflected in our lives as we extend grace, build bridges, and seek justice in our diverse and dynamic world.

We surrender to Your mystery, O God, acknowledging that Your ways are higher than ours. Lead us, guide us, and draw us ever closer to You as we continue to journey in the unfolding narrative of Your salvation plan.

In the name of Jesus Christ, who is the fulfillment of Your promises and the embodiment of Your inclusive love, we pray. Amen.

## Chapter 8

# Foundations of Christian Faith

**Introduction**

**Dear Reader,**

Welcome to the final chapter of your journey—a journey that has led you through the corridors of inspiration, contemplation, and, perhaps, transformation. As we stand at this pivotal crossroad, it is not only a conclusion but a commencement—a beginning of a new and profound understanding of your faith.

In acknowledging your journey, we celebrate the steps you've taken, the questions you've asked, and the yearning that has brought you to this point. Whether this is a continuation of a lifelong exploration or a recent inquiry, your presence here is significant, and I commend you for the courage to seek and the openness to explore.

The pages that follow hold the keys to the foundational doctrines that underpin the Christian faith. These are not mere theological concepts; they are the bedrock on which your spiritual journey will find its sure footing. As a new believer, grasping these foundational truths is akin to unlocking a treasure chest—revealing the richness of God's love, the depth of His redemptive plan, and the profound mystery of your place in His story.

Understanding these doctrines is not a scholarly pursuit reserved for theologians alone; it is a personal expedition into the heart of your faith. These are the pillars that support your relationship with God, the compass that guides your spiritual navigation, and the source of strength in times of uncertainty.

So, let us embark on this expedition together. As we unfold the layers of each doctrine, consider it not as a mere intellectual exercise but as a journey into the very essence of your faith. With each revelation, may your understanding deepen, your convictions strengthen, and your heart resonate with the eternal truths that have shaped the lives of believers throughout history.

This is more than a chapter; it is an invitation to a deeper encounter with the God who loves you, the Savior who redeems you, and the Spirit who empowers you. May the exploration of these foundational Christian doctrines be a transformative and enlightening experience, solidifying the ground on which you stand as a follower of Christ.

Let the journey begin.

Warmest regards,

...................................
Bisaso Julius

## The Trinity

At the core of Christian theology lies the enigmatic concept of the Trinity, a profound revelation that unravels the nature of God in His triune existence. The Trinity posits that God, in His infinite majesty, exists in three persons—Father, Son, and Holy Spirit. These persons, distinct yet inseparable, form a divine community of perfect love and eternal unity. In essence, the Father is not the Son, the Son is not the Spirit, and the Spirit is not the Father, yet there is only one God. This unity in diversity challenges our finite comprehension but reveals the infinite nature of the Almighty.

To unravel the mystery, we turn to the Scriptures, where the Gospel of John elucidates that Jesus is the Word of God. In the beginning was the Word, and the Word was with God, and the Word was God (John 1:1, NIV). This divine Word, inseparable from the Father, is identified as the Son of God. Unlike human birth, God's divine process is beyond our finite comprehension; it involves the eternal existence of the Word within God.

This understanding becomes clearer when we grasp that God does not give birth as humans do. In human terms, birth necessitates a male and a female, but God, in His divine nature, has always been present with His Word within Him. This Word, as the Bible reveals, proceeds from the Father (John 15:26, ESV), providing a clear explanation of the sonship of Jesus Christ to God.

The concept of the Word proceeding from the Father underscores the inseparability of the Word from the Word Bearer. The Gospel of John further illuminates that this Word, through which God created all things visible and invisible, became flesh in the person of Jesus Christ (John 1:14, NIV). God, in His creative act, spoke forth His Word, and that Word, as an extension of His will and imagination, brought into existence all that we behold.

Understanding Jesus as the Word of God becomes paramount. The Word, proceeding from the Father, is not a detached entity but an integral part of God's divine essence. The voice or Word cannot be separated from its owner—the Word Bearer. Thus, Jesus, identified as the creating Word of God, is inseparable from the Father.

The Bible further illuminates our relationship with Jesus, affirming that we belong to Him and He belongs to the Father (John 17:10, NIV). This relational dynamic within the Trinity encapsulates the divine dance of unity, love, and purpose—a dance in which we, as believers, are invited to participate.

*Scriptural Support:*

1. **Matthew 28:19 (ESV):**
   o *"Go therefore and make disciples of all nations, baptizing them in the name of the Father and of the Son and of the Holy Spirit."*
   o *This verse from the Great Commission provides a foundational understanding of the triune nature of God. The three persons are distinct, yet they share the singular name underlining their oneness.*

2. **2 Corinthians 13:14 (NIV):**
   o *"May the grace of the Lord Jesus Christ, and the love of God, and the fellowship of the Holy Spirit be with you all."*
   o *This benediction from Paul beautifully encapsulates the roles of each person within the Trinity. The grace of Jesus, the love of God the Father, and the fellowship of the Holy Spirit exemplify the diverse yet unified actions of the triune God.*

3. **John 14:16-17 (NIV):**
   - *"And I will ask the Father, and he will give you another advocate to help you and be with you forever—the Spirit of truth."*
   - *In this passage, Jesus speaks of His relationship with the Father and the coming of the Holy Spirit. It illustrates the distinct roles within the Trinity—the Son asking, the Father giving, and the Spirit advocating.*

4. **John 1:1-14 (NIV):**
   - *"In the beginning was the Word, and the Word was with God, and the Word was God... The Word became flesh and made his dwelling among us."*
   - *The prologue of John's Gospel beautifully presents the eternal existence of the Son with God and His incarnation as Jesus. This highlights the dual nature of Jesus as fully divine and fully human.*

5. **John 10:30 (NIV):**
   - *"I and the Father are one."*
   - *Jesus declares the oneness with the Father, affirming the unity within the Trinity. This statement underscores the inseparable nature of the Father and the Son, emphasizing their shared divine essence.*

In these passages, we find a tapestry of verses woven together, each thread contributing to the rich portrayal of the triune God—Father, Son, and Holy Spirit. Together, they offer glimpses into the intricate dance of unity and diversity within the Godhead, affirming the foundational truth of the Trinity in Christian theology.

In contemplating the Trinity, we stand at the precipice of the divine, where unity and diversity coalesce in the ineffable nature of God. This understanding invites us into a deeper relationship with the triune God—Father, Son, and Holy Spirit—revealing the richness of our faith and the depth of God's love for His creation.

## The Deity of Jesus Christ

In the depth of Christian theology, the deity of Jesus Christ stands as a central and profound thread. Exploring the nature of Jesus requires delving into the mystery of His dual existence—fully divine and fully human. This paradoxical nature is not a theological puzzle to confound, but a revelation that enriches the understanding of God's redemptive plan.

At the heart of this exploration is the acknowledgment that Jesus is not merely a great moral teacher or a historical figure; He is the incarnation of God, the Word made flesh (John 1:14, NIV). In His earthly sojourn, Jesus exhibited the fullness of deity while experiencing the depth of human existence. This union of divinity and humanity in Jesus is essential for comprehending the breadth of God's love and the efficacy of His salvation.

Emphasizing Jesus' role as the Savior is paramount. The New Testament resounds with the declaration that in Jesus, God Himself entered the human drama to reconcile humanity to Himself. This reconciliation is not a distant act but a personal one, as Jesus, fully divine, bore the weight of human sin on the cross, offering the ultimate sacrifice for redemption.

*Scriptural Support:*

1. **John 1:1 (NIV):**
   o *"In the beginning was the Word, and the Word was with God, and the Word was God."*
   o *The opening verse of John's Gospel unequivocally establishes the pre-existence and deity of Jesus. The Word, identified later as Jesus (John 1:14), existed with God from the very beginning.*

2. **Colossians 2:9 (ESV):**
   o *"For in him the whole fullness of deity dwells bodily."*
   o *The Apostle Paul, writing to the Colossians, articulates the completeness of the divine nature in Jesus. The fullness of God is not an abstract concept but a tangible reality dwelling bodily in Christ.*

3. **Philippians 2:6-7 (NIV):**
   o *"Who, being in very nature God, did not consider equality with God something to be used to his own advantage; rather, he made himself nothing by taking the very nature of a servant, being made in human likeness."*
   o *Paul's hymn in Philippians beautifully captures the humility of Jesus. While being in very nature God, He willingly took on human likeness, illustrating the depth of His love and sacrifice.*

4. **Hebrews 1:3 (NIV):**
   o *"The Son is the radiance of God's glory and the exact representation of his being, sustaining all things by his powerful word."*

o *The Book of Hebrews portrays Jesus as the radiance of God's glory, the exact representation of His being. This imagery underscores the perfect reflection of God's nature in the person of Jesus.*

The deity of Jesus Christ is not an abstract theological concept but a cornerstone of Christian belief. It is a declaration of the God who, in His boundless love, stepped into human history, not in a semblance of humanity, but in genuine and profound identification with our human experience. As believers grasp the depth of Jesus' divinity, they find not just a Savior but the embodiment of God's redemptive love.

**The Holy Spirit**

Within the Trinitarian understanding of God, the Holy Spirit occupies a unique and essential role. The Holy Spirit is not a mere force or influence but a distinct person within the Godhead, co-equal and co-eternal with the Father and the Son. Understanding the Holy Spirit involves delving into the multifaceted nature of His work—guidance, empowerment, and conviction.

The Holy Spirit's role in the Trinity is dynamic and relational. The Spirit proceeds from the Father and the Son, functioning as the Advocate or Comforter promised by Jesus (John 14:16-17). The Spirit is not a passive entity but an active participant in the divine work of creation, redemption, and sanctification.

The guidance of the Holy Spirit is a source of comfort and assurance for believers. The Spirit not only illuminates the Scriptures but also directs and empowers individuals in their journey of faith. The transformative work of the Spirit is evident in the lives of believers, producing the fruit of the Spirit and empowering them for service.

*Scriptural Support:*

1. **John 14:16-17 (NIV):**
   - *"And I will ask the Father, and he will give you another advocate to help you and be with you forever—the Spirit of truth. The world cannot accept him because it neither sees him nor knows him. But you know him, for he lives with you and will be in you."*
   - *In these words, Jesus introduces the coming of the Holy Spirit. The Spirit is the Advocate, the Helper, who will be with believers forever. This promise is a testament to the ongoing presence and work of the Spirit in the lives of believers.*

2. **Acts 1:8 (ESV):**
   - *"But you will receive power when the Holy Spirit has come upon you, and you will be my witnesses in Jerusalem and in all Judea and Samaria, and to the end of the earth."*
   - *Jesus, before His ascension, promises the disciples the empowerment of the Holy Spirit. The Spirit's role is not passive but dynamic, providing the power needed for effective witness and ministry.*

3. **Romans 8:26 (NIV):**
   - *"In the same way, the Spirit helps us in our weakness. We do not know what we ought to pray for, but the Spirit himself intercedes for us through wordless groans."*
   - *Paul, in his letter to the Romans, describes the intercessory role of the Holy Spirit. The Spirit comes alongside*

*believers, aiding them in their weaknesses and even interceding in prayer on their behalf.*

4. **Galatians 5:22-23 (NIV):**
   o *"But the fruit of the Spirit is love, joy, peace, forbearance, kindness, goodness, faithfulness, gentleness, and self-control. Against such things, there is no law."*
   o *The fruit of the Spirit, listed by Paul in Galatians, exemplifies the transformative work of the Holy Spirit in the lives of believers. These qualities reflect the character of God produced within those who yield to the Spirit.*

The Holy Spirit is not an impersonal force but a divine person actively engaged in the lives of believers. His work encompasses guidance, empowerment, and conviction, leading individuals into a deeper relationship with God and transforming them into Christlikeness. As believers yield to the Spirit, they experience the ongoing and transformative work that marks them as children of God.

## The Authority of Scripture

In the vast landscape of Christian beliefs, the Bible stands as the bedrock, the timeless and unerring Word of God. Understanding the authority of Scripture is not merely a theological endeavor; it is an acknowledgment of the divine inspiration that breathes life into its pages.

The Bible is not a collection of human musings but a sacred library inspired by God Himself. Its authority stems from its divine origin, where human authors, moved by the Holy Spirit, penned truths that transcended the limitations of their own understanding. This divine inspiration ensures the Bible's reliability as a guide for faith and practice, illuminating the path for believers across generations.

The significance of the Bible as the guide for faith is profound. It is more than a manual for moral living; it is a narrative that reveals the character of God, the nature of humanity, and the redemptive plan woven throughout history. It serves as a compass, providing direction in the journey of faith and offering solace in times of uncertainty.

*Scriptural Support:*

1. **2 Timothy 3:16 (NIV):**
    - *"All Scripture is God-breathed and is useful for teaching, rebuking, correcting and training in righteousness."*
    - *This verse, penned by the Apostle Paul, encapsulates the divine origin of Scripture. The phrase "God-breathed" emphasizes the unique inspiration that sets the Bible apart as the authoritative Word of God.*

2. **Psalm 119:105 (ESV):**
    - *"Your word is a lamp to my feet and a light to my path."*
    - *This poetic verse from Psalm 119 beautifully portrays the practical impact of God's Word. It is not merely a theoretical guide but a luminous source of direction, dispelling darkness and providing clarity for life's journey.*

3. **Hebrews 4:12 (NIV):**
    - *"For the word of God is alive and active. Sharper than any double-edged sword, it penetrates even to dividing*

soul and spirit, joints and marrow; it judges the thoughts and attitudes of the heart."
- o  The writer of Hebrews vividly describes the dynamic power of God's Word. It is not a static text but a living force that discerns and transforms the innermost recesses of the human heart.

4. **Isaiah 55:11 (NIV):**
   - o  "So is my word that goes out from my mouth: It will not return to me empty, but will accomplish what I desire and achieve the purpose for which I sent it."
   - o  This verse from Isaiah underscores the effectiveness of God's Word. It is not just spoken; it is a powerful force that accomplishes God's purposes, illustrating the transformative impact of divine revelation.

Understanding the authority of Scripture invites believers into a profound relationship with the living Word of God. It is an acknowledgment that, within its pages, we encounter not just ink on paper, but the very breath of God—a guiding light, a discerning force, and a source of enduring transformation.

## Salvation by Grace through Faith

The essence of Christian salvation lies not in human merit but in the unmerited favor and boundless love of God. Understanding salvation by grace through faith is to grasp the foundational principle that, in Christ, God offers the greatest gift—redemption—from the bondage of sin.

Salvation is not earned through human efforts, achievements, or moral uprightness. It is a divine gift, freely given by God out of

His abounding grace. This grace is an expression of God's unconditional love, extended to humanity despite our unworthiness. It is in comprehending this unearned favor that the beauty of salvation becomes most evident.

Faith plays a pivotal role in this divine transaction. It is the outstretched hand that receives the gift of salvation. Faith acknowledges the inadequacy of human righteousness and relies wholly on the finished work of Christ on the cross. It is not a work in itself but a response to the grace that precedes it—a surrender to the benevolence of a God who offers salvation to all who believe.

*Scriptural Support:*

1. **Ephesians 2:8-9 (NIV):**
   - *"For it is by grace you have been saved, through faith—and this is not from yourselves, it is the gift of God—not by works, so that no one can boast."*
   - *This foundational passage from Ephesians underscores the inseparable connection between grace, faith, and salvation. It emphasizes that salvation is not a result of human effort but a gift from God, ensuring that boasting is eradicated.*

2. **Romans 10:9 (ESV):**
   - *"Because, if you confess with your mouth that Jesus is Lord and believe in your heart that God raised him from the dead, you will be saved."*
   - *Paul's letter to the Romans encapsulates the simplicity of faith. Confessing with the mouth and believing in the heart are expressions of faith that lead to salvation. This verse emphasizes the relational aspect of faith—acknowledging Jesus as Lord and trusting in His resurrection.*

3. **Titus 3:5 (NIV):**
    - "He saved us, not because of righteous things we had done, but because of his mercy. He saved us through the washing of rebirth and renewal by the Holy Spirit."
    - The book of Titus emphasizes the undeserved nature of salvation. It is not a reward for righteous deeds but a result of God's mercy and the transformative work of the Holy Spirit.

4. **Galatians 2:16 (NIV):**
    - "know that a person is not justified by the works of the law, but by faith in Jesus Christ. So we, too, have put our faith in Christ Jesus that we may be justified by faith in Christ and not by the works of the law because by the works of the law no one will be justified."
    - This verse from Galatians underscores the futility of relying on human works for justification. Justification comes through faith in Christ, highlighting the centrality of faith in the salvation narrative.

Salvation by grace through faith is the cornerstone of Christian belief. It is a truth that echoes through the New Testament, revealing the heart of God's redemptive plan—an invitation to receive the gift of eternal life through faith in Jesus Christ. This understanding transforms the believer's perspective, fostering humility and gratitude for the unearned favor that flows from God's gracious heart.

## Human Depravity

Human depravity is a foundational concept in Christian theology that acknowledges the inherent sinfulness of humanity. It recognizes that, as descendants of Adam, all individuals are born into a state of sin, separated from God, and in need of redemption. Understanding human depravity is crucial for comprehending the depth of God's grace and the necessity of salvation through Christ.

The biblical narrative traces the origins of human depravity to the disobedience of Adam and Eve in the Garden of Eden (Genesis 3). This rebellion introduced sin into the human experience, resulting in a fallen nature inherited by all subsequent generations. The consequences of this original sin permeate every aspect of human existence, affecting thoughts, desires, and actions.

The acknowledgment of human depravity does not lead to despair but serves as a backdrop against which the brilliance of God's redemptive plan shines. It underscores the universal need for salvation and the inability of humanity to save itself. It is in this recognition of our spiritual poverty that the grace of God becomes not only necessary but profoundly transformative.

*Scriptural Support:*

1. **Romans 3:23 (NIV):**
   - *"for all have sinned and fall short of the glory of God."*
   - *This concise verse from Romans encapsulates the universality of sin. It declares that every individual, without exception, falls short of the glory of God. The emphasis is on the comprehensive nature of human depravity.*

2. **Romans 5:12 (ESV):**
   - *"Therefore, just as sin came into the world through one man, and death through sin, and so death spread to all men because all sinned."*
   - In Romans, Paul articulates the connection between Adam's sin and its impact on all humanity. The universality of sin and its consequences is outlined, emphasizing the inherited nature of human depravity.

3. **Psalm 51:5 (NIV):**
   - *"Surely, I was sinful at birth, sinful from the time my mother conceived me."*
   - David's confession in Psalm 51 reflects an awareness of his own sinful nature from birth. This acknowledgment of inherent sinfulness extends beyond individual actions to the core of human existence.

4. **Ephesians 2:1-3 (NIV):**
   - *"As for you, you were dead in your transgressions and sins, in which you used to live when you followed the ways of this world and of the ruler of the kingdom of the air, the spirit who is now at work in those who are disobedient."*
   - Paul, in his letter to the Ephesians, describes the spiritual condition of humanity apart from Christ. The language of being "dead in transgressions and sins" underscores the severity of human depravity.

Human depravity is not a pessimistic view but a sober acknowledgment of the fallen state of humanity. It sets the stage for the glorious work of redemption through Christ, emphasizing the transformative power of God's grace to lift humanity from the depths of sin to the heights of His glory. Recognizing our need for salvation, grounded in an understanding of human depravity, magnifies the grace and mercy of God in Christ Jesus.

## Justification by Faith

Justification by faith is a foundational doctrine in Christianity, illustrating the gracious act of God in declaring a sinner righteous through faith in Jesus Christ. It is a legal concept, describing the judicial declaration of righteousness, not based on human merit, but on the atoning work of Christ. Understanding justification involves grasping the depth of God's mercy, the role of faith, and the transformative nature of being declared righteous before God.

In biblical terms, justification is not earned through good deeds or religious observances but is a gift from God, received by faith. It involves the imputation of Christ's righteousness to the believer, transforming their standing before God from guilty to justified. This profound act of God's grace is central to the Christian understanding of salvation.

*Scriptural Support:*

1. **Romans 3:28 (NIV):**
    - *"For we maintain that a person is justified by faith apart from the works of the law."*
    - *Paul's declaration in Romans underscores the exclusivity of faith in the process of justification. It emphasizes that righteousness before God is not achieved through adherence to the law but through faith in Christ.*

2. **Galatians 2:16 (ESV):**
   - *"yet we know that a person is not justified by works of the law but through faith in Jesus Christ, so we also have believed in Christ Jesus, in order to be justified by faith in Christ and not by works of the law, because by works of the law no one will be justified."*
   - *In his letter to the Galatians, Paul contrasts justification by faith with justification by works of the law. He emphasizes the exclusive role of faith in the process of being declared righteous.*

3. **Romans 5:1 (NIV):**
   - *"Therefore, since we have been justified through faith, we have peace with God through our Lord Jesus Christ."*
   - *Paul's letter to the Romans highlights the immediate consequence of justification—peace with God. The reconciliation brought about through justification by faith brings a profound sense of peace and harmony.*

4. **Philippians 3:9 (NIV):**
   - *"and be found in him, not having a righteousness of my own that comes from the law, but that which is through faith in Christ—the righteousness that comes from God on the basis of faith."*
   - *Paul, in his letter to the Philippians, emphasizes the shift from self-righteousness based on the law to the righteousness that comes through faith in Christ. Justification is a divine gift received through faith.*

Justification by faith stands at the core of the Christian understanding of salvation. It is a transformative act where God, in His grace, declares sinners righteous through their faith in Jesus Christ. This doctrine accentuates the sufficiency of Christ's atonement and the surpassing value of faith in establishing a right relationship with God.

## The Atonement

The concept of atonement is the heartbeat of Christian theology—a profound and transformative understanding of Jesus Christ's sacrificial act on behalf of humanity. Atonement, at its core, is the redemptive work of Jesus, securing reconciliation between a fallen humanity and a holy God.

Atonement involves the vicarious sacrifice of Jesus as the Lamb of God, bearing the weight of human sin on the cross. This act is an unparalleled demonstration of God's love, mercy, and justice intersecting at the intersection of the divine and the human. In the shedding of His blood, Jesus becomes the bridge that spans the chasm created by sin, allowing humanity to draw near to a righteous God.

The essence of atonement lies in the reconciliation it achieves. Humanity, marred by sin and estranged from God, finds restoration through the substitutionary work of Christ. This reconciliation is not a mere transaction; it is a divine exchange where Jesus takes our sin, and we receive His righteousness. Atonement, therefore, is not just an event; it is the foundation of a renewed relationship between God and humanity.

*Scriptural Support:*

1. **Isaiah 53:5-6 (NIV):**
   - "But he was pierced for our transgressions, he was crushed for our iniquities; the punishment that brought us peace was on him, and by his wounds, we are healed. We all, like sheep, have gone astray, each of us has turned to our own way, and the Lord has laid on him the iniquity of us all."
   - *The prophetic words of Isaiah vividly describe the substitutionary nature of Jesus' atonement. His sacrifice brings peace, healing, and the bearing of human iniquity.*

2. **1 Peter 2:24 (ESV):**
   - "He himself bore our sins in his body on the tree, that we might die to sin and live to righteousness. By his wounds, you have been healed."
   - *Peter's epistle reinforces the atoning work of Christ. Jesus bore our sins, providing not just forgiveness but a transformative healing that liberates believers from the power of sin.*

3. **Romans 5:10 (NIV):**
   - "For if, while we were God's enemies, we were reconciled to him through the death of his Son, how much more, having been reconciled, shall we be saved through his life!"
   - *Paul, in his letter to the Romans, emphasizes the reconciling power of Christ's death. The atonement is not just a one-time event but the source of ongoing salvation through the resurrected life of Jesus.*

4. **Hebrews 9:14 (NIV):**
    - *"How much more, then, will the blood of Christ, who through the eternal Spirit offered himself unblemished to God, cleanse our consciences from acts that lead to death, so that we may serve the living God!"*
    - The book of Hebrews highlights the purity and efficacy of Jesus' sacrifice. His unblemished offering not only cleanses but empowers believers to serve the living God.

The atonement is the focal point of God's redemptive plan. It is a symphony of divine love and justice, echoing through the pages of Scripture and resonating in the hearts of believers. Through the sacrifice of Jesus, humanity finds forgiveness, healing, and reconciliation—an atonement that forever alters the course of human destiny.

## Eternal Life

Eternal life is a central theme in Christian theology, embodying the promise of an everlasting, intimate relationship with God for those who believe in Jesus Christ. This concept stands in stark contrast to the destiny faced by those who reject Christ, highlighting the gravity of the choices individuals make regarding their faith. Understanding eternal life involves appreciating the depth of God's love, the redemptive work of Jesus, and the profound implications of faith in determining one's ultimate destiny.

For believers, eternal life is not merely an endless existence but a quality of life marked by communion with God, righteousness, and fulfillment of God's purpose. This assurance is grounded in the finished work of Jesus Christ, who conquered sin and death, offering the gift of eternal life to all who trust in Him. The concept of eternal life also serves as a stark reminder of the separation that awaits those who reject the salvation offered through Christ.

*Scriptural Support:*

1. **John 3:16 (NIV):**
   - *"For God so loved the world that he gave his one and only Son, that whoever believes in him shall not perish but have eternal life."*
   - *The iconic verse from John's Gospel encapsulates the essence of eternal life. It underscores the inseparable connection between God's love, belief in Christ, and the promise of eternal life.*

2. **Romans 6:23 (NIV):**
   - *"For the wages of sin is death, but the gift of God is eternal life in Christ Jesus our Lord."*
   - *Paul's letter to the Romans articulates the dichotomy between the consequences of sin (death) and the gift of God (eternal life) through Christ. Eternal life is portrayed as a gracious gift, received through faith.*

3. **1 John 5:11-12 (NIV):**
   - *"And this is the testimony: God has given us eternal life, and this life is in his Son. Whoever has the Son has life; whoever does not have the Son of God does not have life."*
   - *The epistle of John emphasizes the inseparability of eternal life from having a relationship with the Son of God. It highlights the exclusivity of this life found in Christ.*

4. **John 17:3 (NIV):**
   - *"Now this is eternal life: that they know you, the only true God, and Jesus Christ, whom you have sent."*
   - *Jesus' prayer in John 17 provides insight into the nature of eternal life—it is a deep, intimate knowledge of God and Jesus Christ. It goes beyond mere duration and encompasses a rich, relational experience.*

Eternal life, as presented in the Bible, is a gift offered to humanity through Jesus Christ. It is not contingent on human merit but is graciously provided by God for those who believe. The contrasting destinies depicted in Scripture serve as a poignant reminder of the eternal implications of one's faith—the promise of life for those in Christ and the sobering reality of separation for those who reject Him.

**Resurrection and Ascension**

The resurrection and ascension of Jesus Christ are pivotal events in Christian theology, marking the culmination of God's redemptive plan and securing the hope of believers. These transformative moments are not mere postscripts to the crucifixion but integral components that proclaim victory over sin, death, and the assurance of an exalted Lord.

The resurrection is the heartbeat of Christianity—a testament to the triumph of life over death. Jesus, who willingly laid down His life on the cross, conquered the grave and rose victorious on the third day. This event not only validates His claims to divinity but assures believers of the power of God to overcome the most insurmountable obstacle: death itself.

The ascension of Jesus further underscores His exalted position. He did not merely rise from the dead to resume earthly life but ascended to the right hand of the Father, assuming a position of authority and honor. This ascension signifies the completion of His earthly ministry and the beginning of His eternal reign.

*Scriptural Support:*

1. **1 Corinthians 15:20-22 (NIV):**
   - *"But Christ has indeed been raised from the dead, the firstfruits of those who have fallen asleep. For since death came through a man, the resurrection of the dead comes also through a man. For as in Adam all die, so in Christ, all will be made alive."*
   - *Paul's discourse in Corinthians establishes the foundational truth of Christ's resurrection. He is the firstfruits, the guarantee of the resurrection for all believers. The victory over death is inaugurated through Christ.*

2. **Acts 1:9-11 (ESV):**
   - *"And when he had said these things, as they were looking on, he was lifted up, and a cloud took him out of their sight... Men of Galilee, why do you stand looking into heaven? This Jesus, who was taken up from you into heaven, will come in the same way as you saw him go into heaven."*
   - *The account in Acts narrates the ascension of Jesus. This event is not a departure but a prelude to His promised return. The angels' message assures believers that the exalted Jesus will one day return in glory.*

3. **Romans 8:34 (NIV):**
    - *"Who then is the one who condemns? No one. Christ Jesus who died—more than that, who was raised to life—is at the right hand of God and is also interceding for us."*
    - *Paul, in his letter to the Romans, highlights the ongoing work of Jesus at the right hand of God. He is not distant but actively interceding for believers, ensuring their security in Him.*

4. **Hebrews 4:14 (NIV):**
    - *"Therefore, since we have a great high priest who has ascended into heaven, Jesus the Son of God, let us hold firmly to the faith we profess."*
    - *The book of Hebrews presents Jesus as the great high priest who has ascended into heaven. This exaltation is the basis for believers to hold firmly to their faith, knowing that their high priest advocates for them.*

The resurrection and ascension of Jesus are not historical curiosities but pillars of Christian hope. They affirm the victory over sin and death, assure believers of a living and interceding Savior, and point to the promised return of the exalted Lord. In these events, Christians find the bedrock of their faith and the assurance of a future secured by the resurrected and ascended King.

### The Priesthood of Believers

The concept of the priesthood of believers is a profound aspect of Christian theology that emphasizes the direct access each believer has to God. It reflects the biblical teaching that, through faith in Christ, every believer becomes a priest, with the privilege and responsibility to approach God personally. Understanding the priesthood of believers involves recognizing the equality of access to God, the call to serve, and the transformative impact this truth has on the believer's identity and engagement in the world.

In the Old Testament, the role of the priest was to serve as an intermediary between God and the people, offering sacrifices and representing the community before God. The New Testament, however, introduces a revolutionary shift where Jesus Christ becomes the ultimate High Priest, and all believers share in the priesthood. This signifies that every believer, irrespective of status or position, has direct access to God and is called to actively engage in a life of worship and service.

*Scriptural Support:*

1. **1 Peter 2:5 (NIV):**
   - *"you also, like living stones, are being built into a spiritual house to be a holy priesthood, offering spiritual sacrifices acceptable to God through Jesus Christ."*
   - *Peter's letter underscores the communal aspect of the priesthood of believers. Believers collectively form a spiritual house, each one serving as a living stone, and together, they constitute a holy priesthood offering acceptable sacrifices to God through Jesus Christ.*

2. **Revelation 1:6 (NIV):**
   - *"and has made us to be a kingdom and priests to serve his God and Father—to him be glory and power for ever and ever! Amen."*
   - *The vision in Revelation acknowledges the transformative work of Christ, who has made believers a kingdom of*

*priests. This verse highlights the dual role of believers—to serve God and to bring glory and power to Him.*

3. **Hebrews 4:16 (NIV):**
   o *"Let us then approach God's throne of grace with confidence, so that we may receive mercy and find grace to help us in our time of need."*
   o *The author of Hebrews encourages believers to approach God's throne of grace with confidence. This reflects the direct access each believer has to God, emphasizing the intimate relationship made possible through Christ.*

4. **1 Corinthians 6:19-20 (NIV):**
   o *"Do you not know that your bodies are temples of the Holy Spirit, who is in you, whom you have received from God? You are not your own; you were bought at a price. Therefore, honor God with your bodies."*
   o *Paul's letter to the Corinthians reinforces the understanding that believers, indwelt by the Holy Spirit, are temples of God. This highlights the sacred nature of believers' bodies and their role in honoring God.*

The priesthood of believers is a revolutionary concept that dismantles the traditional barriers between clergy and laity. Every believer is called to actively serve, worship, and represent God in their daily lives. This truth underscores the dignity and responsibility each believer carries as a priest, contributing to the building of God's spiritual house and participating in the ongoing work of Christ in the world.

## The Second Coming of Christ

The Second Coming of Christ is a central and anticipated event in Christian theology, representing the fulfillment of God's redemptive plan. This concept encompasses the promised return of Jesus for judgment and the establishment of God's eternal kingdom. The Second Coming is not merely a future event; it is the culmination of God's narrative of redemption, bringing both judgment and vindication.

The New Testament resounds with the promise of Jesus' return. This event is not shrouded in mystery but presented as a definitive moment in which Jesus, who ascended into heaven, will return in glory and power. The Second Coming holds profound significance, marking the final chapter of human history, the defeat of evil, and the establishment of God's everlasting kingdom.

*Scriptural Support:*

1. **Revelation 22:12 (NIV):**
    - "Look, I am coming soon! My reward is with me, and I will give to each person according to what they have done."
    - The final chapter of the Bible echoes Jesus' promise of His imminent return. The concept of reward according to one's deeds emphasizes the accountability associated with the Second Coming.

2. **Matthew 24:30 (ESV):**
    - "Then will appear in heaven the sign of the Son of Man, and then all the tribes of the earth will mourn, and they will see the Son of Man coming on the clouds of heaven with power and great glory."

- In the Olivet Discourse, Jesus Himself speaks of His return. The imagery of the Son of Man coming on the clouds with power and glory conveys the majestic nature of this event.

3. **1 Thessalonians 4:16-17 (NIV):**
    - *"For the Lord himself will come down from heaven, with a loud command, with the voice of the archangel and with the trumpet call of God, and the dead in Christ will rise first. After that, we who are still alive and are left will be caught up together with them in the clouds to meet the Lord in the air. And so, we will be with the Lord forever."*
    - Paul's letter to the Thessalonians provides insight into the nature of the Second Coming. The resurrection of the dead and the gathering of believers to meet the Lord in the air emphasize the transformative and unifying nature of this event.

4. **Acts 1:11 (NIV):**
    - *"Men of Galilee, why do you stand looking into heaven? This Jesus, who was taken up from you into heaven, will come in the same way as you saw him go into heaven."*
    - The angelic proclamation at Jesus' ascension assures the disciples of His return in the same manner. The Second Coming is presented as a future event, grounded in the certainty of Jesus' promise.

The Second Coming of Christ is not a peripheral doctrine but a foundational truth that shapes Christian hope and perspective. It signifies the ultimate triumph of God's purposes, the fulfillment of promises, and the consummation of redemption. Believers eagerly anticipate this event, recognizing it as the grand climax of God's redemptive narrative and the dawn of a new, eternal era.

## The Church

The Church, as portrayed in the Bible, is not merely a physical structure or a gathering of people; it is the living and dynamic body of Christ. Its essence lies in being a community of believers who are united in Christ, sharing a common purpose, and collectively participating in God's redemptive mission. Understanding the Church involves recognizing its multifaceted role in worship, fellowship, disciple-making, and the proclamation of the Gospel.

The Church is described as the body of Christ in the New Testament, emphasizing the intimate connection between Christ and His followers. Each member plays a unique role, contributing to the overall health and functioning of the body. The Church is not a human invention but a divine institution established by Christ, with Him as the head.

*Scriptural Support:*

1. **Ephesians 1:22-23 (NIV):**
    o *"And God placed all things under his feet and appointed him to be head over everything for the church, which is his body, the fullness of him who fills everything in every way."*
    o *In Ephesians, Paul describes the Church as the body of Christ, with Christ as its head. This imagery underscores the unity and interconnectedness of believers with Christ as the source of fullness.*

2. **Matthew 16:18 (ESV):**
   - *"And I tell you, you are Peter, and on this rock, I will build my church, and the gates of hell shall not prevail against it."*
   - Jesus' declaration to Peter in Matthew affirms the establishment of the Church by Christ Himself. The imagery of the unyielding gates of hell emphasizes the enduring nature of the Church.

3. **1 Corinthians 12:12-13 (NIV):**
   - *"Just as a body, though one, has many parts, but all its many parts form one body, so it is with Christ. For we were all baptized by one Spirit so as to form one body—whether Jews or Gentiles, slave or free—and we were all given the one Spirit to drink."*
   - Paul's analogy in Corinthians underscores the diversity and unity within the Church. Regardless of individual differences, believers are united by the Spirit into one body, each contributing to the collective mission.

4. **Matthew 28:19-20 (NIV):**
   - *"Therefore go and make disciples of all nations, baptizing them in the name of the Father and of the Son and of the Holy Spirit, and teaching them to obey everything I have commanded you. And surely, I am with you always, to the very end of the age."*
   - Known as the Great Commission, these words of Jesus highlight the mission of the Church. Making disciples, baptizing, and teaching are collective responsibilities, with the assurance of Christ's presence.

The Church, as the body of Christ, is not a passive entity but an active participant in God's redemptive plan. Its purpose extends beyond the walls of a building, encompassing worship, fellowship, disciple-making, and the proclamation of the Gospel. Understanding the Church involves recognizing its identity in Christ, embracing its collective mission, and actively participating in the transformative work of God in the world.

## Baptism

Baptism is a profound and symbolic act within Christianity, representing a believer's identification with Christ in His death, burial, and resurrection. It is not merely a ritual but a powerful expression of faith, publicly declaring one's commitment to follow Jesus. Understanding baptism involves recognizing its symbolic nature and appreciating its significance in the believer's spiritual journey.

Baptism, rooted in the New Testament and modeled by Jesus Himself, signifies a spiritual rebirth and a public declaration of allegiance to Christ. It is an outward expression of an inward reality—a symbolic act of dying to the old self, being buried with Christ, and rising to new life in Him. Baptism is a tangible and visible representation of the believer's union with Christ and the transformative work of salvation.

*Scriptural Support:*

1. **Romans 6:4 (NIV):**
   - "We were therefore buried with him through baptism into death in order that, just as Christ was raised from the dead through the glory of the Father, we too may live a new life."
   - Paul, in his letter to the Romans, articulates the profound symbolism of baptism. The act of immersion in water represents burial with Christ, and emerging symbolizes rising to new life. Baptism is a public declaration of the believer's identification with Christ's death and resurrection.

2. **Matthew 3:13-17 (ESV):**
   - "Then Jesus came from Galilee to the Jordan to John, to be baptized by him... And when Jesus was baptized, immediately he went up from the water, and behold, the heavens were opened to him, and he saw the Spirit of God descending like a dove and coming to rest on him; and behold, a voice from heaven said, 'This is my beloved Son, with whom I am well pleased.'"
   - The baptism of Jesus by John the Baptist is a significant event. Though sinless, Jesus undergoes baptism, setting an example for believers. The divine affirmation from heaven emphasizes the spiritual significance of this act.

3. **Acts 2:38 (NIV):**
   - *"Peter replied, 'Repent and be baptized, every one of you, in the name of Jesus Christ for the forgiveness of your sins. And you will receive the gift of the Holy Spirit.'"*
   - *In Peter's sermon on the day of Pentecost, he connects repentance, baptism, and the forgiveness of sins. Baptism is not a mere ritual but a response to God's grace, symbolizing the cleansing and forgiveness found in Christ.*

4. **Colossians 2:12 (NIV):**
   - *"having been buried with him in baptism, in which you were also raised with him through your faith in the working of God, who raised him from the dead."*
   - *Paul, in his letter to the Colossians, reaffirms the transformative nature of baptism. It is an act of faith in the working of God, symbolizing the believer's identification with Christ's death and resurrection.*

Baptism, as a symbol of identification with Christ, holds profound spiritual significance. It is a public testimony of a believer's commitment to follow Jesus, marking the beginning of a new life in Him. Baptism is not a solitary act but a communal expression of faith, connecting believers across time and cultures in their shared identity with Christ.

## The Lord's Supper (Communion)

Communion, also known as the Lord's Supper, is a sacred and symbolic observance within Christianity. It serves as a communal act of remembrance, commemorating the sacrifice of Jesus Christ on the cross. Understanding Communion involves appreciating its symbolism, acknowledging its significance in fostering a sense of unity among believers, and recognizing it as a continual proclamation of the Gospel.

Communion traces its origins to the Last Supper, where Jesus, on the night before His crucifixion, shared a meal with His disciples. During this intimate gathering, Jesus instituted the practice of breaking bread and sharing the cup as symbols of His body and blood, representing the impending sacrifice for the forgiveness of sins. The act of Communion, rooted in this biblical event, serves as a tangible expression of the Gospel message.

*Scriptural Support:*

1. **1 Corinthians 11:23-26 (NIV):**
    - *"For I received from the Lord what I also passed on to you: The Lord Jesus, on the night he was betrayed, took bread, and when he had given thanks, he broke it and said, 'This is my body, which is for you; do this in remembrance of me.' In the same way, after supper, he took the cup, saying, 'This cup is the new covenant in my blood; do this, whenever you drink it, in remembrance of me.' For whenever you eat this bread and drink this cup, you proclaim the Lord's death until he comes."*

- o  Paul's account in Corinthians emphasizes the central theme of remembrance in Communion. The repeated phrase "in remembrance of me" underscores the significance of Communion as a continual proclamation of Jesus' sacrificial death.

2. **Luke 22:19-20 (ESV):**
   - o  "And he took bread, and when he had given thanks, he broke it and gave it to them, saying, 'This is my body, which is given for you. Do this in remembrance of me.' And likewise, the cup after they had eaten, saying, 'This cup that is poured out for you is the new covenant in my blood.'"
   - o  Luke's Gospel provides an account of the institution of the Lord's Supper. Jesus' words highlight the symbolic nature of the bread and cup, linking them to His body and blood—the elements of the new covenant.

3. **1 Corinthians 10:16-17 (NIV):**
   - o  "Is not the cup of thanksgiving for which we give thanks a participation in the blood of Christ? And is not the bread that we break a participation in the body of Christ? Because there is one loaf, we, who are many, are one body, for we all share the one loaf."
   - o  Paul's words in Corinthians underscore the communal aspect of Communion. The shared participation in the bread and cup symbolizes the unity of believers as one body in Christ.

4. **Matthew 26:26-28 (NIV):**
    - *"While they were eating, Jesus took bread, and when he had given thanks, he broke it and gave it to his disciples, saying, 'Take and eat; this is my body.' Then he took a cup, and when he had given thanks, he gave it to them, saying, 'Drink from it, all of you. This is my blood of the covenant, which is poured out for many for the forgiveness of sins.'"*
    - *Matthew's account reinforces the symbolism of Communion, emphasizing Jesus' body and blood as integral elements of the covenant established through His sacrifice.*

Communion is a sacred observance that unites believers across time and space. It serves as a tangible reminder of Christ's sacrificial love, fostering a sense of gratitude, humility, and unity among the body of believers. Participating in Communion is not a mere ritual but a profound act of worship, proclaiming the Gospel and anticipating the eventual consummation of God's kingdom.

## Conclusion of chapter

As we conclude this exploration of foundational Christian doctrines, it's essential to reflect on the profound significance each doctrine holds in the life of a believer. These truths, rooted in the Bible and woven into the fabric of Christian theology, form the bedrock of our faith, providing a solid foundation for understanding God, salvation, and our role in His redemptive plan.

**The Trinity,** a mysterious and awe-inspiring reality, reveals the intricate nature of our triune God—Father, Son, and Holy Spirit. This understanding invites us into the depths of divine community and challenges us to embrace both the unity and diversity within the Godhead.

**The Authority of Scripture** reminds us that the Bible is not merely a collection of words but the inspired and authoritative Word of God. It serves as our guide for faith and practice, offering profound wisdom, comfort, and direction in our journey of discipleship.

**The Deity of Jesus Christ,** fully divine and fully human, stands as the cornerstone of our faith. Jesus, the Son of God, is the Savior of humanity, and our acknowledgment of His lordship transforms our lives and perspectives.

**Salvation by Grace through Faith** underscores the unmerited favor of God, highlighting that our salvation is a gift received through faith in Jesus Christ. This foundational truth sets us free from the burden of earning our salvation and invites us into a relationship marked by grace.

**The Atonement,** Jesus' sacrificial death for human sin, becomes the source of our reconciliation with God. This act of love reshapes our understanding of justice, mercy, and the profound depths of God's redemptive plan.

**Resurrection and Ascension** declare the victory of Jesus over sin and death. Our hope is anchored in the risen Christ, who ascended to the right hand of God, interceding on our behalf.

**The Holy Spirit** empowers and guides us. This divine presence within believers transforms lives, bringing about spiritual fruit and equipping us for the journey of discipleship.

**Human Depravity** humbles us, recognizing our need for salvation and the transformative work of God's grace in our lives.

**The Second Coming of Christ** propels us forward with anticipation, reminding us of the future establishment of God's eternal kingdom.

**The Church,** as the body of Christ, calls us to worship, fellowship, disciple-making, and the proclamation of the Gospel. We are active participants in God's mission.

**Baptism and Communion** symbolize our identification with Christ's death, burial, and resurrection, fostering unity among believers.

**Justification by Faith** declares us righteous through faith in Christ, emphasizing the foundational nature of our standing before God.

**Eternal Life** assures believers of an everlasting, intimate relationship with God, while also highlighting the separation faced by those who reject Christ.

**The Priesthood of Believers** grants us direct access to God, transforming us into active participants in God's work.

In conclusion, let these foundational truths not be mere theological concepts but living realities that shape your identity and guide your journey of faith. Embrace them with conviction, let them resonate in the depths of your heart, and allow them to propel you into a life marked by love, service, and worship.

As you close this chapter, the invitation is extended—a continual journey awaits. Dive deeper into the richness of these doctrines, explore their implications in your daily life, and discover the boundless depths of God's love and wisdom. May your faith be strong, vibrant, and continually nurtured by the profound truths we've encountered together.

# Book Conclusion:

**IN THE CULMINATION** of this exhaustive odyssey through the realms of belief systems and spiritual landscapes, the tapestry of human spirituality stands unveiled. Across continents, cultures, and eras, we have traversed the ancient chronicles of the Bahá'í Faith, Mormonism, and Jehovah's Witnesses, encountering the eclectic expressions of New Age Spirituality, Atheism, and Secular Humanism. The richness of human creativity is evident, from the satire of Pastafarianism to the extraterrestrial perspectives of Raelism, each contributing to the mosaic of spiritual thought.

This exploration extended beyond conventional bounds, embracing even the irreverent humor of the Church of the SubGenius and the amalgamation of self-help and science fiction in Scientology. From the reverence for nature in Environmentalism to the revival of African Traditional Religions in modern contexts, and the rise of the "Spiritual but Not Religious" movement, our journey spanned the wide spectrum of human thought.

As we conclude this study, it is paramount to acknowledge the beauty in diversity and the resilience of the human spirit to seek meaning. Each belief system, whether ancient or contemporary, contributes to the intricate mosaic of human understanding. The journey doesn't end here; it is poised to enter a phase of rigorous evaluation through a comprehensive five-level criteria. With an open heart and discerning mind, we invite readers to delve deeper into the intricate fabric of faith, contemplating life's profound questions and searching for meaning in the vast cosmos of human spirituality.

The exploration then ventured into the ancient paths and sacred traditions, delving into major Abrahamic religions and unveiling a set of criteria—Origin, Longevity, Relevance, Accuracy of Predictions, and The Power or Evidence of God. The challenges and strengths of belief systems, from the complexities of ancient Eastern philosophies to the monotheistic foundations of Judaism, Christianity, and Islam, were laid bare. Each criterion served as a lens, highlighting the inadequacies in the origin stories of Buddhism, Hinduism, Shintoism, Taoism, Confucianism, and African Traditional Religions.

Relevance emerged as a pivotal factor, urging us to consider a belief system's ability to engage with contemporary issues. Accuracy of Predictions revealed the prophetic depth in the Abrahamic traditions, particularly in the book of Daniel, contrasting with belief systems lacking a well-documented record of fulfilled predictions. The Power or Evidence of God emerged as central, emphasizing the transformative nature of divine encounters.

The comparative analysis aimed not at condemnation but at encouraging exploration and research, urging readers to move beyond inherited beliefs and engage in an open-minded investigation of spiritual truths. The call remains for sincere seekers to embark on their own journey of discovery.

Lastly, the journey ventured into the mystery, unraveling the shadows of the Old Testament and discovering the radiant light of the New. Prophetic shadows, examples, and shadows in the law led us to symbols of redemption and common doctrines. The New Testament echoed and fulfilled these shadows, and the mystery concealed in the Old found revelation in Christ. The foundational doctrines of Christianity, explored in depth, became not just theological concepts but living truths that illuminate the path of faith.

Book Conclusion:

As this book concludes, may these revelations linger, beckoning readers into a lifelong journey of knowing, loving, and following the One who is the Alpha and Omega—the Redeemer of all creation. The echoes of God's covenant invite all to partake in the grand narrative of redemption. May this exploration kindle a fervent desire to delve deeper into the inexhaustible riches of God's Word, discovering afresh the wonders of Christ concealed in every inch of creation.

# Works Cited:

1. "Religion." Oxford English Dictionary, Oxford University Press, 2021, www.oed.com/view/Entry/162864.

2. Alleyne, Richard. "Universe 'Fine-Tuned for Life'." The Telegraph, Telegraph Media Group, 12 Nov. 2010, https://www.telegraph.co.uk/news/science/space/8121484/Universe-fine-tuned-for-life.html.

3. Axelrod, Alan and Charles Phillips. Encyclopedia of Wars. Infobase Publishing, 2013.

4. Barrow, John D., and Frank J. Tipler. The Anthropic Cosmological Principle. Oxford University Press, 1986.

5. Biola Magazine Staff. (2010, May 31). Can DNA Prove the Existence of an Intelligent Designer? *Biola Magazine.* https://www.biola.edu/blogs/biola-magazine/2010/can-dna-prove-the-existence-of-an-intelligent-desi. Retrieved: Nov 25, 2023.

6. Borowski, John. "Has Science Discovered God?" Christianity Today, Christianity Today, 6 June 2016, www.christianity-today.com/ct/2016/june/has-science-discovered-god.html.

7. Charan, Preeti K. "What Happens When We Die? Quantum Theory Sheds Light on Life after Death." The Epoch Times, 15 Dec. 2014, www.theepochtimes.com/

what-happens-when-we-die-quantum-theory-sheds-light-on-life-after-death_1157745.html.

8. Covey, Stephen R. The 7 Habits of Highly Effective People. Simon and Schuster, 2013.

9. Darrin S. Joy. AI Sheds New Light on the 'Code of Life'. May 22, 2023. https://dornsife.usc.edu/news/stories/ai-dna-code-of-life/ Retrieved: Nov 25, 2023.

10. Greenstein, George. The Symbiotic Universe. William Morrow, 1988.

11. Guliuzza, Randy J. "Science vs. God: Has Science Discovered God?" ICR, Institute for Creation Research, 20 Apr. 2017, www.icr.org/article/science-vs-god-has-science-discovered-god/.

12. Ham, Ken. The Lie: Evolution. Creation Science Foundation, 1987.

13. Hameroff, S. (2023, October 12). Stuart Hameroff. In Wikipedia. Retrieved 10:42, November 25, 2023, from https://en.wikipedia.org/w/index.php?title=Stuart_Hameroff&oldid=1179859812

14. Hawking, Stephen. A Brief History of Time: From the Big Bang to Black Holes. Bantam, 1998.

15. Holland, Dan. "Four Revolutionary Discoveries from the Fields of Astronomy and Molecular Biology That Point to the Existence of God." The Sun, The Sun, 29 Aug. 2018, www.thesun.co.uk/news/7117879/four-revolutionary-discoveries-from-the-fields-of-astronomy-and-molecular-biology-that-point-to-the-existence-of-god/.

## Works Cited:

16. Hoyle, Fred. "The Universe: Past and Present Reflections." Annual Review of Astronomy and Astrophysics, vol. 20, 1982, pp. 16-18.

17. Huxley, Thomas Henry. "Agnosticism and Christianity." Collected Essays V. Essays on Education and Kindred Subjects, The Macmillan Company, 1911, pp. 271-306.

18. Jastrow, Robert. God and the Astronomers. W.W. Norton & Company, 1992.

19. Joiret, M., Leclercq, M., Lambrechts, G., Rapino, F., Close, P., Louppe, G., & Geris, L. (2023). Cracking the genetic code with neural networks. *Frontiers in artificial intelligence*, 6, 1128153. https://doi.org/10.3389/frai.2023.1128153

20. Jong, Jonathan. "What is religion?" BBC, 8 March 2018, https://www.bbc.com/future/article/20180323-what-is-religion.

21. Keller, Timothy. The Meaning of Marriage: Facing the Complexities of Commitment with the Wisdom of God. Penguin, 2013.

22. Lennox, John C. God's Undertaker: Has Science Buried God? Lion Hudson, 2009.

23. Lewis, C. S. Mere Christianity. HarperOne, 2001.

24. Maslow, Abraham H. Motivation and Personality. Harper, 1987.

25. McMahon, Paul. "What Is DNA?" Johns Hopkins Medicine, 25 Oct. 2019, www.hopkinsmedicine.org/health/conditions-and-diseases/what-is-dna.

26. Merriam-Webster. "Deity." Merriam-Webster.com, 2023, https://www.merriam-webster.com/dictionary/deity. Accessed 9 Feb. 2023.

27. Merriam-Webster. "Theism." Merriam-Webster.com, 2023, https://www.merriam-webster.com/dictionary/theism. Accessed 9 Feb. 2023.

28. Milne, Edward. "The World of Physics." Philosophical Magazine 43.258 (1952): 269-276.

29. Müller, Max. Lectures on the Science of Language, 4th ed., vol. 1, Longmans, Green, and Co., 1866.

30. Penrose, Roger. Shadows of the Mind. Oxford University Press, 1994.

31. Prothero, Stephen. "Why Religious Conflict Persists." CNN, 5 Apr. 2013, www.cnn.com/2013/04/05/opinion/prothero-religious-violence/index.html.

32. Rimmer, John. "DNA Coding Reveals Intelligence." Catholic Exchange, 8 Feb. 2023, catholicexchange.com/dna-coding-reveals-intelligence.

33. Schaeffer, Francis A. True Spirituality. Tyndale House Publishers, 2005.

34. Smith, John. "The Universe Had a Onetime Beginning." Evidence for God from Science. http://www.godandscience.org/apologetics/universe_has_a_beginning.html.

35. Whittaker, Edmund. "The Beginning of the Universe." The Listener 54.1397 (1955): 370-371.